PENGUIN BOOKS

SRI LANKA'S EASTER SUNDAY MASSACRE

Rohan Gunaratna is Professor of Security Studies at the S. Rajaratnam School of International Studies, Nanyang Technology University, Singapore. He was the founder of Singapore's International Centre for Political Violence and Terrorism Research.

He received his Masters from the University of Notre Dame in the US where he was a Hesburgh Scholar and his doctorate from the University of St Andrews in the UK where he was British Chevening Scholar. A former Senior Fellow at the Combating Terrorism Centre at the United States Military Academy at West Point and at the Fletcher School of Law and Diplomacy, Gunaratna was invited to testify on the structure of al Qaeda before the 9/11 Commission.

The author of twenty books including *Inside al Qaeda: Global Network of Terror* (University of Columbia Press), Gunaratna edited the *Insurgency and Terrorism Series* of the Imperial College Press, London. He is a trainer for national security agencies, law enforcement authorities, and military counter terrorism units, has interviewed terrorists and insurgents in Afghanistan, Pakistan, Iraq, Yemen, Libya, Saudi Arabia, and other conflict zones. For advancing international security cooperation, Gunaratna received the Major General Ralph H. Van Deman Award.

Advance Praise for *Sri Lanka's Easter Sunday Massacre: Lessons for the International Community*

'Rohan Gunaratna's *Sri Lanka's Easter Sunday Massacre: Lessons for the International Community* is yet another masterful work by this world-renowned political scientist and internationally acclaimed expert on terrorism. All of his towering skills come together in this work to lay bare the causes behind one of the most dastardly and devastating terrorist attacks of the 21st century. This book, a riveting exploration of systemic bureaucratic failure, will appeal to all audiences, but will be particularly valuable to those who must deal with the policy challenges of protecting one's society and one's people from the scourge of radicalization, and the extremism and violence that inevitably follow. Dr Gunaratna has done us all a service by highlighting the events of this immensely tragic moment.'

—General (Retd.) John Allen
Special Presidential Envoy to the Global
Coalition to Defeat the Islamic State (2014–2015)
Commander NATO International Security Assistance
Force and U.S. Forces Afghanistan (2011–2013)

'Dr Gunaratna's critical examination of the Islamic-State-inspired Easter Sunday terror attack in Sri Lanka is essential reading for those in law enforcement, intelligence, military, government, and politics who share responsibility for preventing such devastating events. This is much more than a review of another act of terrorism, but rather a step by step assessment of what enabled such an egregious act—perhaps one of, if not the worst since 9/11—missteps that otherwise might have prevented it and, most importantly, essential lessons learned. In many respects, the clarity, depth, and insight Dr Gunaratna brings to bear in tearing apart events and decisions leading up to, during, and after the Easter Sunday events, is comparable in importance to the US government's after-action 9/11 Report. Like that Report, Dr Gunaratna's study of the Easter Sunday attack is must reading for all who deal with the on-going threat embedded in religious extremism.'

—David Cohen
CIA Deputy Director for Operations 1995–1997
NYPD Deputy Commissioner for Intelligence 2002–2014

'Gunaratna explains how exclusivist and extremist ideologies crystallize and manifest in the form of terrorism and political violence. A must read for national leaders, policy makers, and frontline practitioners.'

—Maria Ressa, Nobel Laureate

'Rohan Gunaratna is one of our leading experts on international terrorism. His book on the Easter Sunday massacre in Sri Lanka provides an authoritative and well-sourced account of events leading to those terrible attacks, and the lessons we should all learn from them.'

—Lord Jonathan Evans, Director-General of the British Security Service (MI5), 2007–13

Sri Lanka's Easter Sunday Massacre: Lessons for the International Community

Professor Rohan Gunaratna

PENGUIN BOOKS

An imprint of Penguin Random House

PENGUIN BOOKS

USA | Canada | UK | Ireland | Australia
New Zealand | India | South Africa | China | Southeast Asia

Penguin Books is part of the Penguin Random House group of companies
whose addresses can be found at global.penguinrandomhouse.com

Published by Penguin Random House SEA Pvt. Ltd
9, Changi South Street 3, Level 08-01,
Singapore 486361

First published in Penguin Books by Penguin Random House SEA 2023

10 9 8 7 6 5 4 3 2 1

ISBN 9789814954631

Typeset in Garamond by MAP Systems, Bangalore, India

www.penguin.sg

To the guardians of the state—intelligence, law enforcement, and military—who work day and night to prevent, pre-empt, and counter security threats.

Contents

List of Acronyms

ACJU	All Ceylon Jamiyyathul Ulama
ACTJ	All Ceylon Thowheed Jamaat
ACTM	All Ceylon Thareekathul Mufliheen
AG	Attorney General
BBS	Bodu Bala Sena
CCD	Colombo Crime Division
CIG	Centre for Islamic Guidance
CNI	Chief of National Intelligence
CTB	Counterterrorism Bill
CTID	Counterterrorism Investigation Division
DIG	Deputy Inspector General
DMI	Directorate of Military Intelligence

DMRCA	Department of Muslim Religious and Cultural Affairs
FBI	Federal Bureau of Investigations
HRC	Sri Lanka Human Rights Commission
HRDP	Human Resource Development Programme
IED	Improvised Explosive Device
IGP	Inspector General of Police
INTERPOL	International Criminal Police Organization
IS	Islamic State
ISIS	Islamic State of Iraq and Sham
JASM	Jamiyathul Ansaari Sunnathul Mohomadiya
JMI	Jamiyathul Millathu Ibrahimi Fi Seylani
KTJ	Kattankudy Thowheed Jamaat
LTTE	Liberation Tigers of Tamil Eelam
MOD	Ministry of Defence
NGO	Non-Government Organization
NIA	National Investigation Agency, India

NSA	National Security Adviser
NSAB	National Security Advisory Board
NSC	National Security Council
NSCS	National Security Council Secretariat
NTJ	National Thowheed Jamaat
OIC	Officer-in-Charge
PCoI	Presidential Commission of Inquiry
PSC	Parliamentary Select Committee
PSD	Presidential Security Division
SBI	Special Board of Inquiry
SDF	Syrian Democratic Forces
SDIG	Senior Deputy Inspector General
SIS	State Intelligence Service
SLFP	Sri Lanka Freedom Party
SLISM	Sri Lanka Islamic Student Movement
SLJI	Sri Lanka Jamaat-e-Islami
SLTJ	Sri Lanka Thowheed Jamaat

SOC	Sectoral Oversight Committee on National Security
STF	Special Task Force
TNTJ	Tamil Nadu Thowheed Jamaat
UPFA	United People's Freedom Alliance
VBIED	Vehicle–Borne Improvised Explosive Device
YDP	Youth Development Programme

Easter Sunday: An Extensive Chronology of Events

Pre-2015

26 August 1942—Jamaat-e-Islami was formed by Abdul A'la Maududi in India. Jamaat-e-Islami's ideology started to influence the neighbourhood including Sri Lanka.

1954—Sri Lanka Jamaat-e-Islami (SLJI) was founded by Abdul Cader Jailani Shahib in Colombo.

1980—The SLJI student wing, Sri Lanka Islamic Student Movement (SLISM), was established.

1990—Mohamed Aliyar founded the Centre for Islamic Guidance (CIG), which began propagating Wahhabism. Aliyar was arrested after the Easter Sunday bombings.

29 May 1996—Extremist Wahhabis reportedly launched an attack on the Dhikr Meditation Centre opened by the All Ceylon Thareekathul Mufliheen (ACTM) in Kattankuddy. The leader, M.S.M. Abdullah alias Rah, and other Sufis were targets of shootings, grenade attacks, physical aggression, intimidation, and other threats.

29 May 1998—M.S.M. Farouk Qadhiree, who was said to be a vocal opponent of Wahhabism, was shot and killed by extremist

Wahhabis. A public warning was later issued that the murder was conducted as punishment for those who act against Wahhabism.

29 January 2003—The Oluvil Declaration was proclaimed, claiming that north-eastern Muslims have an identity and a homeland and therefore claim a separate nation.

2004—Mohamed Ibrahim Mohamed Naufer met Zahran at Jamiathul Falah Madrasah in Kattankudy, where both were students studying Islam. Naufer influenced Zahran on Wahhabism. They would play lead roles in the Easter Sunday attack.

31 October 2004—More than 500 extremist Wahhabis reportedly attacked Sufis in Kattankudy. Dhikr Meditation Centre was set ablaze, and the library, homes, and businesses were destroyed. A complaint was filed with the police headquarters and a case was filed at the Sri Lanka Human Rights Commission (HRC) in 2005. The HRC opined in the Sufis' favour.

2005—Zahran was expelled from Jamiathul Falah Madrasah for disobedience and extremist ideology. Naufer Moulavi, Ashfar Moulavi, Rauf, Subair, and Zahran then attempted to infiltrate the Islamic Centre established by Abu Bakr Falahi. After failing to do so, they left to create their own Wahhabi organization.

2006—Daarul Adhar ad Da'iyyah, a Wahhabi organization, was formed in Kattankudy by Zahran and the others. After the Easter Sunday attacks, Daarul Adhar was banned, but it was said that their activities continued.

December 2006—When M.S.M. Abdullah alias Payilvan, leader of ACTM passed away, Kattankudy witnessed several days of rioting and an indefinite hartal. Many Sufi supporters fled the town after receiving death threats while some who remained in town were reportedly forced to renounce Sufi beliefs.

2008—A Supreme Court order allowed over 200 members of the ACTM to return to their original homes in Kattankudy and exercise their freedom to practice religion. It was said that they were obstructed by extremist Wahhabis and armed jihadists.

2009—Following a dispute with the management of Daarul Adhar, Zahran left the organization with a few others. They planned to establish their own Thowheed Jamaat in Kattankudy.

24 July 2009—Traditional and local Islam came under threat when Sufis held a *kanduri* feast in honour of a Muslim saint. In Beruwala, the followers of the Sufi Bukhari Thakkiya Mosque and the Thowheed Mahagoda Masjidur Rahman Mosque clashed. Two people were killed, over forty were injured, and at least 132 were arrested by law enforcement authorities.

16 August 2009—Islamic fundamentalism surged in Kattankudy. Exclusivism, said to have been advocated by extremist Wahhabis and the SLJI, in turn, promoted extremism—the precursor to terrorism.[1]

2011—Kattankudy Thowheed Jamaat was established by Zahran.

2012—Mohammed Zuhair Mohammed Aroos travelled to Australia on a student visa in 2005. He was deported to Sri Lanka in 2012 for overstaying his visa. While in Australia, he attended the notorious Al-Furqan Mosque in Melbourne, where he met Haroon Moulavi. He also built a relationship with Abdul Latheef Jameel Mohamed alias Jameel, the New Tropical Inn suicide bomber. Eventually, Aroos joined the IS and influenced Jameel to strike their home country.

---

[1] Chris Kamalendran, Asif Fuard, and Saman Kariyawasam, 'Unholy Tension In Lanka's Muslim East', *The Sunday Times, Sri Lanka*, August 9, 2019, https://www.sundaytimes.lk/090816/News/nws_23.html.

2012—Bodu Bala Sena (BBS) was established by Venerable Galagoda Aththe Gnanasara.

January 2012—National Thowheed Jamaat (NTJ) was formed by Zahran in Kattankudy. The NTJ was banned after the Easter Sunday attack.

July 2013—The European Union parliament in Strasbourg identified Wahhabism as the main source of global terrorism.[2]

13 August 2013—Mohamed Mushin Ishaq Ahamed was the first Sri Lankan to join the IS. A humanitarian worker in Africa, he left Tanzania for Syria through Turkey. He was accompanied by his wife and five children.

2014—At Ishaq's request, his brother Mohamed Muhusin Sarfas Nilam alias Nilam, met with Jameel at the All Ceylon Thowheed Jamaat (ACTJ) Mosque at Dematagoda. Nilam proceeded to Syria to join the IS.

Meanwhile, an Australian citizen and Qatari University professor, Ahmed Thalib Lukman Thalib, met with the SLJI members. Together with his sons Lukman Thalib Ahmed and Lukman Thalib Ismail, he came under scrutiny after the Easter Sunday attack for facilitating the SLISM national organizer Mohamed Ibrahim Sadiq Abdullah alias Abu Umair to train in Syria.

---

[2] https://www.europarl.europa.eu/thinktank/en/document/EXPO-AFET_ET(2013)457137

This was simply a report/ study—did not result in a resolution—or even a press note - by the EU Parliament. Please check this and qualify the statement accordingly. The report itself contains the following disclaimer:

DISCLAIMER Any opinions expressed in this document are the sole responsibility of the author and do not necessarily represent the official position of the European Parliament.

26 February–22 October 2014—Sufis of the Alhaj Abdul Jawan Alim Waliullah Trust lodged eleven complaints against Zahran and the NTJ at the Kattankudy police station. The NTJ incited hatred and violence against the Sufi community, especially its leader Alhaj A. Abdul Rahumman Mispahi Pasji alias Moulavi Rauf.

1 May 2014—A complaint was made by the Alhaj Abdul Jawan Alim Waliullah Trust to the Eastern Security Forces Commander, Major General Lal Perera, on the grounds that the group was receiving multiple threats from violent Muslim groups, which included the Zahran-led NTJ. Major General Perera summoned and warned Zahran to refrain from inciting hatred and violence, but it was said that the latter continued to do so.

June 2014—Organized violence was carried out in Aluthgama, Dharga town, Welipenna, and Beruwala.

29 June 2014—Abu Bakr al-Baghdadi, then leader of the Islamic State of Iraq and Sham (ISIS), announced the promulgation of a caliphate. It was believed that ISIS, or the IS, influenced Salafi-Wahhabi groups outside Iraq and Syria to travel to theatre. To build a global caliphate, the self-proclaimed caliph reportedly also instructed followers unable to travel to Iraq and Syria to kill non-Muslims in the country or the region where they resided. The IS envisaged controlling territories—including Sri Lanka—by 2020. In its map, Sri Lanka was identified as a part of the Khorasan province.

November 2014—Under the guidance of Ishaq and his brother Nilam, Jameel travelled to Turkey in an attempt to enter Syria but failed. He returned to establish an IS support group in Sri Lanka, Jamiyathul Millathu Ibrahimi Fi Seylani (JMI), by raising funds, recruiting, and mounting attacks. Through the Sri Lankan contingent in Syria, Jameel also linked IS to Zahran.

Late 2014—Islamic fundamentalism and religious extremism allegedly influenced Sri Lankan Muslims to travel to Syria to join the IS.

2015

January 2015—JMI was established by Jameel, Umair Mohamed Iqbal, and Mohammed Imad Ibthisam Fakeer to support the IS. The latter two were inspired and influenced by Jameel.

Early 2015—Save the Pearls, a charity caring for homeless children, was said to have been infiltrated by Jameel and his recruits, Mohamed Ibrahim Mohamed Ilham Ahamed and Mohamed Ibrahim Inshaf Ahamed. All three would become Easter Sunday suicide bombers.

9 January—Maithripala Sirisena assumed office as President and Defence Minister, and Ranil Wickremesinghe as Prime Minister. With the Yahapalana government consolidating power, it was said that national security no longer seemed a priority.

26 January—Abu Mohamed al-Adani, a chief spokesperson of the IS, announced the establishment of Wilayat Khorosan or Khorasan province in South Asia. Hafiz Shahid Khan, a former Tehrik-e-Taliban Pakistani commander, was appointed its *wālī* or governor.[3]

Mid-2015—Naufer, who was working for a law firm in Qatar, started propagating Wahhabism at the Islamic Centre in Qatar. He managed the largest Tamil language Wahhabi website. Operating online, Naufer started to influence Sri Lankan Muslim youth including members of the Jameel-led JMI.

---

[3] Abu Muhammad al-'Adnani, 'Say, "Die in Your Rage!"', January 26, 2015, https://scholarship.tricolib.brynmawr.edu/bitstream/handle/10066/21167/ADN20150126.pdf?sequence=1&isAllowed=y.

12 July—Nilam was killed in an airstrike in Raqqa, Syria, six months after his arrival there. He was the first of the Sri Lankan contingent to die.[4]

26 July—Mahendran Pulasthini of Kaluwanchikudy fell in love with Muhammad Hashtoon Achchi Muhammad, a member of the Sri Lanka Thowheed Jamaat (SLTJ). After converting to Islam, she changed her name to Sara Jasmine and married Hashtoon. Hashtoon would mount the Easter Sunday suicide attack on the church in Katuwapitiya. His widow Sara would later kill herself in a mass suicide attack in Sainthamaruthu.

30 July—Zahran issued an open letter to political parties in Kattankudy contesting the 2015 general elections to abide by the conditions set out by the NTJ. NTJ pledged to support those who agreed with them, and worked against those who opposed their conditions (e.g. SLMC). After M.L.A.M. Hizbullah was nominated for the national list seat from the Sri Lanka Freedom Party (SLFP), his supporters celebrated and attacked the NTJ mosque where Rilwan would suffer head injuries.

22 August—The national organizer of the SLISM, Sadiq Abdul Haq, was removed by the SLJI for fear of segregation within the movement. Although he trained with an al-Qaeda affiliate in Syria, he embraced the IS ideology.

6 October—The then Defence Secretary Hemasiri Fernando referred to Zahran by name at the National Security Council (NSC) meeting. Zahran was identified as an extremist by law enforcement authorities and the security and intelligence community.

---

[4] Chandani Kirinde, 'Galewela: Shocked residents recall principal turned ISIS member', *The Sunday Times, Sri Lanka*, July 26, 2015, https://www.sundaytimes.lk/150726/news/Galewela-shocked-residents-recall-principal-turned-isis-member-158512.html.

8 November—Tamil Nadu Thowheed Jamaat (TNTJ) leader P. Jainulabdeen, or P.J., was prevented from entering Sri Lanka. A proponent of Wahhabism, P.J. visited Sri Lanka in 1989, 1992, 1993, 2001, and 2005. P.J. also visited Kattankudy in 2005, strengthening its surging Wahhabi base.

15 December—NTJ was registered as a social service organization with the divisional secretariat in Kattankudy. Formed in January 2012, the influence of the NTJ steadfastly grew alongside Zahran's own organization.

End 2015—The IS support group in Sri Lanka, JMI, led by Jameel, expanded. Determined to create an IS Sri Lanka branch, Jameel recruited individuals and co-opted the organization.

2016

Early 2016—IS distributed Mohamed Ibn Abd al-Wahhab's book, *Kitāb at-Tawḥīd*, in Iraq and Syria. The IS declared Sri Lanka as part of the caliphate. Zahran promoted these on his Facebook page. Apart from the Counterterrorism Investigation Division's (CTID) regular surveillance, it was said that the Yahapalana government did not take action against Zahran despite intelligence reports.[5] Reportedly, the government also neither proscribed Jamaat-e-Islami nor the Salafi-Wahhabi organizations that promoted exclusivism and extremism.

29 January—Mohamed Sahid Mohamed Mushin and Nurul Inya Sahabdeen, Ishaq and Nilam's parents, returned to Sri Lanka from Syria.

[5] Select Committee of Parliament to look into and report to Parliament on the Terrorist Attacks that took place in different places in Sri Lanka on 21st April 2019, *Report of the Select Committee of Parliament to look into and report to Parliament on the Terrorist Attacks that took place in different places in Sri Lanka on 21st April 2019*, October 23, 2019, https://www.parliament.lk/uploads/comreports/sc-april-attacks-report-en.pdf.

4 March—Zahran held a programme at Meeraode Junction, Valaichchenai under the theme 'The Harm caused to Muslims by the Shia Sect', where he criticised the Shia.

April 2016—Zahran told his wife, Hadiya, about his membership in the IS. Zahran created a Telegram group called 'Ansar Kilafat' (supporters of the caliphate) with more than 200 members. Hashtoon, who visited the NTJ mosque in Kattankudy, assisted Zahran in managing his social media.

19 May—Sara was said to have initially rejected Hashtoon's attempts to radicalize her and travelled to the UAE where her mother was employed. She returned to Hashtoon after four months. With Hashtoon joining the NTJ, she followed him and started working with Zahran. They would eventually embrace the IS ideology and become suicide bombers.

24 June—Naufer returned to Sri Lanka, met with Zahran, and gave him a pen drive containing the IS videos and documents before returning to Qatar.

July 2016—The Inspector General of Police (IGP) was said to have been informed by the State Intelligence Service (SIS) director that Jameel facilitated Sri Lankans to travel to Syria and Iraq to join the IS. With reportedly no decisive action taken against Jameel, he continued to build JMI, radicalize Sri Lankan Muslims, and maintain links with the Sri Lankan IS contingent in Syria.

17 July—The IS ideology would spread within the SLJI and the SLISM despite the removal of Shahid, Sadiq's brother.

31 July—Naufer met with Hayathu Mohamed Ahamed Milhan in Qatar before returning to Sri Lanka with him. They met with Zahran to lay the groundwork to create an IS Sri Lanka branch.

4 September—To promote the IS, Zahran conducted seminars every Sunday at the NTJ mosque in Kattankudy under the theme 'IS and Caliphate', thus openly advocating for the IS ideology.

14–16 October—A group of JMI members, including Jameel and Ilham, attended fellow member Mohamed Ismail Husni Mubarak's wedding in Maruthamunai. In the neighboring Kattankudy, they met the NTJ members, including Zahran, and established rapport.

17 November—At an NSC meeting, the global threat posed by the IS and the radicalization of Muslims in Sri Lanka were discussed. However, reportedly no action was taken during or after the meeting.

18 November—In a speech, Sri Lankan Justice Minister Wijeyadasa Rajapaksa highlighted the ongoing radicalization in the local Muslim community. However, it was said that Muslim politicians rejected and even condemned the minister's warning.

22 November—The United Thowheed Jamaat wrote a letter to the President disagreeing with the Justice Minister's speech on rising Islamist extremism. Others accused him of attempting to drag the country to extremism and incite a bloodbath by igniting racism.

December 2016—After Jameel was identified as a religious extremist, he was placed under surveillance by the Directorate of Military Intelligence (DMI). During this time, members of the JMI attended training camps conducted by Zahran. However, the government reportedly advised the DMI not to conduct ground operations.

9 December—Zahran conducted a sermon on Islam and the caliphate at the NTJ mosque in Kattankudy. The video of this

sermon was shared on YouTube. To recruit other like-minded IS supporters, Zahran employed social media to identify them, got them to visit the Kattankudy mosque, and discreetly indoctrinated them on the IS ideals.

2017

February 2017—With the global resurgence of Salafism and Wahhabism, local and traditional Islam was supplanted. Belgium Coordination Unit for Threat Analysis voiced concerns and warnings about Saudi-backed Wahhabism's spread across Europe. Sri Lanka was no exception to the worldwide phenomenon of *madrasahs*, mosques, and other religious institutions coming under the control of politico-religious ideologies.

2–4 March—Zahran posted letters on his Facebook explaining the concepts of the IS and the caliphate and claimed that it was mandatory for Muslims to wage *jihad.*

10 March—An NTJ meeting/sermon turned into a physical altercation between armed NTJ members and Sufis. This resulted in casualties while eight NTJ members and two Sufi members were arrested. Zahran, his family, and other close associates attempted to flee Kattankudy. Other NTJ members, including Niyaz alias Reporter Niyaz, continued to spread hate online.

13 March—Sufis protested in Kattankudy calling for Zahran's arrest. They handed over a petition at the presidential secretariat and lodged a complaint to the Kattankudy police regarding Niyaz's online post. A week after the Easter attack, Niyaz would be killed by Sri Lankan security forces.

15–16 March—Following the instigation of violence at the Sufi's public demonstration, the then western province governor Azath

Salley, on a TV news report, inquired about the reasons for not arresting Zahran.[6] The NSC, presided over by President Sirisena, reviewed the incident. The issue of Sri Lankan IS advocates was discussed but it was said that no action was taken to mitigate the threat.

27–30 March—The Alhaj Abdul Jawan Alim Waliullah Trust prepared a dossier about Zahran and sent it to relevant government and anti-terrorism agencies. Sufi Moulavi K.R.M Sahlan, representing the Sufi sect, along with Sufi-Islamic leaders in Kattankudy, also claimed to have submitted a written complaint against Zahran's violent extremist conduct.[7] Eventually, the CTID Director Nalaka Silva's request to investigate the NTJ's activities was granted.

17 May—Mohamed Kaleel Mohamed Masfi, an NTJ member accused of giving information to the police about the organization, was shot dead. He was reportedly accused on 10 March, assaulted on 26 March and 2 April, and intimidated on 11 April. This was the first assassination allegedly ordered by Zahran.

25–26 May—IGP was said to have been informed by the CTID Director Nalaka Silva that they sought the Attorney General's (AG) advice on banning the NTJ's online platforms and arresting and investigating those engaged in unlawful activities. Meanwhile, President Sirisena was reportedly informed by the SIS that

[6] Sandun Jayawardana, 'Authorities were warned of Zahran's ISIS terrorism, claim witnesses', *The Sunday Times, Sri Lanka,* June 16, 2019, https://www.sundaytimes.lk/190616/news/authorities-were-warned-of-zahrans-isis-terrorism-claim-witnesses-353779.html.

[7] Select Committee of Parliament, *Report*; Yohan Perera and Ajith Siriwardana, 'We informed Office of Prez, PM and IGP about extremist groups: Sahlan Maulavi', *Daily Mirror,* June 19, 2019, https://www.dailymirror.lk/breaking_news/We-informed-Office-of-Prez--PM-and-IGP-about-extremist-groups:-Sahlan-Maulavi/108-169574.

Galagoda Aththe Gnanasara Thero's conduct could possibly have caused more Muslim youth to move towards the IS ideology.

May 2017—Abu Haytham alias Millah Seylani's plans to send Muslims to Afghanistan as part of Wilayah Khorasan suffered a setback with the arrest of NTJ members following the 10 March clash.

6 June—The SIS reportedly informed President Sirisena of possible attacks against non-Muslims by IS supporters or members. The SIS recommended an increase in security in areas where diplomats and western tourists would gather.

8 June—Members of Jamiyathul Ansaari Sunnathul Mohomadiya (JASM), the oldest Wahhabi group in Sri Lanka, allegedly attacked a cultural centre belonging to Shia Muslims at Meeraode, Valachchenai, injuring three persons and damaging property. Meanwhile, the IS influence would continue to grow in Sri Lanka.

13 June—International and regional expansion of the IS ideology and Buddhist and Muslim extremist groups operating in Sri Lanka were highlighted at an NSC meeting.

22 June—Reportedly, Deputy Solicitor General (DSG) Dileepa Peiris stated that the IGP failed to precisely monitor the NTJ's activities despite being requested to inform the AG's department about the progress of investigations on the NTJ's conduct.[8]

July 2017—It was said that the Defence Secretary was instructed to enhance surveillance on radicalized personnel by focusing more on their 'locations' to detect unusual behavioural patterns and movements.

[8] Select Committee of Parliament, *Report.*

18 August—After Zahran went into hiding, he reportedly reactivated his Facebook account and began promoting violent activities in support of the IS again. Despite drawing criticism, it was said that he persisted in his efforts to radicalize the Muslim community, especially the youth.

November 2017—The government reportedly reviewed the United Nations Security Council Resolution 2253 (2015) to identify mechanisms to counter the IS and al-Qaeda's potential activities in Sri Lanka. However, it was said that there seemed to be little to no progress from Muslim leaders in raising public awareness about extremism. Similarly, there seemed to be inadequate efforts by the government to criminalize the aforementioned entities. Zahran, now a wanted fugitive, Jameel, and other extremists continued to establish the IS and clandestinely ran training camps and seminars throughout the country.

11 November—At an NSC meeting, Zahran was reportedly identified by the SIS director as an extremist preacher motivating Sri Lankan youth towards the IS ideology. The rise of the IS and the threat to reconciliation was also explained to President Sirisena and others in attendance.

13–14 November—Communal violence erupted between a few Muslim and Sinhala groups in the coastal town of Gintota. Three homes were damaged in the attack. It was said that the reprisal by the Sinhalese caused dozens of Muslim homes and businesses to be burned and vandalized.

19 November—It was believed that Zahran attempted to take advantage of the unrest following the Gintota incident by uploading a video on Facebook to speak in favour of the caliphate, *hijrah* or migration, *sharia* law, and jihad.

16 December—Zahran held a seminar at Panda Multi Sports Arena, Malwana to settle a dispute that had arisen within the JMI due to ideological differences.

27 December—Zahran released a video criticising the legislature and judiciary in Sri Lanka. He reportedly declared that Muslims who seek assistance from the courts of non-Muslims rejected Allah and that Muslim judges and lawyers must be murdered. He called this a great act of jihad.

November–December 2017—A segment of Jamaat-e-Islami members joined the IS. Former SLISM leader Sadiq conducted a one-day training in Thoppur where he indoctrinated six trainees and demonstrated assembling and disassembling a T-56.

Late 2017—It was said that the Chief of National Intelligence (CNI), SIS director, and DMI director briefed the Defence Secretary on the possible radicalization of Muslims in Sri Lanka and its future consequences. The CNI was reportedly instructed to compile a report on the issues, identify counter-mechanisms, and bring the matter to the AG to obtain a legal perspective. Meanwhile, it was said that at the NSC, there still seemed to be no policy and decision-making on containing the apparent extremist or terrorist threat.

2018

Early 2018—Reportedly, a deputy IGP from the intelligence service of Tamil Nadu police, mounted an operation to infiltrate the IS Sri Lanka branch. It was said that undercover officer Abu Hind masqueraded as an IS leader and accessed Zahran through Rilwan.

5 January, 4 February—Along with other Thowheed Jamaat factions, Zahran was said to have continued to preach and post online videos against democracy and the parliamentary system while

emphasizing the importance of jihad. The SIS director reportedly recognized Zahran as a threat to harmony in Sri Lanka.

6 February, 12 February—Under his instructions, Zahran and his followers planned to mount attacks. Abdul Majeed Mohamed Farzan, a nominee of the Yahapalana-endorsed National Front, was reportedly attacked with explosives, and his house was damaged. Days later, an election office of the National Front at Marine Drive, Kattankudy was also attacked by bombs.

26 February—Muslim and Sinhalese violence erupted in Ampara in the eastern province after rumors that a Muslim-owned restaurant allegedly served members of the Sinhalese community food laced with chemicals that would affect their fertility. Following this, mobs of Sinhalese Buddhists were reported to have attacked Muslim citizens, mosques, and other properties. After the government imposed a state of emergency, the military assisted the police in affected areas.

28 February—President Sirisena was reportedly informed by intelligence about a Sri Lankan who was connected to al-Qaeda and was involved in plans to launch attacks in South Asia. This individual was said to have been in contact with Abu Abdullah al-Yemeni in Australia.

5–9 March—Rioting erupted in Teldeniya and later spread to Digana and other areas after a forty-four-year-old Sinhalese truck driver was allegedly violently assaulted by four Muslim youths following a traffic accident, resulting in his eventual death days later. Sinhalese mobs reportedly began attacking Muslim properties. It was said that there were widespread damages and casualties despite organized efforts by groups of Sinhalese youth and Buddhist monks to protect the mosques. Police arrested eighty-one persons and noted forty-five incidents of damage to houses, businesses, and four places of worship.

5 March—Zahran, by now the IS Sri Lanka branch leader, was said to have uploaded a video on the rioting incidents in what was supposedly an attempt to exploit communal unrest and recruit Muslim youth. In the video, he reportedly called for jihad, claiming that Islam could not co-exist peacefully with non-believers, and encouraged Muslims to harm those who fought against them. In response, Jamaat-e-Islami youth in Mawanella, led by Sadiq, and the JMI, led by Jameel, were said to have united and begun working with Zahran's group.

16 March—The IGP was reportedly informed by Deputy Inspector General (DIG) Nalaka Silva on the steps taken to report Zahran's Facebook account. Despite doing so, however, it was said that Zahran's social media activities continued unabated.

23–25 March—Zahran conducted his first training camp after the Digana riots to radicalize and recruit new members. Lectures were delivered on topics such as the IS, evading security, and intelligence monitoring. The Tarbiya session reportedly concluded with the demonstration of a T-56. Six of the twenty-five instructors and participants at the camp would eventually participate in the Easter Sunday bombings.

30 March–1 April—Zahran conducted another training camp at the Thashila Holiday Resort with 15–20 participants. It was said that military wing leaders Milhan, Hashtoon as well as Zahran and Naufer delivered lectures on using firearms, making explosives, and the IS, respectively.

2 April—Saudi Crown Prince Mohammed bin Salman Al Saud reportedly stated in an interview that Saudi Arabia had been spreading Wahhabism at the request of its Western allies.[9]

---

[9] Karen DeYoung, 'Saudi prince denies Kushner is "in his pocket"', *The Washington Post*, March 22, 2018, https://www.washingtonpost.com/world/national-security/

8–16 April—The CTID was said to have summoned Jameel to investigate his role in propagating the IS ideology. Days later, the IGP was reportedly informed by the CTID director about Zahran's disappearance from his wife's home in Kekunagolla, Kurunegala. Afterwards, and supposedly intending to transfer the investigations on Zahran to the SIS, the SIS director informed the IGP to conclude the CTID investigation.[10]

May 2018—The Defence Secretary reportedly instructed the SIS director to brief President Sirisena on the IS threat posed and countermeasures taken to curtail it. Meanwhile, the IS Sri Lanka branch military wing members Milhan and Rilwan were said to have procured chemicals from Pettah. It was also said that Hashtoon conducted extensive online research to manufacture bombs and built a collection of bomb-making manuals.

4–27 May—Zahran conducted two more training sessions at the Thakshila Holiday Resort with around 30–35 participants. Reportedly, he also continued to post videos on Facebook about the IS' doctrines, including the merits of jihad.

June 2018—Zahran was said to have furthered his propaganda by focusing on justifying the IS' actions and launching criticisms against peace-loving Muslims. As the IS Sri Lanka branch leader, Zahran also apparently merged both the IS and al-Qaeda affiliate members. It was also said that he co-opted former al-Qaeda-affiliate-trained Sadiq, the former national organizer of SLISM.

8 June—The IS Sri Lanka branch reportedly assassinated Adam Bawa Mohamed Ismail alias Palani Bawa by shooting him at Aliyar Junction in Kattankudy. While some were said to have reported

---

saudi-prince-denies-kushner-is-in-his-pocket/2018/03/22/701a9c9e-2e22-11e8-8688-c053ba58f1e4_story.html.

[10] Select Committee of Parliament, *Report*.

that Palani Bawa was killed for being a police informant, others reportedly claimed that he was selling marijuana.

17–28 June—Zahran continued to post videos and was said to have even released articles to justify the extremist actions of the IS and condemn moulavis who spoke against them.

July 2018—In addition to an International Criminal Police Organization (INTERPOL) blue notice, the CTID reportedly obtained a warrant for Zahran's arrest.[11] Meanwhile, Zahran continued his online propaganda.

4 July—Zahran reportedly shared a letter on his Telegram channel praising Abu Bakr al-Baghdadi for sending his son, Huthaifa al-Badri, who was killed in battle on 2 July, to fight in the battlefields, calling it an example for Muslim leaders. Zahran was believed to have been inspired to raise his son in the same spirit.

7–22 July—The IS expanded its reach to Sri Lanka's deep south. Zahran conducted two separate training camps near Shimla Bakery. Milhan provided theoretical and practical training on firearms and knives while Rilwan provided training on bomb preparations. Zahran and Naufer delivered lectures on the IS. Each training was said to have been attended by 20–30 recruits.

28 July—Zahran conducted a dedicated training programme for women recruits—wives, mothers, sisters, and daughters—at Palamuna Holiday Inn. Reportedly, the training's purpose was to radicalize the women further and compel them to support their husbands, brothers, and/or fathers to participate in the IS Sri Lanka branch activities. The programme was organized with the participation of Zahran, Naufer, and other IS instructors.

[11] Select Committee of Parliament, *Report*.

10 August—Pakistan authorities reportedly shared information with the Sri Lankan High Commission in Islamabad about an IS member's active online planning and preparation of explosives from readily available chemicals. It was said that materials retrieved from the suspect included detailed information on preparing IEDs, encryption key instructions, user guides, and weapon training manuals. During this time, Zahran also posted another video supporting jihad, which he apparently believed was part of Islamic religious teachings and was the shortest path to heaven.

15 August—Zahran reportedly established a small unit to act as a secret investigation group. It was said that the unit, which was led by Milhan and included Sadiq, Gafoor Mama, and Sameer, was first tasked to gather information about police stations in Colombo, the Navy headquarters, and police headquarters. They were also tasked with assassinating two persons who had left Islam.

23 August—In a letter on Facebook, Zahran reportedly called for the protection of caliph Abu Bakr al-Baghdadi and hoped al-Baghdadi would receive assistance from Allah to spread Islam by conquering many countries. The letter was published immediately a day after al-Baghdadi was said to have called on his supporters and sympathisers to launch attacks against non-Muslims.

26–28 August—Zahran conducted another training camp near Shimla Bakery. There were reportedly around 30–40 attendees, and the increased number was believed to have been due to Zahran's persistent propaganda. While Zahran, Naufer, and Hashtoon were conducting the camp, it was said that IS operators tested an explosive device in Batticaloa that caused Rilwan to suffer life-threatening injuries. Rilwan was given first aid, then transported to the Colombo National Hospital the next day.

He was reportedly admitted under the alias 'M.I. Shahid' and under the guise of a gas cylinder blast. It was said that Dr H.K. Chandana and nurse Shiromi Vidyasekara noticed inconsistencies in the injuries. However, allegedly with Dr Chandana's endorsement, the police were not informed accordingly.

31 August—After Rilwan's accident, the NTJ issued a formal letter stating that Zahran and his brother Zaini had been removed, presumably to prevent the disruption of the NTJ's radicalization plans. Zahran was said to have visited the NTJ and remained connected with its leaders and in contact with its members.

1 September—It was said that a raid led by India's National Investigation Agency (NIA) resulted in the arrest of six individuals in the alleged assassination plot against Hindu leaders in Coimbatore.[12] The data retrieved during the raid, which included copies of Zahran's speeches and phone records of Zahran contacting the IS fighters in Bangladesh and Afghanistan, reportedly revealed connections between the Coimbatore cell and Zahran.[13]

15–26 September—Zahran posted a video stating that jihad would soon be waged against non-Muslims, which was followed up by an impassioned letter on the same. He also shared Tamil-language IS propaganda through Telegram under the name 'Ansarul Khilafah'.

---

[12] Press Trust of India, 'NIA files charge sheet against alleged ISIS sympathisers', *Hindustan* Times, February 26, 2019, https://www.hindustantimes.com/india-news/nia-files-charge-sheet-against-alleged-isis-sympathisers/story-4nUJlhf12QMwX80oJmlQXP.html.

[13] Jason Burke and Michael Safi, 'Sri Lanka told of extremist network months before blasts', *The Guardian*, April 24, 2019, https://www.theguardian.com/world/2019/apr/24/sri-lanka-knew-of-extremist-network-months-before-blasts-sources.

October 2018—To develop hatred and instigate a riot between religious communities, Zahran reportedly developed a plan to strike sacred Buddhist, Christian, and Hindu images. After presiding over a meeting with the IS leadership at Abdul Latheef Mohamed Shafee's residence, Zahran instructed Sadiq to break the statues.

6–7 October—Zahran conducted a training camp at the Blue Eye Inn in Blackpool, Nuwara Eliya. It was said that about 20–25 recruits attended.

10–11 October—Zahran reportedly posted a letter on his Facebook claiming that a person named Pakkam Bin Abu was an Indian intelligence agent. The next day, it was said that Pakkam Bin Abu published on his Facebook that Zahran was an Israeli intelligence agent.

17 October—The US-led campaign to dismantle the IS infrastructure in Iraq and Syria continued. According to accounts, several Sri Lankans in Syria continued to be killed. This included Thawzi Thajudeen's wife, Seenathul Arfa Farouk, who was killed in an air strike.

19 October—Presumably committed to causing division, Zahran continued his online campaign of hate, reiterating through social media that Muslims should reject democracy.

23 October—It was said that, at another NSC meeting, Zahran was once again identified as a preacher of the IS' extremist ideology. Although details about the IS-radicalized Sri Lankans were said to have been discussed, there were reportedly no measures taken, once again, to arrest or proscribe the IS. Thus, it was believed that radicalization continued implementing preventive measures or executive action to dismantle the IS Sri Lanka branch and arrest Zahran or his leadership and members.

November 2018—Accounts said that Sri Lankans who travelled to Syria remained in contact with supporters via social media and received funds through a Punjab National Bank account. To address the financial challenge of relocating Sri Lankan foreign fighters trapped in Syria, Zahran reportedly obtained US$ 23,500 to support them. At the same time, the SIS director—presumably unaware that the IS Sri Lanka branch had long been established—informed the Defence Secretary that the IS supporters in Sri Lanka were working towards establishing an IS branch in the country. The SIS director reportedly also told the Defence Secretary that the supporters were possibly planning an attack on foreigners and non-Muslims. However, it was said that no arrests were made.

3–4 November—The IS stepped up its training by conducting indoctrination sessions both in the hill country and the south. Zahran was said to have conducted another training camp near Shimla Bakery with about 25–30 attendees.

13 November—In their meeting, the NSC was reportedly briefed that Zahran was motivating Muslims to launch attacks on non-believers. The spread of the IS ideology in Sri Lanka and radicalization were also said to have been discussed.

16–18 November—According to accounts, the IS carefully selected Jamaat-e-Islami and/or Wahhabi followers to train. Zahran conducted a training camp at the Blue Eye Inn. About 15–20 persons participated in the lectures and training. Zahran allegedly maintained a registry of names where he listed those who were committed to fighting versus those dedicated enough to commit suicide.

30 November—Two police officers were reportedly killed in Vavunativu in an IS operation led by Milhan, which aimed to obtain weapons for the IS Sri Lanka branch.

December 2018—It was reported that then-Defence Secretary Hemasiri Fernando received warnings of an attack by Muslim extremists. The IGP was said to have been informed about taking preventive action. However, there was allegedly neither a national plan by Muslim leaders nor a national strategy by the government. Meanwhile, the IS' influence was steadily growing as evidenced by extremist propaganda material recovered by the NIA during a raid in Tamil Nadu, and the SLJI being infiltrated by Sadiq and his brother Shahid in an attempt to radicalize Muslim youth.[14]

1–2 December—The IS members at Sippikulama organized another recruitment programme. The programme was identified as 'Tarbiya' or 'development and training'. However, it was believed that the programme instead sought to politicize and radicalize Muslims—especially youth—to be exclusivists, extremists, and terrorists.

Early to mid-December 2018—The UK-based Wahhabi Razik Mohamed Faiz alias Police Faiz published a message on Facebook alleging that the defence ministry had deployed special intelligence units to investigate Zahran and his followers and that they were currently collecting information. Police Faiz was said to have been an active member of the *mujahideen* group in the east during the war against the Liberation Tigers of Tamil Eelam (LTTE).

14–18 December—The IS reportedly continued to capitalize on Muslim sorrow and anger after the Digana riots. Sadiq took the lead in recruiting and radicalizing affected Muslim youth to the IS Sri Lanka branch.

[14] Rahul Tripathi and Dipanjan Roy Chaudhury, 'Indian sleuths in Sri Lanka to aid probe into Easter attacks', *The Economic Times*, April 25, 2019, https://economictimes.indiatimes.com/articleshow/69034200.cms?from=mdr&utm_source=contentofinterest&utm_medium=text&utm_campaign=cppst.

23–25 December—IS Sri Lanka branch mounted attacks—led by Sadiq and Shahid—on Buddhist, Hindu, and Christian images in Mawanella, presumably to provoke communal clashes. A dozen Jamaat-e-Islami activists turned the IS operators were said to have been arrested. Accounts said that Zahran enlisted the IS financer Ilham and Naufer's support to approach families in need of legal assistance and to represent those arrested and absconding.

28 December—ASP Kamal Perera, personal assistant to the SP division in Kegalle, was designated as the investigation officer-in-charge (OIC) for the religious vandalism case. ASP Perera reportedly requested information from relevant agencies, including INTERPOL, regarding the perpetrating group's possible international connections.

Late 2018—With the SIM cards and identity cards fraudulently obtained by Rilwan, it was said that the IS prepared to build a secure communication system to mount a series of attacks in 2019. These preparations would continue until the commencement of said attacks.

2019

3 January—Western province governor Azath Salley reportedly met with pertinent government officials, presumably after realizing the danger of a communal conflagration following the religious vandalism case in Mawanella. It was said that Sufi Muslim leaders who realized the looming threat pledged support to find the perpetrators. In addition to the Public Development Minister, accounts also stated that Governor Salley called the IGP and Defence Secretary to hand over evidence.[15] Previously, Governor Salley was said to have contacted the president of All

[15] Chandani Kirinde, 'Warnings about growing extremism went unheeded, Salley and ACJU rep. tell PSC', *Daily Financial Times*, June 12, 2019, https://www.ft.lk/

Ceylon Jamiyyathul Ulama (ACJU), Rizwi Mufthi, and head of the Muslim Council, N.M. Ameen, immediately after the Mawanella incident to discuss the matter. Rizwi reportedly assigned Mohamed Salley Mohamed Thassim, also known as Thassim Moulavi, the ACJU assistant secretary and Seylan Muslim Youth Organization director, to assist.

6 January—According to accounts, President Sirisena was informed by the SIS director about the suspects behind the Mawanella incident, their extremist ideologies, and their close connections with Zahran.

14 January—Reportedly, Sadiq and Shahid were properly identified as suspects in the Mawanella incident, and their connection with Zahran was presented at the NSC meeting. However, once again, it seemed that no swift action was taken to dismantle the IS network, nor were there said to have been specialist resources diverted to arrest the perpetrators.

16 January—Following their investigations, law enforcement officers reportedly discovered land at Wanathawilluwa in the Puttalam district where large amounts of weapons and explosives were stored. After the Criminal Investigations Department (CID) received information that Sadiq and Shahid were in Puttalam, it was said that those who managed the facility were questioned. After this, it was revealed that Zahran and his followers allegedly conducted training sessions there. Officers attached to the SIS, the DMI, and other intelligence services visited the site.

22–25 January—Jamaat-e-Islami Central Committee member Rasheed Mohamed Ibrahim, the father of Sadiq and Shahid, was reportedly arrested and produced in court on 25 January. He

---

front-page/Warnings-about-growing-extremism-went-unheeded--Salley-and-ACJU-rep--tell-PSC/44-679836.

was said to be an ideologue of the IS and served as an instructor during Zahran's training camps. A search of his home led to the discovery of over 390 CDs, an air rifle, documents, and a recording studio, which was used to produce propaganda videos.

23 January—Zahran's name was revealed in connection with the discovery of the explosives and weapons in Wanathawilluwa. To avoid the risk of capture or kill, Zahran expedited his plans for mounting a suicide attack.

29 January—It was said that the CID Director SPP Shani Abeysekara turned down ASP Kamal Perera's 28 December request to enlist INTERPOL assistance to investigate the international dimension of the Mawanella incident. He was said to have claimed there was no information to back such a possibility. On the other hand, the monthly threat forecast prepared by the Institute of National Security Studies Sri Lanka recommended that the group involved in the Wanathawilluwa discovery should be investigated for international connections.

31 January–6 March—Presumably, to sustain his online propaganda campaign, Zahran continued to use his Facebook account to propagate hatred towards non-Muslims, with content demonstrating that Zahran was planning to kill and die in the name of jihad.

2 February—At the NSC meeting, the SIS director reportedly discussed the Wanathawilluwa recovery and its connection with Zahran.

8 February—The investigative plan on the Mawanella incident was said to have been sent to the CID Director SSP Shani Abeysekara. It recommended that the investigation explore the possibility of international assistance behind the group.

19 February—In the penultimate NSC meeting held before the Easter attack, accounts said that the Wanathawilluwa incident was mentioned but not discussed at length.[16]

Early to mid-March 2019—CID officers failed to arrest Army Mohideen and Rilwan despite reportedly being notified of their hiding place by the SIS operatives.

6 March—Youth in Batticaloa, Ampara, and Trincomalee were said to have been motivated by Rilwan to launch the IS style attacks in Sri Lanka.

8 March—Milhan allegedly shot Taslim, coordinating secretary to minister Kabir Hashim, in the early morning while he was at home asleep. Taslim miraculously survived the attack but would remain bedridden and partially paralysed. Taslim was the interpreter attached to the CID team that raided the IS' Wanathawilluwa facility.

15 March—Brenton Harrison Tarrant, a 28-year-old Australian and far-right terrorist, killed fifty-one and injured forty Muslim worshippers in two mosques in Christchurch, New Zealand. This attack, along with the losses in Baghouz and the continued government hunt for Zahran, was believed to have prompted the IS Sri Lanka branch to accelerate their attack plans, with Zahran deciding to strike on Easter Sunday.

18 March—With the discord between Zahran and his deputy leader Naufer growing, the IS Sri Lanka branch split, which disrupted their plans.

19 March—In the aftermath of the Christchurch massacre, and after six months of silence, the IS spokesperson Abu Hassan al-Muhajir released an audio recording calling for retaliatory attacks.

---

[16] Select Committee of Parliament, *Report.*

23 March—IS lost its base in the eastern village of Baghouz in Syria, which was considered the IS' final stronghold.

24 March—Zahran's brother Zaini did not respond to his summons at the CID headquarters in Colombo.

25 March—Following the split in the IS Sri Lanka branch, the rivalry between Naufer and Zahran reportedly prompted the factions to co-opt followers of the NTJ, Jamaat-e-Islami, and the JMI.

26 March—The deputy director of the SIS' Q division, which overlooked Muslim extremism, reportedly sent an internal memo stating that Sadiq, Shahid, and Zahran led the Mawanella attacks. It was said that the first two had been hiding in Wanathawilluwa between late December to early January, manufacturing explosives and launching an IS-style attack in Sri Lanka. The SIS reportedly determined it imperative to arrest them.

27 March—It was said that, during a meeting with his group, Zahran announced he would participate in the attack plans as a suicide bomber. According to accounts, Zahran, Hashtoon, Jameel, and Muaath also invited Sameer to join them.

31 March—At the NSC, the SIS director reportedly shared information on the Christchurch incident in New Zealand.

April 2019—Riyas Abu Bakr and Abu Dujana were arrested during a raid conducted by the NIA in multiple districts within Kerala state and were alleged of maintaining links with Zahran. Abu Bakr reportedly travelled to Afghanistan in 2016 to meet the IS militants and had planned an attack in India. A strong network between Indians from south Kerala and Tamil Nadu, and Islamic extremists in Sri Lanka was also identified.[17]

[17] Nafisa Hoodbhoy, 'India Makes it Easier to Charge Citizens With Alleged Ties to IS', *Voice of America*, August 8, 2019, https://www.voanews.com/a/extremism-

1 April—Presumably in preparation for their suicide attack, Ilham and Inshaf transferred their shares in Ishan Spice Company to their younger brother, Mohamed Ibrahim Ismail Ahamed, through a deed of gift. The would-be suicide bombers were also said to have approached their wives to convince them to commit suicide (along with their children). While Ilham reportedly managed to convince his wife, Inshaf failed to do so.

4 April—SIS Director Nilantha Jayawardena was said to have been informed by an Indian intelligence officer about an impending attack by Zahran and his group. This included information on targets, methods of attack, and group members. The message was reportedly forwarded to pertinent officers in the Q division; then, the SIS director sent a team to the eastern province to investigate the matter.

5 April—According to accounts, India's Research and Analysis Wing representative confirmed the information received by the SIS director from the Indian Intelligence Bureau on 4 April. It was said that the Q division's deputy director sent a report to the SIS director that Zahran, Rilwan, and Shahid had been identified to be hiding in Oluvil, Akkaraipattu. Rilwan was said to have continued visiting his family in Arayampathy while in hiding.

7 April—A letter was reportedly sent by the SIS director to the CNI, which included a copy of the intelligence received by the Indian Intelligence Bureau representative. The subject of the letter was said to have been 'information of an alleged plan of attack'. Meanwhile, an Indian delegation led by the then Indian Defence Secretary Sanjay Mitra visited Sri Lanka to attend the Indo-Sri Lanka defence dialogue. He stayed at Taj Samudra, a five-star hotel that had been selected for attack by the IS Sri Lanka branch.

---

watch_india-makes-it-easier-charge-citizens-alleged-ties/6173455.html.

8 April—Then CNI Director Sisira Mendis reportedly discussed the contents of the SIS' letter with then Defence Secretary Hemasiri Fernando before moving to discuss the matter at the intelligence coordinating meeting scheduled on 9 April. According to accounts, during this time, the investigation team returned from the eastern province and reported to the SIS director.

9 April—Two out of the four suspects found in Wanathawilluwa in January were reportedly released by order of President Sirisena in his capacity as Defence Minister. When questioned during the investigations after the Easter attack, accounts said that President Sirisena maintained that the officers who submitted the document for his signature must take responsibility for it.

9–10 April—Defence Secretary Hemasiri Fernando, SIS Director Nilantha Jayawardena, and CNI Director Sisira Mendis reportedly agreed that the Indian intelligence received was not discussed in the intelligence coordinating meeting. The report by the investigation team identified several IS members and the planned suicide terrorist attack in Sri Lanka targeting important churches. This information was said to have been shared by the SIS director with IGP and other pertinent officials and was noted by the CTID director for action. However, it was said that this was not forwarded to the Presidential Security Division (PSD).[18]

10 April—The threat assessment report sent to the DIG by the SIS director was said to have mentioned there were no threats—in the form of terrorists, extremists, or other groups—to President Sirisena's Batticaloa tour on 12 April. Although he reportedly failed to mention the information from the Indian Intelligence Bureau received on 4 April, the

[18] Bentota Unnanse, 'Easter Sunday bombings and spy agencies in Sri Lanka – Part II', *Daily Financial Times,* June 22, 2019, https://www.ft.lk/opinion/Easter-Sunday-bombings-and-spy-agencies-in-Sri-Lanka-%E2%80%93-Part-II/14-680496.

SIS director did refer to Zahran's Facebook uploads, which talked about the destruction of non-Islamic followers or *kafirs* for the protection of Islam.

During this time, Senior Deputy Inspector General (SDIG) M.R. Latheef, commandant of the Special Task Force (STF), reportedly spoke over the phone with two officials of the Indian High Commission. These were said to have been Intelligence Bureau DIG Santhosh Varma and Security OIC Col Ravindran. According to accounts, they discussed security arrangements for the Indian High Commission and India House in response to the 9 April letter by Indian authorities warning of an attack.

12–16 April—President Sirisena toured Batticaloa before proceeding to India, and thereafter to Singapore with the intention of returning to Sri Lanka on 21 April.

16 April—In preparation for the Easter Sunday attack, the IS Sri Lanka branch conducted a dry run where master bomb maker, Hashtoon, was said to have tested an Improvised Explosive Device (IED) on a scooter in Kattankudy.

17 April—The SIS director was reportedly notified of the 16 April motorcycle blast. Meanwhile, Inshaf, who was assigned to strike Cinnamon Grand, booked rooms at the Kingsbury and Shangri-La hotels in Colombo for the bombers to stay the night before the attack. According to accounts, he also obtained Rs. 34 million from his company, Colossus (Pvt.) Ltd, through his firm's accountant, to pay their families. All assigned bombers were said to have cased their targeted hotels too.

18 April—The PSD DIG reportedly discussed security matters related to President Sirisena with the SIS. It was said that no mention was made of the 4 April threat information, but the

delegation was informed of the NTJ's recent extremist statements and murderous intent. Meanwhile, the SIS director was said to have informed pertinent officials and government agencies about the progress of investigations on the 16 April motorcycle blast. This included the involvement of Zahran and his associates as well as the danger posed by the NTJ and its members. However, according to accounts, local police at the location where the blast occurred were unaware of the intelligence report's content, which noted that the IS was preparing to mount an attack.[19]

19 April—Zahran and his chief financier Ilham visited and mounted surveillance on the Shangri-La Hotel.

20 April—While the IS Sri Lanka branch was preparing its attack, both Indian and Sri Lankan security and intelligence services reportedly tried to get law enforcement authorities to pre-empt the attack or neutralize the threat. However, it was said that neither the military nor the STF was deployed. Instructions to strengthen the security around churches, increase road barriers, conduct raids, and alert necessary teams were believed to have neither been executed nor followed up on too.

According to accounts, all suicide bombers—except for the sole female, Fathima Jiffry—gathered at Span Tower in Mount Lavinia, which the IS operator Reporter Niyaz rented. While Zahran delivered the farewell pledge, the bombers renewed their pledge of allegiance to Abu Bakr al-Baghdadi. Hashtoon recorded the proceedings.

After this, these suicide bombers began checking into the hotels: Mohamed Assam Mohamed Mubarak alias Mubarak at

---

[19] Chandani Kirinde, 'EP Senior DIG in the dark about NTJ activity intelligence reports', *Daily Financial Times,* July 11, 2019, https://www.ft.lk/news/EP-Senior-DIG-in-the-dark-about-NTJ-activity-intelligence-reports/56-681767.

Kingsbury Hotel, Zahran and Ilham at Shangri-La Hotel, Inshaf, under the name Mohamed Assam Mohamed Mubarak, at the Cinnamon Grand Hotel, and Jameel at the Taj Samudra Hotel. It was said that Hashtoon travelled to Negombo and occupied the IS safehouse at Katuwapitiya while Azath travelled to Batticaloa through the night.

21 April—The SIS director reportedly received information from the Indian Intelligence Bureau representative that attacks would be carried out between 6 a.m. and 10 a.m. that day. A Methodist Church in Colombo was mentioned as a target of the operation. It was said that these details were passed on to the western province's SDIG, the Defence Secretary, and the IGP.

Mubarak detonated his bomb at the Kingsbury Hotel's Harbor Court restaurant at 8.47 a.m. where reportedly nine died (including eight foreigners) and twenty-three were maimed and injured (including seven foreigners).

Zahran detonated his bomb at the Shangri-La Hotel's Table One restaurant on the third floor at 8.54 a.m. Ilham detonated his bomb by the lift lobby of the third floor—killing, maiming, and injuring those fleeing the restaurant. According to accounts, the blast resulted in the death of thirty-three persons (including twenty-two foreigners) and injured thirty-four persons (including twelve foreigners).

Inshaf detonated his bomb at the Cinnamon Grand Hotel's Taprobane restaurant at 8.50 a.m. Twenty-one died (including twelve foreigners) and twenty were maimed and injured (including nine foreigners).

Hashtoon detonated his bomb at St Sebastian's Church at 8.47 a.m., resulting in 115 deaths and 302 casualties.

Alawdeen Ahamed Muaath detonated his bomb at St Anthony's Church at 8.45 a.m. where fifty-seven died and 145 were maimed and injured.

Mohamed Nazar Mohamed Azath detonated the bomb at Zion Church at 9.02 a.m. This resulted in thirty-one deaths (the majority being children) and sixty-seven casualties.

Jameel attempted to set off a bomb at Taj Samudra Hotel at 8.51 a.m. but failed and checked into the New Tropical Inn, where the blast occurred at 1.20 p.m., resulting in two deaths and one injured. He left the hotel when he was not successful.

Multiple explosions occurred at Mahawila Gardens, which was Inshf and Ilham's parental residence. Two explosions occurred at 2.25 p.m. and 2.27 p.m. in Ilham's bedroom, resulting in one injury and the deaths of three officers, Ilham's wife Fathima Jiffry, who was pregnant, and their children.

22 April—Then President Sirisena appointed a Presidential Committee, which was reportedly headed by Justice Vijith Malalgoda, to investigate the bombings.[20] At the same time, the booby-trapped van at St Anthony's Church, which Muaath had arrived in, was said to have been brought to SDIG Latheef's attention. After evacuating the surrounding areas, the STF conducted a controlled detonation.

23 April—IS claimed responsibility for the attacks through three written statements and a fifty-nine-second video.

24 April—While investigations on the bombings were underway, police reportedly discovered a paint-firm-turned-safehouse in the

[20] Centre for Society and Religion, 'Commission Report Summary', *Easter Attack Info*, accessed March 6, 2023, https://easterattack.info/commission-report-summery/.

Panadura suburb south of Colombo, where 240 empty packets of quarter-inch steel balls, mobile phones, and different vehicle license plates were recovered. It was said that Riyaz Mohammad, distribution manager at the paint firm, confirmed that Hashtoon stayed at the safehouse and regularly drove the rest of the group around.[21]

25 April—According to accounts, detonators wrapped in a parcel were discovered in Nuwara Eliya near Kandy. Meanwhile, President Sirisena and Prime Minister Wickremesinghe received major backlash from the public, who reportedly wanted security forces to act against the IS operatives and supporters. It was said that security forces took the lead and informed President Sirisena that around seventy out of 130–140 IS suspects were arrested. The intelligence community—particularly the SIS and DMI—reportedly provided the IS operators and supporters lists to the CID and the CTID for arrest. Hitherto, the NSC was said to have still been reluctant to respond to threats of Muslim extremism while the military and intelligence supported the police dismantling of the JMI. Hemasiri Fernando also ceased his office as Defence Secretary.

26 April—In Sainthamaruthu, Zahran's family and the widows of two suicide bombers committed mass suicide. The explosion also killed Zahran's son, parents, two brothers, their spouses and children, one sister, her husband, and their children. Zahran's widow, Hadiya, and their daughter survived the explosion and were rescued by security forces.

---

[21] Robert Mendick, Bill Gardner, and Ben Farmer, 'Revealed: Student days of Sri Lanka bomb plotter at UK university', *The Telegraph,* April 24, 2019, https://www.telegraph.co.uk/news/2019/04/24/abdul-lathief-jameel-mohamed-sri-lanka-suicide-bomber/.

27 April—President Sirisena reportedly banned the NTJ and the splinter radical group JMI following the Easter Sunday bombings.

29 April—In an eighteen-minute video and audio clip released via the IS Telegram channels, Abu Bakr al-Baghdadi made his first video appearance since the height of the IS power in July 2014.[22] He congratulated the group on the attacks while seemingly gloating that 'Americans and Europeans' were among the casualties. According to the recording, he portrayed the attacks as vengeance, particularly for their brothers in Baghouz. The audio further mentioned the global presence of the IS, naming affiliates in Sri Lanka, Mali, Burkina Faso, Turkey, the Democratic Republic of the Congo, Khorasan, Tunisia, and Saudi Arabia. He also told fighters to prepare for a long war and to fight a war of attrition to drain the enemy's capabilities.[23]

Meanwhile, President Sirisena reportedly appointed former army commander Gen. S.H.S. Kottegoda as the new Defence Secretary and DIG C.D. Wickramaratne as Acting IGP. It was said that President Sirisena consulted former defence secretary Gotabhaya Rajapaksa in appointing Gen. Kottegoda. On the other hand, after IGP Pujith Jayasundara refused to resign, President Sirisena was said to have sent him on compulsory retirement amid growing public outrage over the government's failure to act on intelligence reports regarding the attacks.

1 May—Weapons were discovered on the east coast of Eravur.

---

[22] 'Isis chief Abu Bakr al-Baghdadi appears in first video', *BBC,* July 5, 2014, https://www.bbc.com/news/world-middle-east-28177848.

[23] Mina al-Lami, 'Analysis: What al-Baghdadi's appearance tells us about Islamic State plans', *BBC Monitoring,* April 30, 2019, https://monitoring.bbc.co.uk/product/c200s8zz.

5 May—Violence erupted between Negombo's Christians and Muslims. Mob attacks were reportedly carried out on Muslim shops and residences despite a curfew being imposed. The intense anger against Muslims was said to have been diffused by the Archbishop of Sri Lanka, Malcolm Cardinal Ranjith, who vehemently condemned the attacks and simultaneously called for peace and calm, making a distinction between 'brothers' in the Muslim community and the attackers.

12 May—Sporadic violence erupted along the Catholic belt despite the declaration of emergency, deployment of security forces, and the Cardinal's call for calm. In Chilaw, riots erupted between Catholics and Muslims after Sinhalese and Tamil mobs allegedly called to boycott Muslim shops. Muslim face coverings associated with foreign influences were reportedly banned under emergency laws that also empowered police and military to arrest people without warrants and detain them for long periods.

13 May—Anti-Muslim riots broke out in two provinces, with Sinhala and Tamil mobs reportedly on a rampage. Muslim properties were attacked in various localities within the Kurunegala district as well as Minuwangoda town in the Gampaha district. It was believed that the erosion of public trust was amplified when the public found out that all 225 parliamentarians were informed of the pending attack. According to accounts, the angry public wanted them, along with President Sirisena and Prime Minister Wickremesinghe, to step down for failing in their duty to protect the citizens and foreign guests.

14 May—Members of Parliament reportedly presented a proposal to the Sectoral Oversight Committee on National Security (SOC) on the manner in which the Easter Sunday attack occurred, the need for immediate changes in the existing core legal framework to remedy the problematic and chaotic situation that built up,

and to prevent jeopardizing the country's national security even further. After convening with members and non-members, it was said that Committee Chairman Malith Jayathilake met with ministries, departments, and other state and non-state institutions. He apparently concluded that national security should prevail above all other priorities.[24]

22 May–20 September—The Sri Lankan Parliament, through a resolution, reportedly appointed a Parliamentary Select Committee (PSC) mandated with investigating the circumstances surrounding or connected to the Easter attacks, dissemination of information between pertinent agencies, and whether adequate measures were taken to prevent and/or mitigate the attacks. It was also mandated to investigate deficiencies in the state machinery, other factors that contributed to the attacks, the validity of allegations levelled against any member of parliament, governors, or any other persons, and what action should be taken to prevent such attacks in the future. In addition to summoning board members to testify before the PSC, it was said that the board's report was also handed over to the PSC chairman. The PSC was said to have also questioned the Special Presidential Commission of Inquiry (PCoI). PSC's final sitting was on 20 September.[25]

23 May—BBS General Secretary Galagodaththe Gnanasara Thero received a presidential pardon and was released from Welikada prison. Reportedly notorious for his provocative rhetoric against Muslims, he was said to have been arrested on the contempt of

---

[24] Sectoral Oversight Committee on National Security, *Report of the Proposals for Formulation and Implementation of relevant laws required to ensure National security that will eliminate New Terrorism and extremism by strengthening friendship among Races and Religions*, February 19, 2020, https://www.parliament.lk/uploads/comreports/1582610584075624.pdf.

[25] Select Committee of Parliament, *Report.*

court charges in August 2018 and had received a six-year term, to be served concurrently.

31 May—After paying homage to the Temple of the Tooth Relic, Opposition lawmaker Athuraliye Rathana Thero reportedly held a 'death fast' to demand the removal of Industries Minister Rishad Badurdeen and eastern and western provincial governors M.L.A.M. Hizbullah and Azath Salley, both of whom were under the National Unity Alliance. Echoing similar demands, Gnanasara Thero was said to have joined Rathana in stating that he would launch a national protest unless Muslim leaders were sacked by noon on Monday, 3 June.

3 June—Nine Muslim ministers, deputy ministers, and state ministers reportedly resigned. Eleven of the nineteen Muslims in the 225-member Parliament were said to have held cabinet, state, deputy ministerial, and governor positions. While retaining their parliamentary seats, Muslim lawmakers were said to have resigned from their portfolios for a month to accommodate investigations into allegations that some supported the Easter attackers. It was, apparently, the first time since independence in 1948 that the government had no Muslim representatives. It was said that, after a month, they rejoined the government, and investigations revealed that none of them were involved in the attacks.

10 June—Justice Vijith Malalgoda, who also led the Special Board of Inquiry (SBI) Appointed to Inquiry into the Series of Incidents Related to the Explosions that Occurred at Several Places in the Island on 21 April 2019 with former IGP N.K. Ilangakoon and former law and order ministry secretary Padmasiri Jayamanne submitted their report on the bombings.

Late June 2019—A stash of arms and explosives were reportedly recovered by Sri Lankan police in Kattankudy. According to accounts, among those recovered were some 300 gelignite sticks, 1,000 detonators, and nearly 500 T-56 live ammunition. The search operation was said to have been based on information from Mohamed Milhan, one of five suspects deported from Saudi Arabia earlier in June.

11 July—Multiple searches were reportedly carried out by the NIA at seven locations in Tamil Nadu over a suspected link between an IS cell in Coimbatore and Sri Lanka. With the IS ideology spreading and crystallizing, IS cells, networks and groups emerged. This led to the arrest of thirty-two-year-old Mohamed Azarudeen, owner of a tour and travel company in Coimbatore. Azarudeen was said to have been Facebook friends with Zahran, and had also been sharing radical content attributed to Zahran over social media. He also ran a Facebook page 'KhilafahGFX', which had IS propaganda.[26]

25 August—SLJI leader Rasheed Hajjul Akbar was arrested and detained by the Colombo Crime Division (CCD).

22 September—As a more comprehensive investigation was needed, President Sirisena reportedly appointed a PCoI to investigate further and inquire into the Easter Sunday attacks. The PCoI had many mandates, which included receiving public complaints, information, and other materials against public servants/officers, organizations/institutions, or any other persons alleged to have direct or indirect connections to the bombings. It was also mandated to identify acts demanding necessary investigations/inquiries or proceedings from pertinent law enforcement authorities or statutory bodies, make

[26] Kamaljit Kaur Sandhu, 'Islamic State link: NIA arrests TN man who befriended Sri Lanka bomber on Facebook in Coimbatore raids', *India Today,* June 13, 2019, https://www.indiatoday.in/india/story/islamic-state-link-nia-arrests-tn-man-who-friended-sri-lanka-bomber-on-facebook-in-coimbatore-raids-1547696-2019-06-12.

recommendations to rehabilitate or assist aggrieved parties, ensure the safety of the public, and prevent the recurrence of and possible damage to national security and unity by acts of terrorism and extremism.[27]

18 November—President Sirisena stepped down as President and Defence Minister. Gotabhaya Rajapaksa, the former defence secretary who ended the fight against LTTE, campaigned on a national security vote and, with a two-thirds majority, was appointed the eighth Executive President of Sri Lanka.

21 November—Prime Minister Wickremesinghe stepped down from office. He was succeeded by Mahinda Rajapaksa, a former president of Sri Lanka.

2020

February 2020—A counterterrorism operation in Russia reportedly dismantled a Tabligh Jamaat terrorist cell. Seven suspects, both Russian and Central Asian, were arrested. Meanwhile, on 19 February, President Gotabhaya Rajapaksa was said to have advised the NSC to implement the recommendations laid out in the previous government's 'Report of the Proposals for Formulation and Implementation of Relevant Laws Required to Ensure National Security that will Eliminate New Terrorism and Extremism by Strengthening Friendship Among Races and Religions'.[28]

12 March–13 May—The PCoI's work was paused due to the COVID-19 outbreak.

---

[27] The Presidential Commission of Inquiry to Investigate and Inquire into and Report or Take Necessary Action on the Bomb Attacks on 21 April 2019, confidential government report, January 31, 2021.

[28] Sectoral Oversight Committee, *Report.*

2 June–17 July—The AG reportedly appointed a committee of officers to hold a preliminary investigation on the delay in tendering advice on the EER/08/2017 file about Zahran. It was said that their findings recommended that DSG Azad Navavi and State Counsel Azeez should be dealt with disciplinary action under the Establishments Code.

15 August—PCoI visited St Anthony's Church and St Sebastian's Church—two of the sites that were bombed during the Easter attacks.

27 October–12 November—PCoI's work was paused due to mandatory quarantine after an officer attached to the investigating unit reportedly contracted COVID-19.

October 2020—According to accounts, Ahmed Thalib Lukman Thalib and his son Ismail were arrested by the Qatar government for aiding and abetting terrorism.

2021–2022

16 March 2021—IS spokesperson, Abu Hasan Muhajir, reportedly called for attacks worldwide in retaliation to the US-led coalition campaign in Syria against IS.

17 October 2021—During a special webinar organized by the Australia-Sri Lanka Forum for Justice for the Easter Sunday Victims, Archbishop Malcolm Cardinal Ranjith was said to have stated that President Gotabaya Rajapaksa informed him that acting on all the recommendations of the Easter Sunday commission would cost him his popularity.

15 December 2021—At a press conference organized by the presidential media division, Defence Secretary Gen. Kamal Gunaratna reportedly denied allegations made against President

Gotabaya Rajapaksa that accused him of being the 'mastermind' of the Easter Sunday bombings.

4 February 2022—It was said that Malcolm Cardinal Ranjith boycotted the seventy-fourth Independence Day celebration, claiming there was no justice for Easter attack victims and calling for regime change.[29]

21 April 2022—Marking the third-year remembrance of the Easter Sunday attack, Malcolm Cardinal Ranjith was said to have condemned the bombings and alleged it was a plot backed by military intelligence officials for Gotabaya Rajapaksa's ascendence to power. According to accounts, he also claimed that Zahran and his band of attackers were known to be in the pay of the military intelligence.

14 July 2022—President Gotabaya Rajapaksa reportedly resigned following protests that prompted him to flee Sri Lanka. Protesters were said to have attacked the President's House and the presidential secretariat and burnt the private residence of Prime Minister Ranil Wickremesinghe. The protests, presumably driven by the fuel shortages, power cuts, and lack of essential commodities, were assumed to result from the economic crisis precipitated by the Easter attack, the COVID-19 pandemic, corruption, and financial mismanagement. It was believed that the Opposition, both mainstream and fringe, took the opportunity to destabilize the constitutionally elected government. It was said and alleged that the Catholic church, Muslim groups, and Tamil separatists played a frontline role in participating and supporting the protests.

[29] Amani Nilar, 'Cardinal to boycott Independence Day celebrations', *Newsfirst Sri Lanka,* February 3, 2022, https://www.newsfirst.lk/2022/02/03/cardinal-to-boycott-independence-day-celebrations/.

24 July 2022—The new President Ranil Wickremesinghe reportedly made an official request to the UK government seeking assistance from UK law enforcement authorities to investigate the Easter Sunday attack.

31 July 2022—At the festive mass held to mark the annual feast of St James Church in Mutuwal, Malcolm Cardinal Ranjith reportedly claimed that the truth behind the Easter Sunday attacks had been swept under the rug because powerful people in the country were behind them. He further alleged that those who were instrumental in setting off the bombs were still engaged in politics and worked as police officers.

20 December 2022—*Voice of Khurasan*, the official magazine of IS' south Asia province, was said to have featured Zahran as 'the Amir of the Istishhadi knights', or prince of the martyrdom knights, and hailed IS' Easter Sunday attack.

12 January 2023—Sri Lanka's Supreme Court reportedly ordered former president Maithripala Sirisena to pay Rs. 100 million (US$ 850,000) from personal funds to the victims' fund. Ruling on a petition filed by the families of the victims as well as church leaders and activists, Sirisena and four officials were ordered to pay compensation for failing to prevent the attacks.

'The face of terror is not the true faith of Islam. That's not what Islam is all about. Islam is peace. These terrorists don't represent peace. They represent evil and war.'

—Former US President George W. Bush

Introduction

Global Expansion

'The caliphate is gone as of tonight,' said an optimistic US President Donald J. Trump on 21 March 2019.[30] However, exactly a month following the collapse of IS' last territorial stronghold in Baghouz, the 'soldiers of the caliphate' would unexpectedly and emphatically strike with a vengeance in Sri Lanka. The Easter Sunday massacre on 21 April 2019, which involved simultaneous suicide attacks on several luxury hotels and churches around Sri Lanka's capital Colombo, demonstrated the global expansion of IS. The world's most dangerous terrorist movement, known as the 'State' among its followers, unleashed a new wave of global terrorism, extremism, and exclusivism in the country. Outside its heartland of Iraq and Syria, the Easter attack remains one of IS' most lethal attacks to date. Conducted 5,199 km away from Syria, the attack portrayed not only its global reach but the changing complexion of the threat. Mounted by adherents of IS, the attack is a critical milestone in the emerging global threat of transnational terrorism.

The world celebrating the fall of Baghouz and IS was short-lived. IS changed its strategy and re-emerged with a shift from direct and open military confrontation to stealth planning and the

[30] Deb Riechman, 'Trump says IS territory in Syria nearly eliminated', *Associated Press,* March 21, 2019, https://apnews.com/0afa69e5a83a416eb3e3f839fb7badb4.

use of terror. To drive its campaign of revenge and retaliation, IS memorialized the final fight in Baghouz as the 'holocaust by the crusaders'.[31] In the tent city of Baghouz, the Kurdish-led Syrian Democratic Forces (SDF)—supported by American, British, and French airstrikes as well as artillery, special forces, and intelligence operatives—fought from 9 February–23 March 2019. The relentless battle between 17,000 coalition forces and 5,000 IS fighters raged day and night. After precision strikes decapitated high-value targets and firebombed IS positions, coalition forces conducted a series of ground assaults, which included breaching the IS human shield. The mangled bodies of beheaded captives and executed hostages were found in mass graves. Among the victims were Yazidis, a beautiful and ancient people the IS had systematically killed to eliminate non-Islamic influences. The IS' rule up until that point had also been characterized by grotesque public killings, whole-scale slaughter, and sexual enslavement. The besieged fighters, believing they would go to heaven, mounted waves of suicide attacks to defend their last enclave. Their last message to all Muslims was 'to rise against the crusaders and take revenge for your religion'.[32] Thousands of fighters, their families, and civilians perished in the fierce dusk-to-dawn fighting. Retreating along the valley of the Euphrates River to fight another day were hundreds of fighters including the core and penultimate leaders of the IS.

A jubilant President Trump, referring to the IS, tweeted, 'There is nothing to admire about them, they will always try to show a glimmer of vicious hope, but they are losers and barely breathing. Think about that before you destroy your lives and the lives of

[31] 'SDF says assault on ISIS pocket almost over', *Asharq al-Awsat*, March 12, 2019, https://english.aawsat.com//home/article/1630801/sdf-says-assault-isis-pocket-almost-over.

[32] 'SDF says assault on ISIS pocket almost over'.

your family!'[33] Having occupied half of Syria and a third of Iraq in 2014, the IS had become a shadow of itself in its heartland by 2019. With Iraqi, Syrian, and coalition strikes, the battlespace of the IS steadfastly shrunk in Iraq and Syria. While retaining its ideology, the IS morphed from a conventional and semi-conventional force into an insurgent one able to hide, fight, and survive as a terrorist movement in the population. After suffering a decisive military defeat, the IS' adherents entered a protracted phase of unconventional warfare in Iraq and Syria. However, the most threatening aspect is the global expansion of the IS where its potent ideas and practices are replicated globally. The IS is decentralizing its ideological and operational capabilities, creating provinces, groups, networks, cells, and personalities worldwide. With the caliphate receding, a new breed of fighters and terrorists are emerging from the shadows and strike by exploiting gaps and loopholes in national and international security.

Cascading Attacks

Since the proclamation of the caliphate on 29 June 2014, the IS emphasized attacking Christians and their houses of worship. In the IS heartland of Iraq and Syria, and in the 120 countries where foreign fighters originated, the IS directed and inspired a series of attacks against non-Muslims, especially Christians. In fact, before the Easter Sunday bombings, the world also witnessed a global surge of strikes against Christian houses of worship, including attacks in Nigeria in 2015, Egypt in 2016, Pakistan in 2017, Indonesia in 2018, and the Philippines in 2019.

[33] Matt Bradley, 'Battle for Baghouz: White House declares victory over ISIS in Syria, but desperation remains', *NBC News*, March 23, 2019, https://www.nbcnews.com/news/world/battle-baghouz-white-house-declares-victory-over-isis-syria-desperation-n986246.

Some of them attracted global headlines, but the idea that the threat had globalized did not adequately register among national and international security planners, nor did it prompt them to take pre-emptive action. As an effort to disrupt the cascading effect, a multipronged preventive and disruptive strategy was needed—with the most fundamental action being to protect churches and their congregations.

In Sri Lanka, the people were influenced by the island mentality. It seemed that the emerging threat flew in the face of authorities, and government leaders overlooked security concerns. With every major IS attack, the target country changed overnight, and some communities would turn suspicious of their fellow Muslims. Even within the Muslim community, some mainstream Muslims started to suspect, demonize, and alienate conservative Muslims. There was a spike in Islamophobia, even in Indonesia—the most populous Muslim country in the world—where there were instances of Muslims attacking *niqab*-wearing women and men with long beards, questioning their version of preached and practiced Islam.

A Critical Milestone

Prior to the Easter attack, Sri Lanka had no history of Islamist-linked terrorist violence. Distant from the glare of the international media, IS followers in Sri Lanka meticulously planned to stage off-the-battlefield strikes throughout Sri Lanka's twenty-five districts. They were religious zealots in pursuit of 'pure Islam'. Although they lived on Sri Lankan soil, they isolated themselves from most Sri Lankans including the domestic Muslim populace who lived harmoniously with other communities. They clustered, formed enclaves, and refused to integrate.

With neither allegiance to the head of state nor loyalty to the land of their birth, they opposed the Sri Lankan ideal of coexistence. Having abandoned the Sri Lankan Muslim heritage, they embraced the IS ideology, self-labelling themselves with extremist jargon such as the 'slaves of God'. Just like the fighters in Iraq and Syria, they pledged their loyalty to Abu Bakr al-Baghdadi, their self-proclaimed caliph. They took guidance from God's representative on earth, the caliph, and instruction from his representative in Sri Lanka, Zahran Hashim, a charismatic cleric and the IS Sri Lanka branch leader. Obeying God, caliph, and *amir*—the Arabic term for 'prince' used to address Zahran—the followers in Sri Lanka prepared for killing, maiming, and destruction in their homeland.

With the declaration of a caliphate in 2014, the IS proclaimed sovereignty over Muslims worldwide. Of 1.8 billion adherents, 60,000 Muslim recruits and family members migrated to Iraq and Syria under the auspices of serving Allah or God and living under His law or sharia as opposed to man-made law—that is, democracy. Like most who join religious movements and turn violent, it was more piety than personal gain that motivated these Sri Lankan Muslims to travel to the caliphate's heartland while their associates and friends remained in Sri Lanka to serve Allah. Both those who relocated and those who stayed in Sri Lanka wanted to fight the enemies of God (Allah), his faith (Islam), and the faithful (Muslims).

To project their influence in faraway theatres, the IS co-opted their indoctrinated co-religionists. The IS capacitated them to organize to fight against their enemies in their homeland. The convincing power of the narrative was so great that the ideologically indoctrinated were willing to kill their fellow citizens and end their own lives as well. Having clandestinely established a branch in Sri Lanka, the IS directing figures primed their followers to strike non-Muslims—especially Christians, who, for centuries, maintained cordial relations with the country's Muslim, Hindu, and Buddhist communities. Both the IS in Sri Lanka and its parent movement identified Christians, Christianity, and churches with the West. As such, Sri Lankan Christians were identified as primary targets over Buddhists and Hindus, the two largest religious majorities.

The Easter attack was not just driven by domestic compulsions but also, and perhaps mainly, by international drivers—including the recent rise of the IS and Sri Lanka's non-membership in the 'Global Coalition to Defeat ISIS'.[34] Despite being a multicultural nation, the Muslims in Sri Lanka had hitherto suffered from the LTTE, the terrorist group that popularized suicide terrorism globally. Considered the most dangerous terrorist group in the world before the advent of the IS, the LTTE ethnically cleansed Muslims in the north and massacred Muslims in the east.[35] Later on, IS would likewise not spare Sri Lanka; exploiting the vulnerabilities in its security and taking advantage of the turmoil to bring harm to the country.

Isolated incidents occasionally led to communal clashes between different religious communities, but these were never at the scale and level of the IS' attacks. Eventually, as mentioned, the IS would inspire its Sri Lanka branch to attack hotels housing Westerners and Christian and Catholic churches. This demonstrated the international dimension of the attack. To the rage of terror by the IS, no country was immune—the globe was their operating theatre.

Island-Wide Attacks

The IS started to plan for their high-impact attack in Sri Lanka a year earlier. To create widespread panic, fear, and rioting, elaborate

---

[34] US Department of State, Bureau of Counterterrorism, *Country Reports on Terrorism 2019: Sri Lanka,* June 24, 2020, https://www.state.gov/reports/country-reports-on-terrorism-2019/sri-lanka/.

[35] The Federal Bureau of Investigation, *Taming the Tamil Tigers, From Here in the US*, FBI, October 1, 2008, https://archives.fbi.gov/archives/news/stories/2008/january/tamil_tigers011008.

preparations were made to mount coordinated simultaneous attacks in the country's twenty-five districts. However, with the CID detecting an IS arms cache in Wanathawilluwa in western Sri Lanka on 16 January 2019, the IS' capacity to conduct island-wide attacks was vastly disrupted. Nonetheless, the IS was able to rely on their caches in other safehouses throughout the country and rapidly recovered to mount the bombings. Had the police investigators not recovered the 110 kg of explosives, ninety-nine detonators, six 35 kg cans of nitric acid, and nine urea bags in January, Zahran would have carried out an even greater attack. This showed the massive capacity of a team of dedicated followers to inflict mass terror, even without formal training and battlefield experience. They learnt through experimentation, trial-and-error, and by reviewing online bomb-making instruction manuals and videos.

Two pivotal events motivated the decision to target hotels and churches. First, the ferocious fight in Baghouz in January 2019, which killed several hundred IS fighters, including Sri Lankan fighters. Second, Muslims were massacred in two mosques in New Zealand by a right-wing terrorist on 15 March 2019. The objective of this target selection was to punish the West—specifically Christian populations whom the IS viewed as antithetical to the flourishing of Islam in India and Sri Lanka. Apart from hotels and churches, the Indian High Commission in Colombo was a target too, but plans did not materialize. The IS also originally planned to target Independence Day celebrations in February 2019. After which, there would be a follow-up attack against Buddhist targets, including plans to strike the 1,700-year procession of the Temple of the Sacred Tooth Relic in August 2019. Attacking such high-profile events would have created unprecedented chaos.

However, the scale of the operation was narrowed due to constraints and challenges placed on the attackers—including Zahran himself—that limited the Sri Lanka branch from staging an island-wide attack. First, having lost communication with IS' Syrian headquarters in January 2019, operational guidance had to come from the IS Khorasan or its representative in India. Second, Zahran faced threats within the organization because of an internal dispute between him and his deputy Naufer. Finally, Zahran, initially identified as an extremist but not an imminent threat, came under close government scrutiny after authorities discovered the arms cache in Wanathawilluwa.

All these posed increased risks to the IS leadership and the planned attack. In response, Zahran decided to speed up operations and scaled-down the elaborate attack plan, limiting it to the Western and Christian targets. He also compartmentalized his operations to ensure that even if someone important was arrested or betrayed him, the entire operation would not be compromised. In doing so, he minimized the probability of detection and disruption by the government. These, as well as lack of adequate governmental action to track and dismantle the 120 IS targets that were known to be active and operating, allowed Zahran to plan, prepare, and execute the attack.

Eventually, as Easter Sunday was fast approaching, the IS Sri Lanka branch shelved the island-wide plan. Instead, they focused on conducting targeted attacks, with final targets selected in March 2019—the month preceding Easter Sunday.

Signature Attack

On the holiest day of the year for Christians, the IS Sri Lanka branch executed near-simultaneous attacks in hotels in Colombo and churches in Colombo, Negombo, and Batticaloa. The attack shocked the world, and religious and political leaders expressed their sadness. President Trump tweeted, '138 people have been killed in Sri Lanka, with more than 600 badly injured, in a terrorist attack on churches and hotels. The US offers heartfelt condolences to the great people of Sri Lanka. We stand ready to help!'[36] Standing for 'the right to worship safely', New Zealand Prime Minister Jacinda Ardern said, 'New Zealand condemns all acts of terrorism, and our resolve has only been strengthened by the attack on our soil on [15 March]. To see an attack in Sri Lanka while people were in churches and at hotels is devastating.'[37]

Staged when Sri Lanka took the top spot for the best country to visit in 2019, the bombings demonstrated the IS' capacity to clandestinely guide catastrophic attacks. It seemed that the international security and intelligence community—which included Western intelligence alliance Five Eyes—weren't unable to assess the IS threat of global expansion accurately, for many reasons. For instance, relevant information held particularly by Australian, Israeli, and Indian services were fragmented. There was no platform where services could share and exchange their findings. There were insufficient efforts to collate, analyse, and assess their respective information to develop a comprehensive picture of the surging and imminent threat.

Apart from the Indian police and local services, Sri Lanka reportedly did not receive warnings of an imminent attack from other intelligence bodies. Despite advice from the country's own forces, Sri Lankan leaders were said not to have taken relevant action or regulated the religious space in time to prevent the attack. It was believed that some politicians, particularly those influenced by the ideals of western liberal democracies, thought it best not to intervene by reforming religious institutions. Though the terrorist threat had been apparent since 2015, the coalition government (2015–2019), which was dependent on the Muslim vote, did not act swiftly enough to dismantle the pipeline that

---

[36] Telegraph Reporters, '"Easter massacre": How the world reacted to Sri Lanka terror attacks', *The Telegraph*, April 22, 2019, https://www.telegraph.co.uk/news/2019/04/21/sri-lanka-bomb-attacks-sports-stars-world-leaders-express-horror/.

[37] Telegraph Reporters, 'Easter massacre'.

produced radicals. The neglect of national security, in turn, likely led to what was deemed as enforcement authorities' and operational agencies' failure to develop high-quality intelligence. With no priority assigned to national security, the very same military forces, law enforcement authorities, and intelligence services that defeated a terrorist organization like the LTTE failed to rise to the IS challenge.

Killing Civilians

Terrorism is not new to Sri Lanka. As mentioned, Sri Lankan military, law enforcement, and intelligence services fought a thirty-year campaign against the LTTE, the only group to assassinate two world leaders, invent the suicide belt, and conduct the largest number of suicide attacks—until the genesis of the IS.[38] After disrupting its US network, Federal Bureau of Investigations (FBI) also stated that the LTTE's 'ruthless tactics have inspired terrorist networks worldwide, including al-Qaeda in Iraq'.[39] In contrast to past LTTE attacks, the IS attacks deliberately targeted westerners and Christians, two categories of targets the LTTE refrained from striking. The scale, magnitude, and intensity of violence, fear, and hate of the Easter attacks was also unprecedented.

The new wave of religion-inspired terror was significantly different from the ethnicity-inspired terror that Sri Lanka experienced before, mainly because religious-inspired terrorism twisted long-existing teachings so obscenely and grotesquely. For example, the IS' ruling on killing the elderly, women, and children was reiterated in the IS propaganda publications *Rumiyah Issue 5*, in January 2017, before the Easter attacks, and *Sawt al-Hind Issue 8*, in September 2020, after the attacks. This suggested future attacks would include these vulnerable categories. According to

[38] The Federal Bureau of Investigation, *Taming the Tamil Tigers.*

[39] The Federal Bureau of Investigation, *Taming the Tamil Tigers.*

both articles, the IS ideologue argued that non-Muslim women and children may not be deliberately targeted. However, if their deaths are unavoidable, or if the intent was to kill adult males, then said deaths were accepted as collateral damage. 'Therefore, it is permissible to kill the old men, women and children of the infidels with other infidels without any intention, provided that they become targets with the fighters for which they cannot be identified, in such case, it is permissible to kill them.'[40] Such a judgement gave latitude to the IS followers to kill, maim, and injure the elderly, women, and children, which Islam explicitly forbids.

A novel brand of global terrorism, the Easter attack was also Sri Lanka's first experience of Muslim-on-Christian mass violence. In addition to inflicting cruelty and extreme violence, the carnage wiped out entire families, causing generational loss. To date, hundreds of survivors, men, women, and children, suffer from physical injuries and continuing trauma. Their grief and community anger need to be addressed sensitively and handled carefully. Although time has diminished the rage and the sorrow, collective anger against the Muslim community persists. Segments of the Muslim community, their elders, and children, live in fear every day. Without closure or a multipronged preventive and disruptive strategy to address these consequences, the risk of another attack or further communal violence remains large.

Changing Configurations and Conflict Crucibles

Since the Easter attack, the global threat landscape witnessed the IS morphing into a transnational terrorist network and an ideological movement. As its branches and foreign fighters grow, the IS strategy no longer invites recruits to Iraq and Syria. Instead, it urges them to either stay and conduct attacks in their home

[40] 'Ruling on killing infidels, children and the elderly in war', *Sawt al-Hind*, September 18, 2020.

country or travel to other theatres and fight. The restructuring is aimed at transforming the IS from a caliphate-building organization to a global terrorist movement. With the IS globalizing, it is also regionalizing and localizing for better integration and control. The impact of mounting attacks overseas would be greater than attacks in the battlefield, with mass casualties and fatalities outside conflict zones drawing greater global attention and generating worldwide support among the IS followers.

The threat morphs—but no threat group lasts forever. Today, the global threat landscape's two key players are the IS and al-Qaeda. With the depletion of its rank and file, especially the decapitation of its top leadership, will the IS be eclipsed by its mothership, al-Qaeda, and its affiliates? Will al-Qaeda continue to compete and complement the IS in their fight for population and territorial control?

To mitigate the threat of attacks like the Easter bombings, governments should look beyond their own national interests and help stabilize conflict zones. These conflict zones from Afghanistan and Kashmir, Iraq and Syria, Somalia and Libya, Mindanao and Rakhine are crucibles that create the ideologies, fighting, suffering, internal displacement, refugee flows, and production of terrorists. Unless there is resolve from world leaders to work together, the global footprints of threat entities are likely to grow in the coming decade—and return with a greater vengeance.

Emerging Developments

After the Easter attack, the world needs a new strategy to combat two deadly global movements and to manage both radicalization and reciprocal radicalization. Without the relocation of highly motivated, trained, and skilled IS fighters from the battlefield, a remote branch of the IS was able to pull off a catastrophic attack. Unless the global terrorist threat is contained, isolated, and eliminated, the tempo of exclusivism, extremism, and terrorism will increase—precipitating strikes intermittently. Having established a presence throughout the global south, threat entities operate across borders. To keep them under check, governments and partners need to cooperate, collaborate, and build partnerships at multiple levels. As the threat is networked, governments need to build common databases, exchange personnel, conduct joint training and operations, share experiences, expertise and, resources, especially technology. This is especially with the IS infiltrating both the cyber and physical space and influencing Muslim institutions—mosques, madrasahs, associations—to subscribe to their ideology.

We are entering an era where once again religion is used to divide, demonize, and destroy communities and countries. With access to the Internet, an unregulated platform, the capacity of threat groups to connect, engage and groom ordinary people to violence is growing. Even if one percent of the population embraces extremist ideology, it can ruin peace and stability.

With the threats becoming globalized, governments need to develop multipronged, multidimensional, multiagency, multinational, and multi-jurisdictional response capabilities. To grapple with the current and future threat, governments need to develop a robust understanding of the contemporary threat and a full spectrum response. At the heart of managing the threat is working with the Muslim community, their institutions, organizations, and leaders.

Tracing the Events

In order to better understand the Easter attacks, their impact, and what can or should have been done, *Sri Lanka's Easter Sunday Massacre* will trace the genesis, threat trajectory, blowback, government response, and lessons learnt.

The book starts off with a chronology that charts significant events delineating the threat and responses that culminated in the Easter Sunday attack. This is followed by this Introduction, which identifies the general contours of the current and emerging global threat and the challenges of a global response.

The chapter discussions properly go into more intricate detail about the circumstances surrounding the attacks and their aftermath. Chapter 1 recounts the execution of the bombings based on interviews conducted with leaders and members of the IS, government investigators, and eyewitness accounts. Chapter 2 focuses on the life and eventual death of Zahran Hashim, the leader and alleged mastermind of the attacks, while Chapter 3 discusses the threat landscape in Colombo, based on field visits to mosques, interviews with Muslim leaders, and a review of law enforcement and intelligence reports. The book ends with Chapter 4, which recaps the IS threat, reviews governmental response based on interviews with the IS detainees and government specialists with expertise on threat entities, and reflects on recommendations and possible ways forward to mitigate and manage the threat in the time to come.

Four years after the Easter attacks, Sri Lanka is currently undergoing a massive economic crisis and political turmoil. It is imperative that we address pertinent issues and those arising from the current crisis as these could snowball into a nation's chaos and a country's collapse—and hopefully this book helps to do just that.

'The Easter atmosphere of hope and bloom was utterly crushed and shattered by nine suicide bombers backed by a radical ideology of hate and destruction.'[41]

—Rashane Jude Pintoe, a seventeen-year-old Catholic

[41] Rashane Jude Pintoe, 'A Rise from the Rubble: The Sri Lankan Easter Massacre', *A View into Global Affairs* (blog), April 23, 2020, https://rashanep.blogspot.com/2020/04/a-rise-from-rubble-sri-lankan-easter.html.

Chapter 1

The Anatomy of the Easter Attack

The Calm and the Storm

21 April 2019 was a beautiful day. Church linings were adorned with silver-lit candle sticks. Hotels were bustling with springtime tourists. The often ethnically segregated populace seemed harmoniously entwined, with many dressed in their Sunday best to celebrate Easter Sunday. Throughout the island, Catholics attended church services and children decorated Easter eggs. At luxury hotels, families, friends, and even Sri Lankan expatriates, international tourists, and investors sat together for sumptuous festive meals—oblivious to the horrific, needless violence that was soon to follow. The scene was perfectly set for a more insidious agenda; the unassuming social landscape juxtaposed with the subtle, sinister intentions of a select few.

To the unknowing public's shock, nine IS loyalists—eight male and one female—were to commit mass murder and spread senseless terror and chaos. The perpetrators performed an elaborate farce by masquerading as hotel guests, devout worshippers, and an innocuous housewife. In the belief of pleasing Allah, Islam, and the greater Muslim community, this errant faction of extremist predators set their sights on their prey—Westerners, Christians, and security forces; an extension of their century-old war against the West. Highly motivated by indoctrination and tightly controlled by their cult-like leader, each attacker carried a 21 kg explosives-laden backpack they would eventually detonate in target locations. Contrary to orthodox western opinion, this attack was not civilian-led, irregular, or impulsive. Its calculated, cold, and organized nature made it planned terrorism.

A cross-section of Muslims from Sri Lanka's east and west were recruited, radicalized, and poised to commit the attacks. Having abandoned the Sri Lankan way of life, the IS ideology turned them into remorseless killers willing to murder and die in the name of their beliefs. Having endured a civil war against the vicious terrorist group LTTE, Sri Lanka was not alien to ethnic divide. However, the brutality and shock-value associated with Islam-centric terrorism, especially during a religious holiday, was novel.

Retrospectively, it was apparent that the implications of the Easter attacks were two-fold. During the time of the bombings, Sri Lanka boasted a booming tourism sector, was ranked the top country in the world for travel in 2019 by Lonely Planet and was globally considered one of the safest countries in the world.[42] The negative externalities that accompanied the attacks overwhelmed the country's good fortune. The once glistening pearl of the Indian Ocean's spark was subdued by voracious acts of terrorism.

A Defining Moment

The Easter Sunday massacre was a watershed event in Sri Lankan history. Inspired by the IS, suicide bombers mounted

---

[42] Antonia Wilson, 'Sri Lanka ranked top country for travel in 2019 by Lonely Planet', *The Guardian*, October 23, 2018, https://www.theguardian.com/travel/2018/oct/23/sri-lanka-ranked-top-country-for-travel-in-2019-by-lonely-planet.

a series of coordinated attacks across the country targeting Easter Sunday church services, high-end international hotels, and security forces. Often coined by revisionists as the world's deadliest terrorist organization, the leader of The Greater IS or ISIS, Abu Bakr al-Baghdadi, claimed responsibility for the attack. Theorists and political analysts continue to contemplate the devastation of the attack, with many considering it to be the most politically and economically stunting outside Iraq and Syria. Similarly, the bombings are also colloquially classified by Christian institutions as one of the deadliest attacks on Christianity in neo-classical history.

Sri Lanka was an easy target. As reflected in nearly 350 government intelligence reports and hundreds of interviews with the IS operators, supporters, and family members, the insidious ideology of the IS crystallized into a network of terror that was facilitated by Sri Lanka's unassuming behavior. As mentioned previously, the Sri Lankan government is said to have overlooked security threats, alerts, and warnings of a catastrophic attack. Country leaders, many of whom were electorally dependent on the Muslim vote, were also reportedly hesitant and politically unable to take immediate action against radical or violent Muslims.

No terrorist attack had killed so many civilians in Sri Lanka including during its thirty-year history of extremist Sinhala insurgency and simultaneous terrorist campaign by the LTTE. The suicide attack by the IS Sri Lanka branch, led by Zahran Hashim, killed more than 200, including the bombers themselves. The attack maimed and seriously injured more than 500 persons. The count is likely to be much higher with those suffering minor injuries and psychological trauma. The table below presents a quantitative overview of locals and foreigners injured or killed during the attacks. A total of forty-two foreigners died while twenty-eight were injured, effectively classifying the event as an act of international terrorism.

Details of victims who died or got injured from the easter attacks on 2019.04.21

Place of Incident	Deaths										Injuries									
	Local					Foreign					Local					Foreign				
	Male		Female		Total	Male		Female		Total	Male		Female		Total	Male		Female		Total
	Elder	Child	Elder	Child		Elder	Child	Elder	Child		Elder	Child	Elder	Child		Elder	Child	Elder	Child	
St. Anthony's Church, Kochchikade	19	6	29	3	57	-	-	-	-	-	65	15	53	12	145	-	-	-	-	-
St. Sebastian's Church, Katuwapitiya	24	9	59	23	115	-	-	-	-	-	158	38	80	26	302	-	-	-	-	-
Kingsbury Hotel	1	-	-	-	1	8	-	-	-	8	15	-	1	-	16	6	-	1	-	7
Shangri La Hotel	6	-	5	-	11	13	3	2	4	22	15	1	6	-	22	7	2	1	2	12
Zion Church, Batticaloa	8	6	9	8	31	-	-	-	-	-	18	9	32	8	67	-	-	-	-	-
Cinnamon Grand Hotel	5	1	3	-	9	6	1	4	1	12	5	2	4	-	11	2	-	7	-	9
House in Mahawila Gardens, Dematagoda	3	3	-	-	6	-	-	-	-	-	1	-	-	-	1	-	-	-	-	-
Tropical Inn	2	-	1	-	3	-	-	-	-	-	-	-	-	-	-	-	-	-	-	-
Total	68	25	106	34	233	27	4	6	5	42	277	65	176	46	564	15	2	9	2	28

Casualties, fatalities, and injuries computed by the Sri Lankan government[43]

Although there are statistics for casualties, there is no comprehensive assessment on the impact of the attack, including the social and economic costs. Though, it goes without saying that the main pillars of the economy—namely, tourism and investments—were indeed affected.

As indicated in the graph above, foreign tourist arrivals declined from 252,033 in February 2019 and 244,328 in March 2019 to 166,975 in April 2019 and 37,000 in May 2019. However, perhaps the greatest damage was on the post-war harmonious nature of intra-state relationships, particularly between the country's religious communities. Muslims had been hitherto a model community in Sri Lanka. However, Zahran unfairly became the community's poster child, after the bombings. This, in turn, effectively shattered Sri Lanka's integrated ethnic landscape, further tearing through layers of political and social reconciliation and jeopardizing the social infrastructure with extremist fervor.

---

[43] Institute of National Security Studies Sri Lanka, 'Easter Sunday Attack Casualties', 2021.

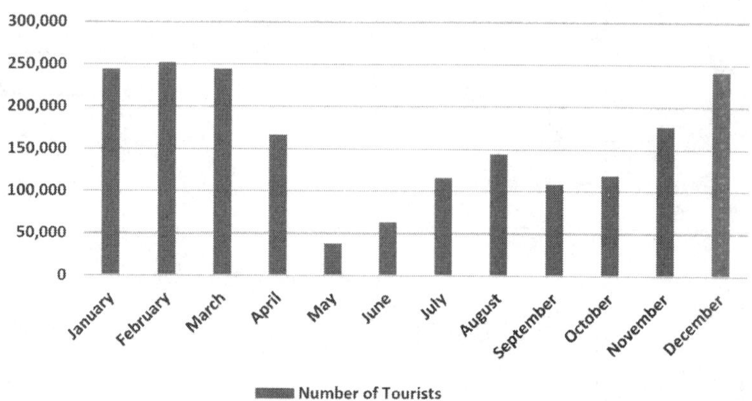

Impact on tourist arrivals in Sri Lanka by the Sri Lanka Tourism Development Authority[44]

Revenge and Fury

Neither Zahran nor his followers were ordinary criminals. They killed and destroyed not for personal gain, but as cogs orchestrated into a larger ploy; deeply influenced by fundamentalist religion and politics. Demonstrating his commitment to faith and Allah, Zahran always addressed his followers as, 'Dear Brothers in Islam and Servants of Allah!'[45] To him, Islam united them, and together they served God. In his final words, Zahran said, 'O' Muslims and servants of God! Today, we have gathered to fulfil a noble form of worship for the sake of Allah known as Istishhad. Istishhad means offering our lives for the sake of Allah.'[46]

Influenced by global and domestic developments, Zahran exploited the lax security environment in Sri Lanka to disseminate the IS ideology. In his farewell video, Zahran's motive to strike

---

[44] Sri Lanka Tourism Development Authority, *Annual Statistical Report 2019*, January 20, 2020, https://srilanka.travel/SLTDA_documents/ASR%202019.pdf.

[45] Zahran Hashim (IS Sri Lanka branch leader), 'Farewell Video', private video recording, April 20, 2019.

[46] Hashim, 'Farewell Video'.

was enshrined in his message both to his followers and enemies. To explain why he mounted 'a heroic death attack' in Sri Lanka, Zahran invoked the spirit of *istishhad* or 'martyrdom'—that is, sacrificing one's life to kill kafirs or disbelievers who were branded as the enemies of Allah, Islam, and Muslims.[47] In his video, Zahran explains the core of this ideology—Al Wala or love for Muslims, and Wal Bara or hatred for non-Muslims:

'We believers are united by ideology. We are not divided by countries, by demarcations drawn by kafirs. If a Muslim in the north is hurt, it will hurt the Muslim in the south; this is the "Al Wala" that the religion teaches. The core of our ideology, our faith is to love and hate for the sake of Allah. We don't differentiate people by country of colour; a Muslim in America is our brother, a kafir who is in Sri Lanka is our enemy. Dear brothers, the fundamental reason for us to carry out this attack is, firstly, "Al Wala"; the love we have for believers.'[48]

In the same video, Zahran also referenced the battle in Baghouz, Syria. The village was the last territorial stronghold of the IS where its fighters—including Sri Lankan fighters—were killed by western-backed forces. Zahran was in direct contact with the Sri Lankan contingent leader, Aroos, in Syria—until their communication was disrupted amid the fray in January 2019. The IS used terms like 'genocide' and 'slaughter' to describe the intense fighting and Muslim losses in conflict zones, especially Baghouz.[49] Zahran did the same. In explaining why Westerners in hotels and Christians in churches were targeted, he brought to attention 'the dogs who worship idols [that] killed the Muslims'

[47] Hashim, 'Farewell Video'.

[48] Hashim, 'Farewell Video'.

[49] IQRA' Media Foundation, 'Slaughter of the Muslims—The Mass Murders by the Crusaders in the 20th Century', August 23, 2021, 26.

in Baghouz and the killings at the 'New Zealand mosque' or the Christchurch mosque attacks—both of which were recent acts of violence against Muslims at the time. In Zahran's eyes, he lived in a zone of war. To Zahran and his followers, the Easter attack was but part of a battle to avenge the suffering of Muslims worldwide, especially in the name of 'blessed Syria'.[50]

Unlike past threat entities that recruited discreetly, IS believed in the mass radicalization of Muslims. The IS, through proponents like Zahran, exploited social media to reach out, radicalize, and recruit. Zahran's strategy was to disseminate his propaganda, crowdsource to assist in fast mobilization and identify the most impressionable and committed within the Sri Lankan populace. Afterwards, he would personally engage and build rapport with them, heighten their interest, and turn them into killers that would destroy the 'enemy'. The culmination of Zahran's decade-long prejudice, resentment, hate, and anger resulted in a violent, combustive wave of violence that Easter Sunday.

Attack Sequence

The devastating carnage took place between 8.45 a.m. and 9.12 a.m. on 21 April 2019. The suicide bombers in Sri Lanka carried out the attacks using IEDs—homemade bombs made to destroy infrastructure and incapacitate people. This type of explosive tends to have a wider shrapnel circuit and is popular with juvenile extremists for the convenience of finding the required apparatus to construct the bomb.

The attacks successfully targeted six principal targets—three Christian churches and three luxury hotels—and first responders visiting the Mahawila Gardens residence, which will be further

[50] Hashim, 'Farewell Video'.

discussed in succeeding passages. The churches and hotels and the time the bombs were set off are listed below:

1. St Anthony's Church, Kochchikade, Colombo 8.45 a.m.
2. St Sebastian's Church, Katuwapitiya, Negombo 8.45 a.m.
3. Zion Church, Batticaloa 9.05 a.m.
4. Kingsbury Hotel, Colombo 8.47 a.m.
5. Shangri-La Hotel, Colombo 8.54 a.m.
6. Cinnamon Grand Hotel, Colombo 9.12 a.m.

As touched on previously, the original attack plan of the IS Sri Lanka branch was to strike twenty targets, but the plan scaled-down considerably due to the detection of the 'Martyr Abu Shurayh al-Seylani camp' in Wanathavillu in January 2019.[51] The scaled down attack plan originally included four luxury hotels: Kingsbury Hotel, Shangri-La Hotel, Cinnamon Grand Hotel, and Taj Samudra Hotel. However, Jameel was unsuccessful in detonating the suicide backpack at the Taj Samudra in Colombo. Thus, the intended attack on the fourth hotel failed.

The IS Sri Lanka branch suicide bombers are listed below. Of the nine involved, one was a woman—Fathima Mohamed Jiffry, wife, and later widow, of Ilham, the Shangri-La bomber.

1. Alawdeen Ahamed Muaath alias Muaath, born 6 January 1997 - St Anthony's Church.
2. Muhammad Hashtoon Achchi Muhammad alias Hashtoon, born 15 February 1995 - St Sebastian's Church. Hashtoon was identified as the primary bomb maker.
3. Mohamed Nazar Mohamed Azath alias Azath, born 5 November 1985 - Zion Church, Batticaloa.

---

[51] Mohamed Ibrahim Mohamed Naufer (IS Sri Lanka branch deputy and ideologue), interview by author, Sri Lanka, March 15, 2020.

4. Mohamed Cassim Mohamed Zahran alias Zahran Hashim born, 19 July 1986 - Shangri-La Hotel.
5. Ilham Mohamed Ibrahim alias Ilham, born 31 August 1986 - Shangri-La Hotel. He was responsible for the second explosion.
6. Inshaf Ahamed Mohamed Ibrahim alias Inshaf, born 5 May 1983 - Cinnamon Grand Hotel. He was Ilham's brother.
7. Mohamed Assam Mohamed Mubarak alias Mubarak, born 29 November 1987 - Kingsbury Hotel.
8. Abdul Latheef Jameel Mohamed alias Jameel, born 18 December 1982 - Responsible for the failed Taj Samudra attack and the accidental explosion at the New Tropical Inn.
9. Fathima Mohamed Jiffry alias Jiffry, born 10 February 1992 - Mahawila Gardens, Dematagoda.

To carry out the attacks, the IS planned to deceive security forces and divert them from the scene by having Ilham register at the Shangri-La under his own name and address, which was his parental residence in Mahawila Gardens, Dematagoda. That way, security forces would attempt to track him down at the address—unaware it was a trap. Unbeknownst to them, Ilham and his wife Fathima had planned for the latter to kill the security personnel and die with their children. They did this believing they would be rewarded with a passage to heaven if they killed 'unbelievers'. Three law enforcement officers would be killed in the bomb blast at Mahawila Gardens.

Attacking Island-Wide

In preparation for mounting the island-wide attacks, Zahran conferred with Naufer, his ideologue, Sadiq, his Syrian-trained deputy military leader, and Rilwan, his brother who specialized in explosives. They initially aimed to carry out the attacks in 2020. However, the timelines shifted. The fall of Wanathavillu in January 2019 and the fragmentation of IS Sri Lanka branch in March 2019 prompted Zahran to scale down and fast-track the operation.

The quantum of explosives and precursors recovered in Wanathavillu was colossal. The base and the camp were to support operations not only in Sri Lanka, but in India and Maldives too. Named in honour of Mohamed Muhusin Sarfas Nilam, the first Sri Lankan foreign fighter to die in Syria and Iraq, the bomb-making facility in Wanathavillu was on Sri Lanka's west coast and had access to the Indian Ocean, including the Arabian Sea.

Chief Inspector Marasinghe, who raided the camp, said, 'The camp had 110 kg of urea nitrate, ready-made explosives. In addition, there were nine bags of urea each weighing 50 kg totalling 450 kg and six cans of nitric acid each weighing 35 kg totalling 210 kg. Each of the bombs used in the Easter attack weighed 500 g. The IS had the potential to manufacture 1,140 bombs with 660 kg of raw material and 110 kg of processed explosives.'[52] Considering the death toll and destruction from just the nine bombs used during the actual attacks, the impact from 1,140 bombs would have been monstrous. Despite the dismantlement of the training facility, the seizure of explosives, firearms, and ammunition, and the Naufer-Zahran split—the IS Sri Lanka branch carried on with its efforts. Although depleted physical and human resources rendered the original plan unfeasible, the threat persisted.

In the face of adversity, reality dawned. In March 2019, the changing circumstances were eventually harnessed by Zahran. His strategy was to remain lean and mean, go dark, and 'to get closer to Allah'. After the losses in Wanathavillu and breakup with

[52] M.M.N.K. Marasinghe (Sri Lanka Police CID chief inspector), interview by author, June 11, 2022.

his deputy Naufer, Zahran decided to turn ultra-secret, lead the attack, and commit suicide.

Timing of the Attack

After the detection of the Wanathavillu terrorist base camp, Zahran became the priority target of both intelligence agencies and investigative authorities. Although hitherto known, he was reportedly not actively hunted by authorities. The police seizure of weapons and explosives in Wanathavillu might have been a body blow but Zahran recovered and re-established two safehouses to hide and manufacture explosives. Nonetheless, he knew that he could be captured or killed at any moment.

Zahran's second body blow was his leadership dispute and eventual split with Naufer, which created two factions within the group. Zahran was said to have been resilient in his leadership and managed to 'recover' rapidly. Despite the division of assets, Zahran had sufficient capabilities to pull off a limited attack. Within a month of the raid on Wanathavillu, Mubarak, who coordinated the logistics, leased two safehouses in Negombo and in Panadura in February 2019. The IS bomb makers who manufactured the bombs for Easter Sunday lived and worked in these safehouses.

Having burdened Naufer with building the organization, Zahran devoted his time, resources, and energy to prepare for attacks. The IS Sri Lanka branch had built the ideological resources and physical infrastructure since its formation on 9 July 2017. An attack was being planned since at least March 2018 when its support group in Colombo built a database of churches. In stages, the support and operational infrastructure was oriented to recruit-and-radicalize, train-and-rehearse, source precursors and equipment, manufacture-and-test, and case-and-strike.

As mentioned in the Introduction, two external events in Syria and New Zealand created an impetus to hasten the attack. The decision to strike on Easter Sunday was taken immediately after the Christchurch attack on 15 March 2019, which occurred in the backdrop of the loss of Baghouz, IS' last territorial hold in Syria. This was further compounded by the anti-Muslim riots in Dharga and Digana as well as the desire to avenge the loss of life of the Sri Lankan contingent in Iraq and Syria—ultimately resulting in Zahran's 'do something' mindset and belief that Muslims should retaliate for these series of events. Against the backdrop of these losses and violence, there was no opposition to Zahran's call for revenge and retribution. Within Zahran's group, the idea of striking swiftly with a vengeance gained momentum.

Scaling Down

Impact-driven, the IS Sri Lanka branch was determined to hit the country's east, west, and centre. Would-be-suicide bomber Inshaf was dispatched by Zahran on a surveillance mission to Nuwara Eliya to source a target in the centre of the island. Inshaf travelled with his family under the guise of a vacation between 14–16 April 2019. Ultimately, however, he did not find a sufficiently large population of foreigners in any of the locations to recommend an attack there. After spending three days in Nuwara Eliya, Inshaf eventually returned to Colombo at 10 p.m. on 16 April 2019. Once back in Colombo, Ilham, the would-be Shangri-La suicide bomber, would enlist his brother Inshaf's support to attack the Cinnamon Grand Hotel. Ilham had convinced both his wife, Fathima, and Inshaf to join him in his 'journey to paradise'. Inshaf did not want his brother to go on his own, so he agreed.

Ilham and Inshaf hailed from one of the most respectable Muslim families in Sri Lanka. Their father Al-Haj Mohommed Yusuf Ibrahim alias Ibrahim Hajjiyar was Sri Lanka's richest spice trader. He was a philanthropist and it was said his generosity was known to many communities. However, unlike him, his sons Ilham and Inshaf turned into religious fanatics. Not only did they carry out the attacks on Shangri-La and Cinnamon Grand hotels, but they also became the principal financiers of the Easter attack. As they were from the capital city of Colombo, they knew to physically blend in and played a vital role in the attack planning.

Attack Plan

A catastrophic attack of the scale, magnitude, and intensity launched by the IS Sri Lanka branch required meticulous planning, preparation, and execution. An insight into the attack planning based on interviews with the perpetrators and access to their electronics reveals that the IS followed the classic attack cycle. After studying a series of suicide attacks, including those on hotels and churches in capitals and cities, Zahran developed a concept for mounting coordinated simultaneous attacks. His most trusted lieutenant, twenty-four-year-old Hashtoon, operationalized the plan supported by Ilham, the thirty-two-year-old financier. In addition to sacrificing their lives, Ilham and his thirty-five-year-old elder brother, Inshaf, provided Zahran and the group with sustained finances, technology, and a network of human resources—that is, suicide bombers.

A meticulous planner and voracious reader, Hashtoon was the de facto operations commander. With a better command of English, his passionate wife, Sara, assisted him at the onset. Having mastered his understanding and knowledge largely online, Hashtoon guided Zahran from A to Z through six steps:

1. Operational security: Every leader, member, and supporter of the IS would receive code names. Within the organization, they were forbidden from revealing their true identities, jobs, and places where they worked or lived. They would communicate using encrypted platforms such as Threema.
2. Casing targets: After surveilling three dozen targets, the feasibility of striking, relative impact, and strengths and weaknesses of security systems would be assessed.

3. Supply chain: Simultaneously, the procurement team would establish a supply chain after identifying supply sources.
4. Manufacturing explosives: After precursors and components were transferred to safehouses, the explosives would be manufactured, and bombs would be prepared.
5. Rehearsal: The bomb devices would be tested, and the bombers would practice.
6. Coordination: In the context of a complex attack that involved simultaneously striking many targets in different locations, an attack plan and strategy would be developed.

The succeeding sections below will take a closer and more comprehensive look at the rationale for and execution of these six steps, which eventually proved crucial in mounting the high-profile, high-impact attacks.

Operational Security

IS' technology chief Hashtoon advised the rank-and-file on both physical and communications security. After the March 2017 clash between NTJ members and Sufis in Kattankudy, Zahran understood that secrecy determined his personal and organizational survival. As they established capabilities to hide and clandestinely mount operations, Hashtoon established a series of protocols.

Most threat groups train their rank-and-file to protect themselves. In the case of IS Sri Lanka branch, Zahran understood this and implemented Hashtoon and financial chief Ilham's advice. Ilham introduced Threema, a Swiss-made, paid, open-source, and end-to-end encrypted instant messaging application for iOS and Android. The software is based on the privacy-by-design principles as it does not require a phone number or other personally identifiable information.

As communications security was a high priority, using Threema became mandatory for all leaders, members, and active supporters of the IS Sri Lanka branch. Hashtoon conducted classes on operational security for the group, including recruits training in Aruppola, Hambantota, and Nuwara Eliya.

The group's activities were also compartmentalized to further protect the organization. The centrally directed organization functioned in clusters of cells. Only dedicated members and supporters of the cell knew their activities. For instance, only the designated team that would attack the hotels would surveil said hotels. To maintain operational security, the IS leadership believed that all those who planned, prepared, and executed the attacks should die. That way, all organizational secrets—from the identity of operators and supporters to their assets—would be preserved. The few suicide bombers that pulled out at the last moment were said to have been threatened with death. They had to commit to secrecy, which was a promise they kept. Reportedly, Zahran also threatened his wife, Hadiya, and told her that she or any of their family would be killed if they betrayed him.

Zahran was protected twenty-four-seven. Ever since he went underground in March 2017, he always kept a firearm in his bag. He did not wish to be captured alive. Zahran was willing to fight to death. The safehouse of the IS leader was also considered top-secret and his schedule was known only to him. He constantly varied his routine. In all the safehouses he resided in, there was a security system installed by Hashtoon, and the CCTV was monitored by both Hashtoon and Sara. Sara and Hashtoon's bedroom, which served as the security monitoring room, would always be next to Zahran's as well. The doors of these two rooms and that of the house were always locked. The house was only opened to allow select occupants to enter, leave, or converse with the house owner. There was virtually no communication with the neighbors and Rilwan, Zahran, and Hadiya were never exposed to anyone outside the house. Constantly learning, Zahran developed a good sense of security to protect himself and his organization.

Concealing the True Identities

As mentioned in passages above, Zahran was determined to conceal the true identities of his rank-and-file. If anyone was arrested, he knew that the authorities would be able to trace and track the others. As such, he followed the model developed by the Muslim Brotherhood, al-Qaeda, IS, and likeminded groups to adopt nicknames or aliases—in other words, pseudonyms. Referred to as *kunya*, all leaders, members, and supporters carried the name starting with 'Abu', which means 'father of', which is then followed by a proper name given by Zahran. The names were given at the end of training sessions by Zahran, on occasion after consultation with the newly joined member.

Zahran himself embraced three names. The first was Abu Mukathil, which he eventually gave to his brother Zaini after the latter was released from prison.[53] After this, Zahran gave himself a new name, Abu Muharik, which he operated with from late 2017 to 19 April 2019.[54] Zahran's third and final name was Abu Ubaidah, which he was known by during and after the Easter attack (even if he went by Abu Muharik for most of his IS career). Apart from his three names, and as the leader of NTJ and, later, the IS Sri Lanka branch, Zahran was also addressed as 'Sheikh' or 'Amir' by his followers. Both are honorific titles in Arabic, with the former meaning leader or member of a royal family and the latter meaning commander or prince.

---

[53] Mohamed Ibrahim Mohamed Naufer (IS Sri Lanka branch deputy and ideologue), interview by author, Sri Lanka, January 18, 2020; Mohamed Ibrahim Mohamed Naufer (IS Sri Lanka branch deputy and ideologue), interview by author, Sri Lanka, March 14, 2020.

[54] Naufer, interview, January 18, 2020; Naufer, interview, March 14, 2020.

A few other notable figures in the IS Sri Lanka branch and their pseudonyms were:

- Naufer alias Abu Sarim alias Sinna Sheikh
- Jameel alias Abu Hamza
- Sanasdeen alias Abu Misan
- Hashtoon alias Abu Mohamed
- Rilwan alias Abu Qital
- Milhan alias Abu Sila
- Riskan alias Abu Thari
- Ilham alias Abu Bara
- Inshaf alias Abu Buhari
- Mubarak alias Abu Abdullah
- Azath alias Abu Mokhtar
- Hilam alias Abu Haitham
- Shahid alias Abu Falah
- Sadiq alias Abu Umar
- Sajith alias Abu Naja
- Gafoor alias Abu Hadeed

Zahran addressed them by their aliases and reprimanded anyone who did not follow the IS code, which, as discussed, forbade rank-and-file from discussing personal information such as their real names or any other identifiers. Since they were Sri Lankan, their assumed names ended with 'As Seylani', meaning 'from Sri Lanka'. For instance, especially if they were overseas, Gafoor alias Gafoor Mama would be known as Abu Hadeed As Seylani. When communicating with Abu Hind to meet in Malaysia or Pakistan about procuring arms, Zahran and Rilwan referred to their rank-and-file as As Seylani. Likewise, Milhan, who was scheduled to travel, was referred to as Abu Sila As Seylani. Zahran's wife, Hadiya, who used to listen to the IS leader's phone calls or read messages, said, 'I found it difficult to fathom who he was referring to as he always addressed them or referred to them by their [Abu name].'[55] Thus, the use of codenames worked; secrecy was maintained.

Casing Targets

Zahran promised to turn Sri Lanka into a 'bloodbath' after the February to March 2018 Digana riots, where Sri Lankan Muslims and establishments were targeted. In the year and months leading up to the Easter attack, the IS' plans and targets grew. Eventually, they wanted to attack hotels and churches.

Thorough surveillance was the first step to a successful attack, which was why IS operatives mounted surveillance on a range of targets. To get the maximum kill, they actively searched for and focused their efforts on large gatherings. There were two key events in Sri Lanka the IS initially considered for attack. The first was the celebration of Sri Lanka's Independence Day on 4 February 2019. During this event, VIPs would gather at the Independence Square while citizens would be at the Galle Face Green. The IS Sri Lanka branch engaged in long range planning and preparation by casing targets as early as twelve months before, during the 2018 Independence Day celebration. Independence Square was surveilled by Riskan, Mubarak, and Hashtoon. Galle Face Green was surveilled by Riskan, Hashtoon, Milhan, and another operator.[56]

---

[55] Abdul Cader Fathima Hadiya (widow of IS Sri Lanka branch leader Zahran Hashim), interview by author, January 20, 2020; Abdul Cader Fathima Hadiya (widow of IS Sri Lanka branch leader Zahran Hashim), interview by author, January 27, 2020.

[56] Mohamed Anwar Mohamed Riskan (personal staff of IS Sri Lanka branch leader Zahran Hashim), interview by author, February 15, 2020; Hayathu Mohamed Ahamed Milhan (IS Sri Lanka branch military wing leader), interview by author, February 15, 2020.

The second event was the annual Kandy Esala Perahera in August where the Sacred Tooth Relic of Buddha, a highly revered Buddhist object housed in the Sri Dalada Maligawa or the Temple of the Tooth, Sri Lanka's most important Buddhist temple, would be taken in procession. Zahran and his team discussed attacking Asia's grandest and most colourful pageant—with 100 caparisoned elephants and 1,000 dancers symbolising the rich Sri Lankan culture and heritage over two millennia—on the final day. The would-be suicide bomber who pulled out at the last moment, Riskan, said, 'While staying in the Mayura Place flat, they discussed the plan. They said attacking the Perahera would kill a lot of people. The first attack was supposed to be on the final night. Since people would be transported to the hospital, they were going to explode the bomb in a bike. They were going to see if it could be done in a van as well.'[57]

To drive terror and fear, the targeting group—Zahran, Hashtoon, Jameel, Ilham, and, later, Inshaf—discussed attacking primary and secondary targets. When the injured and dying were being transported to hospitals, they planned to attack both emergency services and hospitals. The group also wanted both vehicle—bikes and vans—and human-borne suicide attackers.

The targeting was curated not only for disrupting social order but also to cripple the economy. Consistent with the IS ideology, Zahran advocated attacks against hotels, churches, and casinos, which were places with high volumes of people and, according to them, kafirs.[58] While tourism was a principal target, they also discussed striking oil storage facilities and the Ceylon Electricity Board, which would result in blackouts, disrupt transportation, and affect different industries.

---

[57] Riskan, interview.

[58] *Statement before Mount Lavinia Magistrate Court in front of the Additional Magistrate C.H.P. Liyanage*, June 25, 2020, (statement of Khalid Sameer, former IS Sri Lanka branch operator).

To paralyse the country, the target selection ranged widely from police stations and headquarters, armed forces, to schools. Zahran tasked Khalid Sameer to map military and law enforcement targets from Colombo 1–15. Zahran also targeted the Kegalle police for objecting bail to IS Sri Lanka branch members who vandalised Buddhist, Hindu, and Christian statues in December 2018.[59] In addition to surveilling CID and CTID officers investigating the IS, Zahran also deterred Muslims that cooperated with the authorities.

Apart from large-scale targets, the IS Sri Lanka branch also looked to attack individual targets that threatened their operations. After the religious images were vandalised, Highways and Investment Promotion Minister Kabir Hashim requested that his coordinating secretary, Mohamed Razik Mohamed Taslim, support the police. After Taslim supported the CID in raiding the IS base in Wanathavillu, he was also identified by the IS as an enemy. 'Since Taslim was the first on the list, they were discussing how to kill him,' said Riskan, who was one of Zahran's personal staff at the time.[60] The group's plan to make contact with Taslim began when Zahran was informed by planning team member Shahid alias Abu Falah that, 'Taslim delivers murruku to shops and sells goats' in his free time.[61] Gafoor and Milhan were then instructed by Zahran 'to approach Taslim on the pretext of buying goats from his farm and then kill him'.[62]

The location of Taslim's home was known to brothers Shahid and Sadiq. As office bearers of SLISM, they knew Taslim, who was also a community worker. Taslim even said, 'Shahid and his

---

[59] *Statement before Mount Lavinia Magistrate Court*, (statement of Khalid Sameer).

[60] Riskan, interview.

[61] Riskan, interview.

[62] Riskan, interview.

brother, Sadiq had visited my home.'[63] Upon procuring Taslim's personal details from the brothers, IS planners contacted Taslim, and the plan was set in motion. Believing that they wanted to buy goats, Taslim met Milhan and Gafoor in person at Sampath Bank in Mawanella. After IS operators entrusted with surveillance confirmed his identity during that meet-up, Milhan shot him when he was asleep at home at 4.20 a.m. on 10 March 2019.[64] Although Taslim survived, he was paralysed and remains crippled to this day.

Target Selection

Initially, the IS wanted to attack all nine provinces of Sri Lanka at the same time. Their intention was to create a high-impact attack that would truly ravage the country and incur long-term ramifications on several sectors: human, social, and economic. As briefly discussed in the section above, the lofty plans of the IS Sri Lanka branch originally included critical infrastructure damage to the Independence Day celebrations and the Kandy Esala Perahera. The sheer magnitude of the attack plan demonstrated the IS' machinations to destabilize Sri Lanka. In keeping with its ideology, IS also cased many targets—from individual or liberal Muslims like Rizwin Ismath, to the aforementioned Muslim Taslim, and security forces personnel. IS would also use social media platforms like Facebook to collect primary information before casing targets on foot or by vehicle. However, when it came to implementation, Zahran eventually realised that it was not practical to manage an operation of such scale.

Although over a hundred recruits were trained in Aruppola, Nuwara Eliya, and Hambantota by the IS from 2017–2018, not

[63] Mohamed Razik Mohamed Taslim (Highways and Investment Promotion Minister Kabir Hashim coordinating secretary), interview by author, June 16, 2022.

[64] Milhan, interview.

all wanted to kill and die. The bandwidth for coordination and the group's operational capabilities were inadequate for conducting island-wide attacks. Both human resource constraints and logistical challenges shaped and influenced the target selection and target choices. Operational and ideological considerations would eventually prompt IS to strike Christian—including Catholic—targets over Buddhist and Hindu targets.

With the IS Sri Lanka branch's grand plans, the targeting group reaching a consensus. They decided to focus on striking the multiethnic and religious capital, rife with hotels and churches, where the kill ratio would be high, and two other towns: the predominantly Catholic Negombo in the west coast and the predominantly Tamil Batticaloa in the east coast.

Supply Chain

Procuring sufficient resources is another key step in mounting successful attacks—and this was something the IS Sri Lanka branch had been doing from the get-go. To support creating the formal IS structure, the first contribution came from Ilham, a member of JMI, an IS support group in Colombo. Introduced by Jameel, Ilham emerged as the financier of Zahran when, in November 2016, he gave Zahran the very first donation to promote the IS ideal and establish an IS branch.[65] Up until that point, Zahran's plans to establish an IS branch in Sri Lanka were futile due to lack of resources. Ilham's donation thus empowered Zahran to implement his stalled plans, which included attacks on the populace.

However, the IS was cheated in its first weapons transaction. Due to their own lack of understanding of firearms, they found out too late that they received defunct weapons. Attempts to procure weapons from overseas were unsuccessful too.

[65] Hadiya, interview, January 20, 2020; Hadiya, interview, January 27, 2020.

The inability to procure weapons in Sri Lanka and overseas prompted Zahran to move in two directions: first, to manufacture explosives. Second, to attack security forces and acquire their weapons—an idea supported by Milhan, who had served Mohamed Faiz, alias Police Faiz, the leader of a jihad group in Eastern province that fought against the LTTE incursions.[66] This operation was mounted successfully on 30 November 2018.

Eventually, the IS also gained access to an almost unlimited supply of funds from Ilham and his brother Inshaf, which allowed Zahran to plan for an island-wide attack proper.[67] The IS procured supplies, including detonators, for manufacturing explosives, which they stored in their facilities. Of the 100 detonators purchased from the Eastern province, ninety-nine were recovered by authorities in Wanathavillu. Although the IS had another reserve of detonators stored outside the Wanathavillu training facility, which they would eventually use to mount both a dry run in the east and the Easter attack proper, they still had to replace the ones that were seized.

In addition to urea and nitric acid, IS attempted to procure sulphuric acid and toluene too. Initially, Zahran assigned an IS procurement team consisting of Hashtoon, Riskan, and Abdullah to make the purchases. After much difficulty trying to secure a large amount, the team was instructed by Zahran to procure whatever quantity was available for purchase. The team would go on to purchase 25 kg of urea and store it at the safehouse in Panadura.[68] Zahran kept the purpose of all these transactions a secret from his wife, Hadiya.

---

[66] Milhan, interview.

[67] Samanth Subramanium, 'Two Wealthy Sri Lankan Brothers Became Suicide Bombers. But Why?', *The New York Times*, July 2, 2020, https://www.nytimes.com/2020/07/02/magazine/sri-lanka-brothers-bombing.html.

[68] Riskan, interview.

Targeting Hotels

The IS gathered its data by three principal means: insiders, observation on foot, and online research. The IS gathered intelligence from its open operators, while supporters working in target locations planned for strike or, at least, contributed to attack plans. For instance, referring to a founding member of the IS from Medawachchiya, Riskan said, 'Shafi, an electrician, had already worked as a laborer in the Shangri-La Hotel and one of the hospitals.'[69] Investigations also suggested that Shafi worked in One Galle Face, the property adjacent but with access to Shangri-La. However, it was not conclusive if Shafi functioned as an insider by providing information or insights on Shangri-La to designated attackers Zahran and Ilham, or Hashtoon, who was one of the planners.

Similarly, Khalid and Hassan Zavahir were tasked by Zahran to travel to Nuwara Eliya to surveil tourist targets on 30 March 2019. After coming up with alibis for their respective families, Khalid and Hassan visited, among other places in Nuwara Eliya, Lake Gregory, a reservoir in heart of the tea country hill city, and Damro Tea Factory, which was renowned for premium teas. Although there were tourists, Khalid and Hassan, who were reluctant to conduct attacks, reported there were only one or two.

As detailed above, IS operators conducted surveillance in multiple steps. The physical surveillance of intended targets for attack adhered to the following process:

1. First was the initial observation to understand the layout of the target, identify where most people were gathered, and note security features and measures.
2. After the initial surveillance, IS operators planned how to conduct the operation with the least resistance,

[69] Riskan, interview.

overcoming the security impediments. After which, they prepared accordingly.

3. Lastly, a final observation would be carried out by the operator or operators staging the attack.

As surveillance on foot was expensive and could gather inaccurate data due to fluctuating crowd volumes, online research was initiated to build efficiency. This was conducted by Hashtoon. In addition to extensive computer searches, Hashtoon, who was a specialist in surveillance photography and videography, also built a database of photos and video clips. He was assisted by his wife, Sara, an equally talented backend operator. A convert with no understanding of mainstream Islam, Sara was as or even more radical and violent than Hashtoon. Skilled and committed, Hashtoon's influence gripped her right until the end of her life. Bilingual and internet-savvy, Sara wrote articles in Tamil and English promoting the IS. Even after Hashtoon's death, Sara continued to study targets online and built a target deck for Rilwan, the operational successor to Zahran, prior to committing mass suicide on 26 April 2019.

The IS' plans to build capabilities to target hotels started incrementally. At its inception, the IS had zero knowledge of how to surveil, which was a prerequisite for effective targeting. On foot, they started with beaches and then checked into hotels outside Colombo to develop familiarity. The preliminary surveillance of tourist targets in general started in 2018 and in the first quarter of 2019. Surveillance focused on hotels in Colombo over the first three weeks of April 2019. In the lead-up to the attack, surveillance intensified, and the focus shifted to designated hotels. After extensive online research by Hashtoon, Zahran gradually deployed operatives on the ground. They were to case both coastal and hill country targets to build experience and confidence in the operations.

Along the coast, tourist sites cased by the IS operators were Mirissa, Matara, Hikkaduwa, Unawattuna, Weligama, and Negombo. Leading the effort personally, Zahran and the team blended into the tourist environment by altering their appearance through haircuts or outfit changes. The original team that cased beaches included Ilham, Inshaf, and Jameel, who were from Colombo and possessed knowledge and understanding that was vital for the IS to build its operational capabilities and sharpen their readiness to strike the area. Eventually, the team gained experience and expertise and, after realising that there were not enough tourists at the beach, they decided to target restaurants in five-star hotels instead.

According to Riskan, Americans were targeted at caliph Abu Bakr al-Baghdadi's behest, who implored the IS to take revenge 'because they were attacking Syria'.[70] The surveillance team checked hotels and hospitals in the aforementioned areas, and hotel rooms facing the seaside as points to observe tourists on the beach. Just like before, they changed their dress and appearance to suit their potential target location. In between surveillance, Zahran also conducted meetings in the field with operators, supporters, and others. Data on tourist flows ultimately varied, thus the team adopted the IS methodology of taking the average of reported tourist sightings and selecting targets for maximum kill threat.

Targeting Churches

Khalid Sameer, the first IS operator to surveil churches, was born into poverty. He lived a life of hardship until he worked for Abans in Rajagiriya. Educated in a Sinhala Buddhist school, Khalid was the ideal candidate for operating in Colombo and in Sinhala areas to gather data.

---

[70] Riskan, interview.

With the rise of the IS in 2014, Khalid joined the IS support group JMI in Colombo and, after training, the IS Sri Lanka branch proper. After he was indoctrinated, Khalid was given a tested assignment in early 2018 by Ilham and Jameel to 'identify and enter every church in Sri Lanka into a database'.[71]

Immediately after attending the IS training from 24–25 March 2018, Zahran provided Khalid with a monthly salary, personal equipment including a motorbike, and a dedicated phone with Threema for encrypted communication, among other benefits like financial support for his family—if Khalid continued his surveillance. 'On August 15, 2018, I met Zahran, Naufer, Milhan, Hashtoon. Milhan said, he wanted to find out the information about everything from Colombo 1–15; houses, buildings, mosques, churches, temples, police stations, the headquarters of the three forces, schools, and other targets. He said that if there was a problem in Sri Lanka in the future, they would need this information.'[72]

In the lead-up to the Easter attack, another IS member, Muaath, who lived close to St Anthony's Church, impressed Zahran. During one of the group's preparatory meetings, Muaath informed Zahran that he was familiar with St Anthony's Church, which he always passed by whenever he travelled home to Mattakuliya. With his enthusiasm surging, Muaath added, 'You do not need to look for places. We will see and inform you the places.' To which Zahran responded, 'You will not reach Ramadan fasting this year. Your time will start from today.'[73] This brought Zahran and Muaath to a point of no return. With Muaath's commitment, Zahran would eventually designate him to attack St Anthony's Church.

---

[71] *Statement before Mount Lavinia Magistrate Court*, (statement of Khalid Sameer).

[72] *Statement before Mount Lavinia Magistrate Court*, (statement of Khalid Sameer).

[73] *Statement before Mount Lavinia Magistrate Court*, (statement of Khalid Sameer).

Manufacturing Explosives

Prior to the Easter attack, the pace of activity in the organization, especially that of Zahran's, his family's, and functionaries', increased. The mobility of the IS leaders and operatives stepped up in the month preceding the attack, especially after the IS leadership began to suspect that authorities were conducting searches. Zahran and his family moved discreetly between safehouses, eventually relocating to an apartment in Lucky Plaza on 3 April 2019. Located in Kollupitiya, Colombo's centre, this also became one of the group's safehouses. During this period, Hashtoon, one of the principal bomb makers who would eventually attack St Sebastian's Church, also shifted bomb manufacturing activities between safehouses to avoid detection.

As Easter Sunday drew near, the two weeks preceding the attack became the busiest period for the IS functionaries, especially Hashtoon and Rilwan. Both led the crafting of explosives, with assistance from other members, armed with malicious intent and extremist fervor. Until mid-day on 19 April, the IS leadership remained in the Lucky Plaza safehouse. Meanwhile, the Katuwapitiya and Panadura safehouses were used to store, manufacture, and rig the explosive devices. There, the IS explosives manufacturing team used fans to dry explosives in the living room and prepared sheets of explosives with ball bearings for the bombers to wear.

However, despite the group's efforts, the IS safehouses also faced intermittent threats and risks. For instance, the owner of the Panadura safehouse, who was unaware that his house was being used to store and manufacture bombs, visited his property unannounced at mid-day on 3 April 2019 to check if it was being well looked after by his tenants.[74] Although he was

---

[74] Lahiru Fernando, 'CID officer tells PCoI probing Easter Sunday terror attacks: Suicide bombers purchased backpacks from Battaramulla, Grandpass shops', *Daily*

effectively deterred by Riskan, it was apparent that the IS agents were unprepared for such instances. These routine checks and the spontaneity of them being found out was an agitating distraction and incredibly stressful in the lead-up to Easter Sunday.

Zahran was immediately informed by the procurement, storage, and manufacturing team that it was 'not safe' to store the precursors in the Panadura safehouse. Realizing the danger of detection, Zahran acted promptly; he did not want a repeat of what happened in Wanathavillu. Zahran immediately instructed the transfer of the explosive precursors to the Katuwapitiya safehouse on 4 April. To reduce the risk of the vehicle being stopped and searched, Zahran said the precursors should be transported during rush hour. He personally oversaw the operation and remained with the explosives manufacturing team, including Hashtoon, for three days to demonstrate strong leadership after the close call; only returning to Lucky Plaza once the situation stabilized. On the eve of the Easter Sunday attack, the makeshift bomb-making factory was moved back to the Panadura safehouse.

When the IS bomb makers successfully manufactured the explosive, urea nitrate, Zahran immediately instructed them to make two types of bombs. The first were explosives-laden backpacks for human-borne attacks and the second were explosives-laden vehicles for vehicle-borne attacks. Once prototypes were manufactured, Hashtoon advised Zahran to conduct a dry run before mounting the Easter attack proper.

Hashtoon, Rilwan, Mubarak, and Sanasdeen, were thus assigned by Zahran to return to IS ground zero—Kattankudy. They selected an isolated field located in a forty-three-acre piece of bare land in Palamunai, 200 m from the beachfront, to conduct the dry run. At Hashtoon's recommendation, the explosives

---

News, October 29, 2020, https://www.dailynews.lk/2020/10/29/local/232579/suicide-bombers-purchased-backpacks-battaramulla-grandpass-shops.

device would be tested on a motorbike, which the team procured from other IS members. Prior to its execution, the team also came up with backup plans in case there would be casualties among them during the trial.[75]

The dry run was conducted on the night of 16 April 2019 during a thunderstorm. Although the timer attached to the motorbike failed on the first attempt, the second attempt was a success. The deafening explosion had even alerted a nearby military camp and would prompt the owner of the land to lodge a police report at the Kattankudy police station the very next day, 17 April. After the successful trials, the team would return and Hashtoon would continue the construction of backpack bombs at the Panadura safehouse.

Coordination

After the successful dry run, Zahran convened a meeting at the Panadura safehouse four days before the Easter Sunday attack to assign targets. Zahran and Ilham led and made key decisions for the plans. As they had to coordinate the attack, the bombers remained together at the safehouse until Easter Sunday. Zahran instructed that rooms be booked for 20 April in the four upmarket hotels designated for attack: Cinnamon Grand, Taj Samudra, Shangri-La, and Kingsbury. To avoid detection, Inshaf, who was assigned to do the bookings, used Kingsbury bomber Mubarak's personal details.

At the same time, after their return from the dry run, Hashtoon and his team prepared to deliver the manufactured bombs, which were to be used at the target locations. Together with the IS' principal financier, Ilham, Mubarak returned to the safehouse in Panadura on Thursday, 18 April, with ten backpacks,

[75] Interview by author with a detainee, Colombo, Sri Lanka, March 2020.

hats, pants, shirts, and shawls.[76] The explosives charges were to be placed in the backpacks, which would then be transported to target locations in polo trolly bags.

Ground Zero of Easter Sunday

On Friday, 19 April 2019, Zahran left the Lucky Plaza apartment at around 6.00 a.m. with Ilham. Hadiya watched Zahran leave but claimed to be unaware of the plot and uninvolved with the plan. CCTV cameras recorded the two would-be-suicide bombers walking to Shangri-La Hotel, which they were preparing to turn into ground zero.

Zahran and Ilham arrived at the Shangri-La at 7.28 a.m. They had breakfast at Table One on the third floor and sat in the main lobby, blending into the foam of unsuspecting hotel visitors and biding their time. Shangri-La was, at the time, a newly constructed luxury hotel. Classified as one of the most popular and sought-after hotels, the beautifully decorated lobby of marble, which reflected the sparkle of the overhead chandelier, was a surreal sight—and one that would be forever tarnished by the horror that was soon to follow.

In their final surveillance mission, Zahran and Ilham wanted to see the targets personally and figure out how to create maximum impact. The lobby was not crowded, which was why they decided to strike the Table One restaurant instead. On Easter Sunday, they envisaged, Table One would be fully packed. They planned for the 'Sheikh' to strike inside the restaurant and when the survivors ran out, Ilham would blast its entrance. Before they left, Zahran and Ilham studied the security features and mapped out where western visitors gathered. After which, they returned to the Lucky Plaza safehouse to change their clothes at 9.50 a.m.

---

[76] Fernando, 'CID officer tells PCoI'.

Shortly after, Zahran and Ilham travelled to Panadura and joined the rest of the Easter attack team. There, a few hours later in the afternoon on the same day, 19 April, Ilham assisted Hashtoon in rigging the bombs, which included a purpose-built device for Ilham's wife, Fathima Jiffry. Zahran blessed Fathima's desire to be a *mujahida* or female fighter for Allah—and her eventual wish to sacrifice her life and that of their children to serve Him.

Such resolve was also seen in the likes of Inshaf, who, on the morning of 19 April, lied to his wife, Fathima Shifka, claiming he needed to travel to Zambia that night on business. This was a difficult necessity especially since Shifka, who came from a mainstream Sri Lankan Muslim family and maintained both Muslim and non-Muslim friends, had rejected Inshaf's attempts to radicalize and recruit her. In the early afternoon at 3 p.m., Inshaf's family accompanied him to the Bandaranaike International Airport, where Inshaf would hand two USB storage devices to Shifka that contained audio recordings for his family and associates, as well as extremist and terrorist materials.

The mindset of the suicide bombers is reflected in these audio recordings, which are not available to the public. Said recordings identified what motivated Inshaf and other bombers to conduct the attacks. Considerable online falsehoods and manipulations formed the content exploited by IS ideologues, propagandists, and preachers such as Zahran, Jameel, and the like. Indoctrinated and radicalized by the IS, members such as Inshaf and Ilham believed that Islam should be spread by war and that it was the obligation of every Muslim to wage jihad or holy war against unbelievers.

Once Inshaf's family left the airport, he travelled to Dematagoda where, at 10 p.m., he visited his parents' home and told them he was traveling to Cyprus on business. This would be his final call to his parents and siblings, who were not involved in the operation. After this, Inshaf, Ilham, and Jameel would meet one last time at about 10.25 p.m. at DineMore, Jameel's favourite restaurant.

The three would-be suicide bombers met to reminisce about what they believed was the difficult path they had chosen. In their eyes, they had chosen to abandon their parents, wives, and children for their ideology and to fight mercilessly against the enemies of Allah. Indoctrinated, they could not reflect beyond the confines of the ideological framework through which they perceived the world. They were prisoners to their own beliefs, marching down a path of carnage, ceaseless destruction and, no return.

Parting of Ways

As seen above, dealing with their families was the greatest challenge for the suicide bombers, including Zahran. Although Zahran let the bombers meet their families, he forbade them from telling their loved ones that they would be mounting attacks. On the night of 18 April, when Zahran and Hashtoon returned to Lucky Plaza after the bomb-making facilities were stable again, Zahran reportedly showed a particular closeness to his loved ones. Zahran planned for Hadiya, the children, and the families of the mujahideen to return to the eastern province in twenty-four hours, where he believed they would be protected—especially in the wake of the devastating attack that was to take place. In the predominantly Muslim east, Zahran trusted that the families would be well cared for especially by relatives who believed in the same ideology.

As Easter Sunday drew near, Zahran was likewise said to have been unusually kind to the children. It was recorded during Hadiya's testimony that one of the final conversations between her and her husband were regarding his arrest warrant and a possibility of a better future elsewhere for her and the children—in other words, a glimmer of hope.

Zahran used the term hijrah, which meant 'entering another path [elsewhere]', to describe his journey. Hadiya often questioned

Zahran regarding the location of this 'elsewhere', to which Zahran would respond, 'Do not ask when and where we are going.'[77]

Zahran's destructive agenda was rooted in his belief that he would reach the entrance of Jannat-ul-Firdaus—the fourth heaven, where the companions of the prophet lived. As he contemplated his self-perceived martyrdom, he must have known the dangers that would befall his parents, brothers, sisters, their families, and his own family but he believed that they would all eventually join him in heaven. Similarly, in Zahran's eyes, the wives of the mujahideen were to be respected for performing their duties to their husbands for sacrificing their lives for Allah, Islam, and Muslims. As such, at the Lucky Plaza apartment, Zahran told Hadiya in confidence, 'You will be looked after by parents and brothers, and our son will be looked after by Rilwan.'[78]

Inspired by Abu Bakr al-Baghdadi's son, Huthaifa al-Badri, who was killed in battle in Syria on 2 July 2018, Zahran likewise raised and wanted his son to grow up as a *mujahid* or a male fighter for Allah.[79] To ensure his son's allegiance, he tasked his brother and successor to guide the boy's spiritual journey. While opting to send his wife to his parental home, Zahran hoped to deter her from linking up with her parents, justifying his actions by warning her, 'If you return home, the CID will arrest you.'

Zahran also developed post-attack plans for the mujahideen's wives, including his own wife Hadiya, with Hashtoon's assistance, who was a meticulous and intuitive planner. These plans included *idda*—a four or five-month mourning period after a death or divorce where the woman is not to marry. In connection with this, Zahran also arranged for funds to be disbursed through

---

77 Hadiya, interview, January 20, 2020; Hadiya, interview, January 27, 2020.

78 Hadiya, interview, January 20, 2020; Hadiya, interview, January 27, 2020.

79 'IS leader Abu Bakr al-Baghdadi's son "killed in Syria"', *BBC*, July 4, 2018, https://www.bbc.com/news/world-middle-east-44710004.

the suicide attackers to their wives (and eventual widows), which would allow them to buy light or white coloured clothes to wear after the bombings. In one of his final conversations with Hadiya, Zahran sounded ambivalent when he said, 'We are going on hijrah. We are going to another place. If you hear we died, mourn by expressing sorrow and wear white clothes. If we are alive, we will return.'[80]

Zahran's Successors

With Zahran's desire to 'get closer to god', the IS leader split the team into two: the A team that would kill and die on Easter Sunday, and the B team that would relocate to the east. The former was directly under Zahran, while his operational successor and brother Rilwan was nominated as the guardian and protector of the latter. Zahran also entrusted Rilwan with harnessing the resources passed down to him—including explosives and precursors, technology, and substantial funds—to mount a second strike in August 2019.

On the eve of the Easter attack, Rilwan was to leave for the eastern province with the suicide bombers' wives. Moving to the east, hiding the families, building up IS infrastructure and their new operating base, and planning, preparing, and executing a second strike—all of these comprised his first assignment as the group's new operational chief. Before leaving, it was said that Rilwan embraced all the bombers, including Zahran, whom he embraced last and the longest. This was believed to be a sign of affection, especially since the brothers understood each other more than others. When Zahran became a fugitive, Rilwan stood by him, and Zahran did the same when Rilwan was severely injured. As they bid farewell, the brothers likely believed that they would meet soon in heaven.

[80] Hadiya, interview, January 20, 2020; Hadiya, interview, January 27, 2020.

Back in the safehouse, the IS operational council sat with the bombers in the living room. Zahran led the prayer with the bombers and bomb makers, after which, the bombs were assembled through the night. Of the nine bombers, only eight were present at the safehouse—all males. The last and only female bomber, Fathima Jiffry, could not be in a hall full of male bombers; this would be considered haram under the IS' teachings. Instead, as discussed in succeeding passages, she was given specific instructions and would participate in the attack separately—at Mahawila Gardens. Other than the male suicide bombers, only IS operators Riskan and Sanasdeen were present at the safehouse. Apart from assisting in preparing the IEDs, they also helped secure the safehouse and provided travel support. They played a vital role in providing the attack team with food and other essentials too.

Final Preparations

In the early hours of the morning on 20 April, the bombers reviewed the final surveillance conducted against their targets in the following venues:

Zahran - Shangri-La Hotel, Colombo
Ilham - Shangri-La Hotel, Colombo
Inshaf - Cinnamon Grand, Colombo
Mubarak - Kingsbury Hotel, Colombo
Jameel - Taj Samudra Hotel, Colombo
Muaath - St Anthony's Shrine, Kochchikade, Colombo
Hashtoon - St Sebastian's Church, Katuwapitiya, Negombo
Azath - Zion Church International, Batticaloa

At the safehouse, Zahran and his team spent the last few hours planning meticulously for the attack. To strike effectively, the bombers had to gain access to the restaurants in the luxury hotels and the churches holding Easter mass. To do so, they had to physically blend into the target environment. Thus, they once again trimmed their beards and dressed unsuspectingly in shirts and trousers.

Each suicide bomber also received a backpack from Zahran.[81] In addition to his own backpack, Ilham carried an extra backpack and a bottle laden with explosives. As mentioned previously, Ilham's wife Fathima also expressed her interest in joining her husband with their children and unborn child. Thus, unlike the others who had moved to the eastern province with Rilwan, Fathima remained in Colombo at Mahawila Gardens, where she would carry out her attack. However, in her state of pregnancy, Fathima could not move around easily, let alone carry a heavy backpack. Hence, a one-and-a-half litre explosives-laden plastic bottle, which was easier to handle, was prepared for her.

On 20 April, the bombers brought their IEDs and moved from their safehouse in Panadura to Span Tower on Templers Road in Mount Lavinia, which was their staging location. Two flats at the complex were rented between 12–21 April by Mubarak, the Kingsbury Hotel bomber. From there, they planned to relocate either to their designated hotels or, at least, closer to their assigned locations. Meanwhile, Sanasdeen and Riskan remained at Panadura safehouse to empty it and load the IS' belongings—including the makeshift bomb factory—into a cab lorry before travelling to Ampara, the new IS headquarters. The group's fledging infrastructure in the east included eight safehouses and items purchased in Colombo to equip the Easter bombers and the second wave of attacks.[82]

---

[81] Fernando, 'CID officer tells PCoI'.

[82] Fernando, 'CID officer tells PCoI'.

Farewell Video

Before staging the bombings, Zahran prepared to deliver his farewell message with his seven mujahideen and renew their oath of allegiance to caliph Abu Bakr al-Baghdadi. At the Span Tower, the suicide bombers changed into black tunics and monochrome headscarves or *keffiyehs* before gathering at the makeshift studio that Hashtoon prepared to start their recording. In the video, Zahran held a T-56 firearm while three others held daggers. All the bombers, apart from Zahran, covered their faces.

The one-and-a-half-hour message gives further insight into the mindset of Zahran and the suicide bombers. All those featured in the video wholeheartedly embraced the IS' politico-religious ideology and believed that they were 'fighters of God'. They believed that they were waging jihad and seeking martyrdom. They had been conditioned to kill and die for their cause, for Allah. Each one was convinced that they would reach Firdaus, the fourth level of Jannah or paradise, for what they perceived to be their heroic act.

In the video, Zahran emphasized the Easter operation was 'not a suicide attack' but was 'a gift [given] by attacking. This [was] a blessed Honourable transaction that [was] done with Allah. Allah Almighty [said] in the Holy Quran "Indeed, Allah has purchased from the believers their lives and their properties [in exchange] for that they will have Paradise."[83]' The climax of the video was when the attackers pledged their oath of allegiance to caliph Abu Bakr al-Baghdadi. Their exact words were, 'We pledge to leader of the believers and the caliph of the Muslims Ash-Sheikh Abu Bakr al-Baghdadi Al Qurashi, Al Hussaini to listen and obey him in difficult and ease.'[84]

[83] Quran 9:111.

[84] Hashim, 'Farewell Video'.

The pledge, or *bayah*, was administered by Zahran. Tracing back to the era of the Prophet Muhammad, bayah was of utmost importance; breaking one was akin to 'breaking a promise to God'.[85] It was said that if the rulers, including caliph or amir, took a decision contrary to Islam, the bayah could be reneged.[86] However, despite blatant and repeated violations, including killing civilians, the IS Sri Lanka branch members and supporters remained committed to their cause and pledge.

Eve of Easter Sunday, 20 April 2019

As Sri Lankan Christians prepared to celebrate Easter Sunday, Zahran and his group of terrorists were planning to strike terror into the heart of the populace. One of the IS' most committed followers, Jameel, checked into the Taj Samudra Hotel at 4.52 p.m. Jameel departed the hotel at 5.39 p.m. with no luggage and travelled to the Panadura safehouse, where he stayed until 7 p.m. before traveling to the Span Tower.

During this time, Inshaf checked into the Cinnamon Grand hotel at 7 p.m. before leaving at 8.26 p.m. and hiring an Uber vehicle to take him to Span Tower. Later, Inshaf and Jameel returned to the Panadura safehouse, where they spend their final night before the attack.

Meanwhile, Zahran and Ilham arrived at the Shangri-La Hotel at 7.56 p.m. The taxi they used came from the IS' Panadura safehouse. They brought two explosive-laden traveling bags with them. The hotel staff offered to take the bags to their room, but they refused the service. With a light travelling bag, Ilham left

[85] Stewart Bell, *The Martyr's Oath: The Apprenticeship of a Homegrown Terrorist*, (Mississauga: John Wiley, 2015).

[86] Carlos Igualada and Javier Yagüe, 'The Use of Bay'ah by the Main Salafi-Jihadist Groups', *Perspectives on Terrorism* 15, no. 1 (2021): 39–48, https://www.jstor.org/stable/26984796.

the hotel and took a taxi to the Span Tower. At the rented room, functioning as a safehouse, Ilham met his older brother, Inshaf, and Jameel. After they embraced each other one last time, Ilham collected the explosives-laden backpack and other IEDs prepared for his wife Fathima. From the Span Tower, he visited his parental residence in Mahawila Gardens in Dematagoda in the wee hours of the morning for the final time.

As for the other bombers, Mubarak checked into the Kingsbury Hotel at 7.47 p.m. He remained in his room until 9 p.m. before leaving the hotel with one bag. Mubarak made his way to his Kolonnawa residence where he met with and handed the bag over to two men on a motorbike. Mubarak then went home to bid goodbye, where he stayed from 9.35 p.m. until 11.05 p.m. After which, he made his way back to the Kingsbury Hotel.

The IS operators with designated targets outside Colombo left for their destination too. Hashtoon returned to the Negombo safehouse after 8.40 p.m. In preparation to strike the Zion Church in Batticaloa, Azath boarded a bus in Maradana, Colombo, with a backpack and a small bag at 8.45 p.m.

Easter Sunday, 21 April 2019

Shangri-La Hotel

As mentioned briefly above, Ilham arrived at his family residence in Dematagoda at 1 a.m. on 21 April to bid his family a final goodbye. Although he was planning to commit mass murder, Ilham, in his self-delusion, must have perceived this as a gallant act. It was said that after giving Fathima the two IEDs, Ilham embraced his wife and both assured each other that they would all meet in heaven. Ilham reportedly wept as he carried and embraced their children too and was believed to be the only bomber to show physical sadness prior to unleashing mass destruction. Afterwards, Ilham departed for

Hotel De Pilawoos on Galle Road, where he purchased Zahran's food before returning to the Shangri-La at 1.46 a.m.

There, both Zahran and Ilham ate their final meal. They spoke, rested, prayed, and left wearing the same clothes they came to the hotel with. Zahran and Ilham arrived at the lift lobby on the sixth floor later that morning at 8.50 a.m., then made their way to the Table One restaurant on level three. The restaurant was packed with Sri Lankans and foreigners at breakfast—and with that, the scene was set.

After signalling to Zahran, Ilham left the restaurant at 8.53 a.m. Zahran detonated his backpack bomb immediately after at 8.54 a.m. With Zahran turning into a ball of fire, guests who were able to flee attempted to exit the restaurant. Using the escalator, Ilham returned to the level three foyer and detonated his bomb at 8.55 a.m. Many of those fleeing, who were in shock, injured, or maimed, received the full blast. Many children who were quick enough to escape the restaurant died in the foyer before their parents, who immediately arrived after hearing the first blast.

Kingsbury Hotel

Mubarak arrived back at the Kingsbury Hotel on 20 April after visiting home for the last time. At 8.47 a.m. the next day, Mubarak arrived at the Kingsbury's Harbor Court restaurant on the ground floor. International and local guests were having breakfast when he detonated his backpack bomb. The deafening screech of the bomb pierced the peaceful normalcy of Easter Sunday brunch; the fury of shrapnel scratching, tearing, and exploding in a blast of hate, delusions, and horrifying intent. As the ambulances were overwhelmed, the hotel transport moved the injured and dying to hospitals. The magnitude of the bomb was so great that corpses lined the corridors and lobbies of hospitals and hotels alike, transforming the latter's once glistening floors into a harrowing zone.

It is also worth noting that Mubarak, in particular, had no social profile. He was not known to law enforcement and was not as well educated or wealthy as the other bombers either. As such, his details were often used by other IS operators for booking hotel rooms and safehouses. Mubarak could operate and accomplish tasks without drawing attention to himself. Thus, because he avoided detection easily, he was the perfect choice to facilitate plans and preparations for the group.

Cinnamon Grand Hotel

Inshaf and Jameel arrived at Span Tower from the Panadura safehouse at 6.30 a.m. on 21 April. After which, they departed together in an Uber. Inshaf was dropped off at the Cinnamon Grand at 7.05 a.m. He went to his room and stayed there until 8.45 a.m., at which point he went to the hotel's Taprobane restaurant.

Between 8.46 a.m. and 8.58 a.m., Inshaf remained inside Taprobane. There were many Muslims and a few westerners. He was said to have been very distraught and kept his head on the table. Reportedly disinterested in the breakfast, Inshaf ate lightly.

He left Taprobane shortly after at 8.58 a.m., going back to his room before returning to the restaurant at 9.07 a.m. There, Inshaf moved to the front of the buffet bar and detonated his backpack bomb at 9.11 a.m.

Taj Samudra Hotel and New Tropical Inn

After Inshaf was dropped off at the Cinnamon Grand, the same Uber continued to the Taj Samudra where Jameel was dropped off at 7.17 a.m. He was in possession of an explosives-laden backpack when he arrived at his room. Following failed attempts to detonate it, Jameel left the Taj Samudra at 8.45 a.m. and made his way to the New Tropical Inn after asking to be taken to a hotel in Dehiwala.

Zahran had developed a plan B if any of the bombers could not successfully carry out an attack. He instructed them to come to Masjidur Rahman Jumma Masjid at Ebenezer Place. A known rendezvous point, the mosque, more commonly known as the Ebenezer Mosque, was used by the IS members to pray. Anticipating that the attack would lead to a Muslim-Sinhalese riot, Zahran had arranged for Riskan to receive bombers at the mosque. Riskan was to direct them to Ahammadu Lebbe Mohamed Niyaz, the IS' most trusted operator in the east. They would then support Niyaz in planning for the second strike.

However, Riskan failed to turn up at the mosque. When Riskan went to the safehouse in Wattala led by Naufer, he was mistakenly informed that all the bombs had exploded. With no IS operator at the Ebenezer Mosque to receive Jameel, he was said to have been highly agitated. A review of CCTV footage at the mosque showed Jameel looking panicked and stressed, further proving this. Following the unsuccessful detonation at Taj Samudra, Jameel went to the local New Tropical Inn where he tried to rectify the malfunction in the device. It was there that the bomb detonated at 1.30 p.m., prematurely killing two lovers who were at the site.

St Anthony's Church

Muaath left the Span Tower at 8 a.m., driving himself to and then parking 80 m from St Anthony's Church. Designed to kill first responders, the Vehicle–Borne Improvised Explosive Device (VBIED) remained unnoticed. After disembarking from the car carrying a grey backpack, he waited for six minutes to synchronise the attack timing. As instructed by Hashtoon, Muaath entered the church at 8.42 a.m. and detonated his backpack bomb shortly after at 8.45 a.m.

St Sebastian's Church

Hashtoon departed for the Negombo safehouse on foot at 8.25 a.m. With a large explosives-laden backpack, he walked in the direction of St Sebastian's Church. He walked east, away from St Sebastian's church along Colombo-Negombo Road at 8.33 a.m., before turning around and walking towards the church through the north side's middle entrance. As he approached the target, it was said that a little girl planning to attend the service almost bumped into him. He reportedly patted her on the head and smiled kindly before continuing to make his way into the church. At 8.45 a.m., Hashtoon stepped into the building, nodded at the priest, looked at the audience, and detonated his backpack bomb.

Zion Church, Batticaloa

Mohamed Nazar Mohamed Azath travelled to Batticaloa in eastern Sri Lanka on the night of 20 April. His target, the Zion Church in Batticaloa, was in the neighboring town of Kattankudy, across a lagoon. From a bus stop near Zahira College in Maradana, Colombo, he boarded the Kalmunai bus at 8.20 p.m. There were no checkpoints, so Azath was able to transport his explosives-laden backpack while traveling 300 km cross country. He was then seen on CCTV arriving in Batticaloa at 2.07 a.m. on 21 April.[87]

From the town, Azath travelled to Jami us Salam Jummah Masjid. Also known as Town Mosque, the Tabligh Jamaat mosque was located at the heart of Batticaloa. Azath was taught not to visit non-Thowheed mosques and especially not to pray with or behind non-Thowheed followers, but he needed a place to pass the time until he mounted his attack. As there were police patrols in the vicinity, identifying himself with the mosque would have kept him from arousing suspicion.

The mosque was closed when he arrived, so he kept the luggage near the main entrance. A police car drove up at 4.42 a.m., but the

---

[87] Deborah Haynes, 'Exclusive: Footage shows final hours of Sri Lanka suicide bomber', *Sky News*, April 30, 2019, https://news.sky.com/story/exclusive-footage-shows-final-hours-of-sri-lanka-suicide-bomber-11707268.

officers inside reportedly did not seem to suspect him. When the mosque opened its gates at 5.42 a.m., he left the luggage inside the mosque, took a phone call, and headed to the bathroom for ablution. On 'several occasions', he was also observed to be 'quite restless'.[88] After a brief conversation with the worshippers, perhaps done to blend in, Azath joined them at 6 a.m. to pray. He eventually slipped out of the mosque at 6.18 a.m., seemingly taking time to reflect alone before mounting his attack. He prayed alone between two plastic chairs. There was a dark irony to the situation—the suicide bombers hoping for a moment of peace before unleashing a devastating attack.

Later, at 8.31 a.m., Azath went to the bathroom to change his clothes before carrying out the plan. At 8.45 a.m., he departed by foot, walking towards Zion Church and reaching at around 8.51 a.m.—in time for the main mass scheduled at 9 a.m. When Azath arrived, Sunday school service had just finished, and the children were playing and enjoying breakfast. When he attempted to enter the church, Azath was stopped and questioned by two church officials, Ramesh Raju and Rasalingam Sasikumar, as he was not in appropriate attire. Stating that two men were both trying to stop the attacker from entering, Rajeevkaran Vimalaretnam, a thirty-eight-year-old sound technician for the church, said, 'I saw a man standing there with two bags wearing a cap and a t-shirt. His dress code—cap, the bag—all of this looked out of place.'[89] It was unusual for a churchgoer to enter with a rucksack, thus Azath was inquired about his bag, to which he said he wanted to film the church service. When the church officials said they needed to ask the pastor's permission first, Azath turned back. Standing

---

[88] Buddhika Samaraweera, 'Zion Church Bomber Travelled 300km With Suicide Pack', *Ceylon Today*, June 6, 2020, https://archive.ceylontoday.lk/print-more/57922.

[89] Rebecca Wright, Sam Kiley, and King Ratnam, 'The Sunday school children: The little-known tragedy of the Sri Lankan Easter attacks', *CNN*, May 4, 2019, https://edition.cnn.com/2019/05/04/asia/zion-bombs-sri-lanka-intl/index.html.

next to a nearby power generator, he detonated the IED in his backpack at 9.05 a.m.—killing twenty-six and injuring seventy. Among the dead were Ramesh and Rasalingam, better known as Sashee, who held Azath outside for almost twenty minutes, and fifteen children who were having breakfast in the church portico or playing in the garden.

Had Azath entered the church, the blast would have killed 200–300 of the 550 people sitting inside waiting for Easter Sunday service to begin. Of the 550, 150 were children attending Sunday school. In addition to the children inside, there were approximately 400 adults. The impact of the detonation would have been far more severe had he achieved his goal. The suspicion he raised to adult members of the congregation prevented an even greater scale of death and destruction.

Mahawila Gardens, Dematagoda

From the Shangri-La's guest booking system, the police identified Ilham's residential address, which was a stately mansion at Mahawila Gardens in the suburb of Dematagoda. This was part of an elaborate plan to lure the police into a trap—and one where they took the bait.

The police team immediately headed to the residence and when they arrived, Ilham's parents, two daughters-in-law, and grandchildren were on the ground floor. Ilham's wife, Fathima Jiffry, must have known at this point that her husband had killed himself at the Shangri-La. She is said to have remained with the children in their room on the first floor. Fathima sent her mother, who was reportedly comforting her, down to join the rest of the family. She also gave Ilham's farewell audio to the rest of the family. CCD Police Sergeant Wasantha Sisira Kumara said all residents of the house were likely aware of the Easter Sunday attack and the fate that befell Ilham and Inshaf by then, with the news being made public.[90]

As mentioned previously, Ilham had also discreetly brought two bombs—an improvised backpack bomb and an improvised water bottle bomb—to the residence the previous night for Fathima.[91] Without much convincing and heavily radicalized herself, Fathima was ready to follow in Ilham's footsteps. Though ready to sacrifice themselves, Ilham and Fathima also loved their children. Thus, rather than leave them orphaned, they decided to conduct a family attack. Ilham reportedly gave Fathima two bombs as a precaution; assuring her that if one failed, the other would explode and instructed her to keep both within reach when security personnel approached. Details regarding the construction of these devices suggest the backpack was like those used by the other suicide bombers, while the water bottle was manufactured using a different method to ensure its function.

By providing their address when checking into the Shangri-La, Ilham was confident that security forces would pay them a visit to conduct a search or question Fathima. The plan worked and the unknowing police, who were considered to be 'Thogud' or devils by the radical and violent IS, would become targets. Sergeant Kumara said that, on the instructions of a senior police officer, a team led by Sub-Inspector Rohana Bandara had left to inspect the house. 'Six police officers including me were deployed for the inspection,' he added.[92] Bandara was the only armed officer. 'Then, we entered the house and there were a few men and women in the basement. At the time of entry, we saw a group of women

---

[90] Interview by author with CCD officers in Colombo, Sri Lanka, March 2020.

[91] Interview by author with a detainee and investigators in Colombo, Sri Lanka, March 2020.

[92] 'Ibrahim, family stood nonchalant despite blasts: Witness', *Daily Mirror*, June 4, 2020, https://www.dailymirror.lk/breaking_news/Ibrahim-family-stood-nonchalant-despite-blasts-Witness/108-189546.

crying in one of the rooms. Later, Bandara and two other police constables went upstairs to investigate,' Kumara said.[93]

There, the officers would find Fathima, who was in a room with her two children. When the officers knocked on the door, Fathima and her children did not open it. Anticipating that they would forcefully enter the room, Fathima was believed to have tightly embraced the children and recited the Quran before detonating one of the bombs at 2.25 p.m. The blast killed the three police officers along with Fathima, her unborn child, and two children. A second explosion occurred at 2.35 p.m., where the wall collapsed on a few officers who were trying to get to the three officers upstairs.

After the explosion, Senior DIG Latiff said Ibrahim Hajjiyar did not show any grief despite losing two sons, a daughter-in-law who was pregnant, and two grandchildren. As the father was neither shocked nor disturbed, authorities believed that the family must have been prepared for or aware of the attack. On the other hand, Ibrahim Hajjiyar's wife was grieving the loss of Inshaf, Ilham, Fathima, and her grandchildren, and it was deemed unlikely that she supported the attack.

After the first explosion, STF, military personnel, and firefighters had arrived at the scene. After the second one, the mangled bodies of Bandara and two other police constables were taken to the hospital by ambulance. Fathima and her children's physical remains were also found.

St Anthony's Church, Second Bomb

As mentioned in one of the preceding sections, IS operator Muaath had parked a VBIED outside St Anthony's Church in Kochchikade on 21 April, which should have exploded within an hour of his IED detonation. The VBIED had been

93 'Ibrahim, family stood nonchalant', *Daily Mirror*.

constructed with a one-hour timer and two trip wires. However, it malfunctioned and did not go off.

On 22 April, the unattended vehicle was discovered and searched by the police. Investigators found one of the trip wires had been partly covered under a blanket by several rupee notes of different denominations. This must have been done to entice an unsuspecting person to lift the blanket to take the money and trigger the explosion. The VBIED was rendered safe through controlled detonation. After which, Muaath's license was found on the ground next to the vehicle. This set-up suggested that he had intended to kill first responders and members of the public. Had the bomb detonated, the church structure would also have collapsed, and would thus have multiplied the death toll and destruction.

IS Claim

Outside Iraq and Syria, the Easter attack was one of the worst ideologically-inspired terrorist attacks by the IS. Inspired by Nilam, the first Sri Lankan fighter to die in Syria, Zahran wanted to be the first IS fighter to die in Sri Lanka. Although Zahran had neither met nor spoken with Nilam, he was in contact with Jhudi Thajudeen, Nilam's widow.

Through Jameel, Zahran was also in contact with Nilam's successor and previously mentioned Sri Lankan contingent leader, Mohammed Zuhair Mohammed Aroos alias Abu Asia until January 2019. As non-Arab foreign fighters in Syria, neither Nilam nor Aroos were ranked high in the IS. Although Aroos sent an audio recording acknowledging Zahran as the IS Sri Lanka branch's amir, neither Aroos nor Zahran had access to the IS central leadership. This meant that neither the regional leadership of the IS nor the IS central knew of the attack in Sri Lanka. Hence, the IS did not claim the attack immediately.

After Zahran entered an operational phase in Sri Lanka in January 2019, the western-led forces pulverized foreign fighters in

Baghouz and communication with the Sri Lankan contingent in Syria was severed. The Easter attack was organized afterwards by Zahran's group without any contact with the IS or with members of the Sri Lankan contingent in Syria.

Eventually, on 23 April 2019, the IS' official channel, Amaq News, would claim responsibility for the Easter Sunday bombings. 'Those who carried out the attack that targeted citizens belonging to the alliance countries and Christians in Sri Lanka are fighters with the IS,' are the exact words that were said.[94]

When Amaq News staked their claim, the government focused on determining how the farewell video was disseminated to the IS central. Investigations identified Qatar-based Sri Lankan Fasrool, originally from Matale, as the connector. Also known as Matale Zahran and Podi Zahran, Fasrool had shared Zahran's farewell video with an IS media group in Indonesia who went on to share it with Amaq News. Fasrool had no direct links with Amaq News, but enjoyed low-level links to the IS supporters. Fasrool reportedly believed that he was in touch with the IS Sri Lanka branch when he was, in fact, communicating with an SIS operator called Sonic Sonic.

Fasrool operated independently from Zahran's group and had become an admirer after watching Zahran's propaganda videos over the years, Fasrool was desperate to meet him personally. An online admirer of Zahran, Fasrool travelled to and arrived in Sri Lanka on 10 April 2019 hoping to meet the IS Sri Lanka branch's leader, but was unable to do so. Although Fasrool lost the opportunity to meet Zahran who would go on to perish in the

[94] Meghna Chakrabarti, 'IS Claims Responsibility For Sri Lanka Bombings', *WBUR On Point,* April 23, 2019, https://www.wbur.org/onpoint/2019/04/23/sri-lanka-bombings-easter-terrorism; Amarnath Amarasingam (@AmarAmarasingam), 'As expected, ISIS has just released video of the attackers in #SriLanka giving bayah (oath of allegiance) to Baghdadi…', Twitter, April 23, 2019, https://twitter.com/AmarAmarasingam/status/1120715960464347137?t=DF-JdkatghCcUhOQfqeIOw&s=19.

Easter Sunday bombings, it was said that Fasrool still wanted to pay homage to his 'idol'. Fasrool reportedly believed it was a waste for an attack of Easter Sunday's magnitude to be overlooked by the State or the IS central leadership. Thus, Fasrool attempted to contact Zahran's team and eventually received the video from IS propagandist turned operator, Ahammadu Lebbe Mohamed Niyaz alias Reporter Niyaz.

Located in Kattankudy, Niyaz worked as a reporter for Puvi Rahamathullah, and was editor of a weekly newspaper, *Varaoraibal.* Niyaz is believed to have started managing Zahran's media portfolio after being enticed by Zahran's speeches. He also ran a mobile repair shop in Kattankudy and was said to have temporarily employed Hashtoon too, another follower of Zahran. Although he left to work in Qatar, he reportedly remained a steadfast supporter of Zahran and returned to Sri Lanka on 14 March 2019. Niyaz was highly trusted by Zahran. He had supported the Easter Sunday attack project and helped develop the group's infrastructure by renting vehicles and property for the intended second wave of attacks. Niyaz would eventually die fighting for and defending his leader's family. His lasting contribution was to make Zahran's legacy live on.

Like Niyaz, who promoted Zahran's Salafi-Wahhabi ideology and later the IS ideology, Fasrool also promoted Zahran's thoughts and work. Both believed in mobilizing and radicalizing Muslims and driving fear and terror into the ranks of supposed 'enemies'. They wanted to influence and shape the human terrain. Reportedly, Fasrool made Zahran a larger-than-life personality by bridging the IS Sri Lanka branch and the IS central. He made the Easter Sunday attack headline news. Like Nilam and his brother Ishaq connected Sri Lankans in Iraq and Syria, Fasrool wanted to do the same for Sri Lankans in Afghanistan and Pakistan. Together with a relative, Fasrool wished to travel to Nangahar in Afghanistan, where the IS Khorasan had established a presence and where he is said to have believed 'pure and pristine Islam' existed. Zahran never met Fasrool, but he indirectly influenced and recruited him; building a momentum in Fasrool, the end of which we have not yet seen. Fasrool apparently resembled Zahran in his charisma and global reach, thus IS followers named him 'Podi Zahran', meaning Little Zahran—another Zahran-in-the-making.

Zahran's legacy and his masterpiece, the Easter attack, is likely to inspire and instigate the next generation of followers and fighters. By staging it, Zahran, a global jihadist living in Sri Lanka, put global jihad into practice on Sri Lankan soil. A practice often likened to that of breaking ground, Zahran's project unleashed his fury and opened the gates to an army of similar wayward individuals disillusioned by a false ideology gap. Unlike his predecessors Ishaq, Nilam, and Aroos, who went to Syria, Zahran and his followers accomplished their goal while living in Sri Lanka. This further suggests inadequate national security apparatus in countering such attacks. Many terrorism experts have reportedly classified the Easter Sunday attacks as a call to fester in Sri Lanka not just as a place to express extremism, but also, more terrifyingly, to breed like-minded devotees. Irrespective of geography, the entire world has now become terrorist groups' theatre of operations. Like Zahran, others may wage global jihad in their own countries—unless the threat is effectively curbed and addressed in a timely manner.

Scenes from Shangri-La Hotel following the attack
Source: STF

Scenes from St Anthony's Church, Kochchikade, following the attack
Source: STF

Scenes from Dematagoda following the attack
Source: STF

'If someone robs, his hand should be amputated and if someone commits adultery, the person should be stoned.'[95]

—Zahran to Hadiya, advocating sharia to be implemented in Sri Lanka

[95] Hadiya, interview, January 20, 2020; Hadiya, interview, January 27, 2020.

Chapter 2

Life and Death of Zahran Hashim

Messiah Complex

As is apparent by now, the key events leading up to the Easter Sunday attacks can be traced back to Zahran Hashim. A fiery orator and a meticulous planner, Zahran founded the IS Sri Lanka branch and staged one of the IS' worst attacks outside Iraq and Syria. Zahran's story provides insights into the genesis and evolution of an alien ideology implanted in Sri Lanka and its consequences. It routes the birthplace of extremism and how it was sown within Sri Lanka's socio-political nexus.

The seeds of the 'messiah complex' were planted in Zahran's mind early in his life.[96] Over the years, his desire to redeem himself, his family, friends, and followers grew. Deeply indoctrinated, Zahran and his followers believed they were serving Allah, Islam, and Muslims; they were convinced their thoughts and actions were inspired by Allah. This culture of hatred and violence culminated and manifested into the Easter Sunday massacre.

Zahran's persona was reportedly one of arrogance, aggression, and zeal; a potent combination that led to an acutely narrow and jaded path of no return. Cognitively inflexible, Zahran stuck

[96] Darren Kelsey, *Media and Affective Mythologies: Discourse, Archetypes and Ideology in Contemporary Politics*, (Cham: Palgrave Macmillan, 2017), p. 155.

to his beliefs. Even when proven wrong, he did not concede. Crude and confrontational, he was contemptuous of other faiths. Zahran blamed other Muslims, Christians, Buddhists, and Hindus for the ills of the world. Eager to occupy a position of power, Zahran was forceful and persevered. His web of thinking and planning reflected grandiosity. Narcissistic, Zahran demonstrated a sense of self-importance, projected an image of how good he was, and harbored an unrealistic sense of superiority. Surrounding himself with people willing to affirm him, he exploited others without guilt and shame. Lacking in empathy, he was oblivious to interpersonal manipulation, and possessed a harsh incapability of understanding foreign worldview. He never feigned to sympathize with those outside his circle and undoubtedly met opposition with defiance and rage.

Born to Poverty

All this begins in Kattankudy, a township on the eastern coast of Sri Lanka, where Zahran was born on 19 July 1986 at Kattankudy Hospital, a government hospital offering free healthcare. Today, it is known as the District Hospital in Arayampathy. He was the oldest followed by two brothers, Zaini and Rilwan, and two sisters, Mathaniya and Hindaya. Except for Mathaniya, Zahran's parents, brothers, Hindaya, and their entire families would eventually perish in a mass suicide in Sainthamaruthu on 26 April 2019, five days after the Easter Sunday attack.

Zahran's parents were from the eastern province of Sri Lanka. When Zahran was born, his father, Hayathu Mohamed Cassim Mohamed, a businessman from Batticaloa, was twenty-two while his mother, Abdul Cader Sitti Sameema from Kattankudy, was only eighteen. The family was Sri Lankan Moor in ethnicity, but they practiced Islam.

Zahran was raised along Mohideen Palli Road, or al Aqsa Palli Road, in New Kattankudy. They lived in extreme poverty and, to support his family, Cassim sold packets of food on the street. Abdul Cader Sitti Sabina, one of Zahran's maternal aunts, had this to say about the family's situation: referring to Cassim, 'The father sold retail items and the family ate for the day. There were days, the family did not eat until 5 p.m.'[97] Eventually, Cassim would even 'turn to petty thievery; he was called "Kallan Hashim" those days'.[98] In a private source file on Zahran, it was said that, 'Two years after Zahran was born, Cassim robbed a push cycle in Kattankudy to feed the family. The village people assaulted him. They placed the cycle around his neck and asked him to carry it saying, "I am the bicycle thief."'[99] Up until that point, Zahran and his family did not follow religion. After this incident, the family joined Tabligh Jamaat and Cassim went on a three-day *jamaat* or missionary retreat. When he returned, he would guide his family to observe the group's religious practices and behaviors.

Apparently, Zahran did not help with his father's business or his mother's housework. Apart from his siblings, he reportedly had no childhood friends and often spent his days in the company of his parents or bothering his brothers and sisters. Due to resource scarcity and poverty, Zahran was said to have been raised in an environment full of family tension and conflicts. This included a long, drawn-out fight between his family, maternal grandmother, and his aunt Sabina over a shared plot of family land, where Cassim was said to have '[taken] over [Sabina's] house and then

---

97 Abdul Cader Sitti Sabina (maternal aunt of IS Sri Lanka branch leader Zahran Hashim), interview by author, December 2020.

98 Lakshmi Subramanian, 'Mastermind of Sri Lanka Blasts—Maulvi Zahran Hashim: Was he a half-baked theologian or a committed Salafi-Wahhabi militant?', *New Age Islam*, May 4, 2019, https://www.newageislam.com/islamterrorism-jihad/lakshmi-subramanian/mastermind-sri-lanka-blasts——maulvi-zahran-hashim-half-baked-theologian-committed-salafi-wahhabi-militant/d/118611.

99 Intelligence Community, confidential source file on Zahran shared with author, 2022.

[their] land too.'[100] After Cassim sold the family land and took the money, the family's relationship with their maternal relatives would become estranged.

Zahran and his family's financial situation would eventually improve after the formation of the NTJ. As a Salafi-Wahhabi cleric and preacher, he steadily built a devout and fanatical following that financed his activities to promote a puritanical version of Islam. However, he was said to have been so religious that he was careful not to spend the funds donated by devotees on himself or the family. As such, Zahran could never go on pilgrimage to Mecca because he lacked the money for it. Unlike his brother Zaini, who was invited to recite the Quran at a contest in Mecca, Zahran could not even visit Saudi Arabia, the land of the two holy mosques. Financial honesty was not just a boiling point of frustration cracking the peace within his family, but a particular point of contention for Zahran as it hindered his ability to effectively practice his faith.

Changing Landscape

Zahran was politicized, radicalized, and mobilized in three phases of exclusivism, extremism, and terrorism. His terminal phase was his exposure to the Islamic caliphate ideology, and, with it, he brought death and destruction to family, friends, followers, and fellow citizens. Kattankudy transformed from a mono-religious enclave to a Salafi-Wahhabi epicentre, and eventually a jihad hub. The most vicious byproduct of Kattankudy, Zahran reflected a new face of religious politics and militancy. Under the cover of religious passion and loyalist fervor, he orchestrated the most damning Islamic terrorist attack Sri Lanka had experienced.

Zahran's transformation was cultivated over time growing up in the densely populated Kattankudy, which hosted the country's

---

[100] Sabina, interview.

largest Muslim settlement. Spanning 3.9 square km, the township was home to forty-five mosques. A bastion of traders and religious preachers, the 'main street of Kattankudy would be turned into a carnival site with food and game stalls, music and entertainment' during the two Eid festivals.[101] Muslims in Kattankudy celebrated the 'birth of the Prophet over twelve nights, by reciting *mawlood* or panegyric poetry after the evening prayer, and which ended in distribution of free food, mostly rice cooked with ghee, to all participants.'[102] Mawlood continued to be celebrated during the third month of the Islamic calendar. Celebrating the Prophet's birthday was a 'religious ritual' and a 'social occasion where people, young and old, gathered and dispersed with happy feelings'.[103]

Similarly, during the eighth Islamic month, multi-volumes of Imam Bukhari's *hadith* collection were recited by clerics in the two big mosques, which would likewise end in food distribution. Although Bukhari recitals continued, some Wahhabis allegedly began attacking Sufi mosques and their leaders, driving fear into the Sufis. Like the Hindus that fulfil their vows by offerings, Sri Lankan Muslims 'donate food or oil or even chooks and goats to the mosques, a part of which were auctioned, and money went to the mosque fund'.[104] Some Wahhabis were said to have opposed these practices including visitation and donation of funds on the eve of a wedding or circumcision at the town's Mawlana Kaburady shrine. The ACJU reportedly did not regulate the religious space strategically or on a daily basis at the time. In turn, these disagreements pre-dating Zahran built up and reached a crescendo during his teenage years.

---

[101] Ameer Ali, 'Kattankudy needs new leadership and direction', *Daily Financial Times*, May 14, 2019, https://www.ft.lk/columns/Kattankudy-needs-new-leadership-and-direction/4-678101.

[102] Ali, 'Kattankudy needs new leadership and direction'.

[103] Ali, 'Kattankudy needs new leadership and direction'.

[104] Ali, 'Kattankudy needs new leadership and direction'.

Historically, the local and traditional Islam was openly practiced in Kattankudy. Zahran himself had been raised to become a traditional Muslim as well. However, after establishing a foothold, resistance and threats from the extremist Wahhabis gradually grew and started to penetrate the social, educational, economic, and political sectors.

Defining Event

Though Sri Lanka is believed to be a tranquil island, this was not always the case, and Kattankudy is one such example. In its thirty-year war, the LTTE conducted the worst massacre of Muslims in the township. When Zahran was five years old, three dozen terrorists disguised as Muslims crossed the lagoon of his town on 3 August 1990. In one of the most brutal attacks staged, the LTTE butchered 147 Muslim men and boys prostrating in Isha prayers at the Meer Jumma and Hussainiya mosques.

With the relentless onslaught from the LTTE, Kattankudy emerged as the hub to defend Muslim villages and towns. Growing up, what Zahran witnessed was very similar to that of a conflict zone. In its project to ethnically cleanse the Muslims in the north and east, the LTTE intermittently killed hundreds of Muslims in Kattankudy and its neighboring areas. The Sri Lanka Army and home guards reportedly enlisted the support of both Wahhabi-Jamaat-e-Islami and Sufi youth to defend Kattankudy.

The 1990 mosque massacre was a turning point. It dissipated the sense of safety and security in the township. To pre-empt another onslaught, it was said that the government armed Muslim groups to protect Kattankudy, with some Wahhabis at the forefront of the fight. The memory of these gruesome attacks were supposedly never forgotten by the Muslims in Kattankudy. For nearly two decades after the LTTE first struck Kattankudy in 1990 until the end of the war in 2009, it was believed that no Muslim could move without an armed military escort. As the Kattankudy Muslims became more isolated, they became increasingly vulnerable to exclusivist and extremist ideologies too. Wahhabi and Jamaat-e-Islami followers formed jihad groups to fight the LTTE, and these same groups reportedly began to target the Sufis—and eventually Sri Lanka.

The massacre in Kattankudy was likely indelible in Zahran's formative phase; the very narrative lived and defined the town. Violence and the idea of attacking places of religious worship to exact revenge was ingrained in Zahran.

Zahran's Education

Despite coming from a poverty-stricken family, Zahran had full access to free education from kindergarten to university as provided by the Sri Lankan government. When he was six years old, his father, Cassim, accompanied him to Al-Ameen Maha Vidyalaya, a mixed government school in Kattankudy. Cassim was not educated, but he valued education and enrolled all the children at school. After being enrolled in 1992, Zahran studied at Al-Ameen from grades one to five, completing his primary education in Tamil, Mathematics, Islam, Environmental Studies, English, and Sinhala.[105]

When Zahran was eleven, Cassim enrolled him in the all-boys Kattankudy Central College, the first Muslim Central College in Sri Lanka. Zahran was an average student at school, but Cassim had other plans. After becoming religious, Cassim preferred that Zahran study in a Tabligh madrasah where he would memorize the Quran and learn sharia. As such, Zahran completed only one year (grade six) of his secondary education at Kattankudy Central College.

105 Interview by author with a schoolteacher, June 1, 2022.

At twelve years old, Zahran left the government school to enroll at Jamiathul Falah Arabic College in Kattankudy. Zahran did well at school—until his younger brother Zaini, who excelled in Quran recitation, also joined the same madrasah. A private source file on Zahran noted the following, 'Arranged annually by the Kingdom of Saudi Arabia through their foreign missions, the students who best recite the [Quran] were invited to compete in Mecca. Zaini was judged the second best. In Saudi Arabia, Zaini received copies of the books of Hadith. After reading the books on Hadith, Zahran started to question the Tabligh clerics at the Falah Madrasah. Without understanding the Sri Lankan context, Zahran said, "What you are teaching is wrong." They cautioned young Zahran and, as punishment, sent him home twice.'[106]

This was the brothers' first foray into Wahhabism, the form of political Islam that was allegedly propagated by Saudi Arabia to rival its geopolitical adversaries. While studying at the madrasah, Zahran and Zaini converted their parents Sameema and Cassim from Tabligh Jamaat to Thowheed Jamaat in 2004. Cassim suffered from ill health and sickness after years of hard work. Because their father was weak, Zahran gradually became more assertive both at home and in school. Together with Zaini, Zahran started to convert their relatives and friends to Wahhabism.

Though Jamiathul Falah Arabic College was established as a Sufi madrasah, Tabligh and eventually Wahhabi influence gradually crept in. When reflecting on Wahhabism in Kattankudy, the M.C.A. Hameed Hajiyar Trust had this to say: 'Kattankudy had Sufis in majority before 1980. Aliyar Riyadhi got selected [to study in] Saudi Arabia on a scholarship [before returning] to Kattankudy and [starting] Centre for Islamic Guidance (CIG). This [was believed to be] the commencement of Saudi infiltration. He [reportedly] convinced other moulavis [to convert to the] Wahhabi ideology.

[106] Intelligence Community, confidential source file on Zahran.

[He also] converted Sufi Alims, [persuading them to] spread Wahhabi ideology in Kattankudy madrasahs. We recall [how at the] Madrasahthul Falah—[the] only madrasah in Kattankudy—Boys Arabic College, [the] syllabus was replaced with Wahhabi ideology *kithabs* (books) by Aliyar Riyadhi. [T]hose who were opposed to this move were [allegedly] bodily attacked or bribed to keep silent. We can name a few moulavis here who were [reportedly] targeted by Aliyar Riyadhi. Athalebbe Moulavi, Aliyar Moulavi, Ameen Moulavi, Zainudeen Moulavi, and Buhari Moulavi [were a] few [of those] who functioned as main *imams* in Grand Jummah Mosque Kattankudy, graduated as Falahi from Madrasahthul Falah Arabic College, Kattankudy, and later became Wahhabis.'[107]

Simply put, teachers and students were believed to have been exposed to Wahhabism at the CIG, a Saudi-funded institution providing resources. While enrolled at the madrasah, the student population including Zahran and Zaini, were gradually radicalized. Apart from the CIG library, the brothers were also said to have been exposed to Wahhabism propagated by the Islamic Centre, another institution in Kattankudy. Their conversion would have grave implications for Sri Lanka's Muslim community. It was said that the extremist Wahhabis intermittently attacked Sufi homes, businesses, and their mosques and shrines. As the Wahhabis' influence in south India and Sri Lanka grew, the Thowheed ideology would eventually penetrate the educational institutions, reportedly making the *hijab* compulsory for women, wearing jewelry forbidden, and growing a beard compulsory for men.

First Wahhabi Organization

With no mechanism to regulate the religious space, Wahhabi mosques, Islamic schools known as *madaris*, and other Islamic

[107] M.C.A. Hameed Hajiyar Trust, 'Some Aspects of Infiltration of Wahhabism in Kattankudy', December 28, 2021.

organizations proliferated. A feature of Sri Lankan Wahhabi organizations was that they were meticulously registered, and they operated openly. For instance, the CIG was incorporated as an Act of Parliament on 4 June 1998, registered at the district secretariat in Batticaloa on 30 March 1992, registered with the Department of Muslim and Religious Cultural Affairs (DMRCA) on 4 November 2004, and registered as Ahadhiya school on 1 October 2007.[108] The general objects of the corporation are listed below:

> '(a) to prepare and guide Muslims to lead and conduct their spiritual and material lives, according to correct Islamic precepts;
> (b) to propagate the preachings of the Holy Quran and the traditions of the Holy Prophet [(peace be upon him)];
> (c) to open, operate, and close bank accounts, and to borrow or raise money, with or without security;
> (d) to invest the funds vested in, or belonging to, the Corporation in adequate securities or in the purchase or acquisition of such movable or immovable property as may be proper or necessary for the purposes of the Corporation; to erect or cause to be erected, any building or structure on any land belonging to the Corporation.'[109]

Aliyar Riyadhi was a member of the board of Jamiathul Falah Arabic College, the madrasah where Zahran was studying.

---

[108] Moulavi Mohamed Aliyar Riyadhi, interview by author, November 9, 2020; Department of Muslim Religious and Cultural Affairs, *Registration of Muslim Religious Institution*, accessed March 6, 2023, https://muslimaffairs.gov.lk/wp-content/uploads/2019/05/Associations-Copy.pdf.

[109] Centre for Islamic Guidance (Incorporation) Act, No. 30 of 1998, Parliament of the Democratic Socialist Republic of Sri Lanka § 3 (1998), https://www.srilankalaw.lk/YearWisePdf/1998/CENTRE_FOR_ISLAMIC_GUIDANCE_(INCORPORATION)_ACT,_NO._30_OF_1998.pdf.

Aliyar was appointed President in 2015 and continues to hold that appointment today. Funded by Saudi Arabia and Kuwait, the CIG expanded into a mosque, religious school, and library with 30,000 books. As the CIG library had the best collection of Islamic books in Arabic and Tamil, Zahran and others often frequented it to read about Wahhabism. Zahran's favourite book was *Kitāb at-Tawḥīd* or *The Book of Oneness*.

P.J.'s Indelible Influence

Another stream of Wahhabi influence in Sri Lanka originated from Tamil Nadu, where 6 per cent are Muslims and the sermons of the most prominent Wahhabi cleric of India and the TNTJ founder, P. Jainulabdeen, or P.J., started to galvanize a tiny segment of Muslim youth. Considered a 'genius' by his followers in Sri Lanka, and known for his powerful memory, especially when demonstrating his deep knowledge of Islamic scriptures, P.J. was admired by the likes of Zahran, Zaini, and Naufer.

He influenced the creation of a series of Thowheed organizations in Sri Lanka. Among the Salafi-Wahhabi leaders and groups in Sri Lanka, P.J. was said to have been the model and his organization the template. Although Zahran went beyond the ideology articulated by P.J., in a fast-escalating rise of radicalization, P.J. was still believed to have been the catalyst in Zahran's formative phase, and that of other youth in Tamil Nadu. P.J. travelled to Sri Lanka in 1989, 1992, 1993, 2001, and 2005. During his last visit in 2005, he spoke in Kattankudy where he influenced then nineteen-year-old Zahran who would go on to join and create Thowheed organizations with others.

The indelible influence in Sri Lanka of the Tamil Nadu Thowheed strain is evident. After it created a footprint in Sri Lanka's eastern and western provinces, where a third of the country's Muslims live, it likely paved the way for a deadlier strain; the IS

Sri Lanka branch emerged in Batticaloa, Ampara, and Colombo through these two hubs. In the western province, Thowheed organizations proliferated in Dematagoda, Maligawatte, and other neighboring suburbs of Colombo. In the eastern province, they were rife in Kattankudy, Batticaloa, and Kalmunai in Ampara. As such, the TNTJ, under P.J., was believed to have radicalized a generation of youth—several of whom would go on to join the IS.

Growing Up

As seen by now, Kattankudy was a heavily charged township and residents, including Zahran, experienced two phases of conflict: the separatist threat and the religious extremist threat. As discussed, Zahran grew up amid a culture of violence and experienced the cycle of attacks, vengeance, retribution, and revenge during the almost two-decade war with the LTTE. Kattankudy residents may have remained resilient, choosing not to abandon their town. However, a good number of them also reportedly succumbed to the threat from within—that is, the rise of Islamic extremism. Extremist Muslims were said to have exploited the fragile security situation. They allegedly inflicted violence and spread propaganda in an attempt to supplant Sufism, thus clashes between the two factions were frequent.

Zahran was too young to join the first phase of violence perpetrated by the extremist Jamaat-e-Islami and Wahhabi followers. However, he was influenced and later identified with the group's exclusivist ideology. A year before Zahran became a teenager, on 29 May 1998, Kattankudy suffered from its first extremist Wahhabi assassination. On the eve of Zahran's twelfth birthday, Farooq Maulvi, who was at the forefront of battling the Wahhabi ideology, was assassinated. The town's main clerical body, Jamiat-ul-Ulema, was infiltrated too. With this, intra-Muslim rivalry surged in Kattankudy. '…the Kattankudy mosque federation and Jamiat-ul-Ulema, came together under the name Eemaniya Nenjangal. The members of this group began telling the Sufis to convert to Wahhabism.'[110]

The seeds of distrust were thus sown in Kattankudy during Zahran's teenage years. With the introduction of political Islam, notably Salafi-Wahhabism and Jamaat-e-Islami, the Muslim community in Kattankudy and elsewhere started to fragment. The clashes and skirmishes grew. Even when the champion of Sufism, Pailwan, died, it was said that some Salafi-Wahhabis wanted to fight his ideas and followers. Vehemently opposed to local and traditional Islam, they reportedly took the opportunity to retaliate against the Sufi community. Not only did some Salafi-Wahhabis allegedly attack Pailwan's burial site, but they also did the same to Sufi homes and establishments. When Zahran was twenty, it was reported that 'On 31 October 2004, at 12.30 p.m., 500 Wahhabis organized under the title 'Jihad' [and] set the Meditation Centre ablaze, destroying its library, along with homes and businesses owned by Sufis.'[111]

A Muslim whose two homes in Kattankudy were burnt down lamented, 'We do not believe in propagating Islam with a sword or a gun. This is against Islam, and we have been a peaceful community of Muslims. We are now helpless in the wake of the Thowheed-backed jihadi group.'[112] The extremist Salafi-Wahhabi-and-Jamaat-e-Islami-supported jihadi groups were said to have been ruthless and relentless in their onslaught. They allegedly planned to decapitate the Sufi leadership, dismantle their infrastructure and disrupt the lives of their followers.

---

110 Subramanian, 'Mastermind of Sri Lanka Blasts'.

111 Stephen Schwartz and Irfan Al-Alawi, 'The Wahhabi Invasion Of Sri Lanka', *Colombo Telegraph*, March 27, 2013, https://www.colombotelegraph.com/index.php/the-wahhabi-invasion-of-sri-lanka/.

112 Kamalendran, Fuard, and Kariyawasam, 'Unholy tension in Lanka's Muslim East'.

Thus, exacting revenge, targeting key religious leaders, and attacking each other's places of religious worship became even more common. Fearing for their lives, hundreds of Sufi followers reportedly converted to Wahhabism in Kattankudy, in November 2004—and many others followed suit in the succeeding years.

As such, it comes as no surprise that the intra- and inter-religious fighting, clashes, and tension where mosques and shrines, homes and businesses were attacked from 2004–2009 had an indelible impact on Zahran's ideation.

A Jihad Hub

The arguably most virulent strain of Salafi-Wahhabism, the doctrine of Thowheed or 'Oneness of God', took root in Sri Lanka at the turn of the century. It was said that this branch of Wahhabism called only to worship Allah and deemed all others His enemies. Thowheed followers were also reportedly more susceptible to embracing the ideologies of al-Qaeda, the IS, and other threat actors. In several instances, they had allegedly called for violence against non-Thowheed Muslims and non-Muslims, attacks against other faiths and followers, and labelled their gods idols.

Zahran started to develop a keen interest in global affairs after al-Qaeda mounted attacks in the US on 11 September 2001. To Zahran and many others, 9/11 was an exhibition attack. Likeminded threat groups worldwide were emboldened to mount attacks against the US and its allies after the US forces intervened in Afghanistan. It was believed that they admired Osama bin Laden, a Salafi-Wahhabi and the architect of the attack. With Muslims suffering in Afghanistan, Palestine, Kashmir, Chechnya, and Somalia, Zahran eventually rejected Tabligh Jamaat, which reportedly opposed Muslim involvement in politics. Zahran decided to embrace Salafi-Wahhabism instead—which allegedly promotes jihad—or, as Zahran would likely have put it, the right to defend Muslims and attack when under threat.

With Salafi-Wahhabism sweeping through Kattankudy, Zahran began to despise its enemies: the west, their allies, and friends. On their target board were the Sri Lankan government and non-believers. Having rejected democracy, which Wahhabis reportedly considered man-made law, Zahran only followed what he believed was Allah's law. It was said that Zahran and his younger brother Zaini—who were both influenced by the CIG—would eventually develop a deep hatred against Sri Lankan Islam, which had evolved through centuries of multireligious interactions.

After committing the Quran to memory and learning sharia, firsthand accounts claimed that, at fifteen, Zahran started arguing with his teachers. At nineteen, he began openly confronting and challenging them, with such incidents peaking in his fourth academic year. After a series of futile warnings, Zahran was reportedly expelled in 2005 for rebellious behavior. When Cassim was informed, he was distraught. Cassim appealed but was ultimately unsuccessful. He was told his son had gone too far. 'Our teaching is based on the Quran and Hadeeth, but Zahran had different views. We felt he was trying to bring a "Naveena Markam" or a new religion. We wear the skullcap when we pray, but he opposed this practice. We pray twenty units of "Taraweeh" prayers during Ramadan, but he argued that we should pray only eight units,' were Vice Principal As-Sheikh Mohammed Aliyar Falahi's exact words.[113]

Elaborating on Zahran's pattern of quarreling with the teachers, Vice President Aliyar, who was also a trustee at the Mohiuddin Meththai Grand Jumma mosque in Kattankudy,

---

113 Ameen Izzadeen and Abdullah Shahnawaz, 'Lightning, thunder and a blast: On the trail of terror leader', *The Sunday Times, Sri Lanka*, April 28, 2019, https://www.sundaytimes.lk/190428/news/lightning-thunder-and-a-blast-on-the-trail-of-terror-leader-347130.html.

detailed Zahran's anti-institution mentality, 'He fought with the elders on our ways of prayer. He caused confusion among youth and exhorted them not to wear [skullcaps]. He certainly knew how to foment trouble.'[114]

Jamiathul Falah Arabic College was in transition at the time. The madrasah was Sufi, then Tabligh, but Salafi-Wahhabi teachers and administrators gradually infiltrated it. A number of its radicalized students and graduates—including Zahran—would eventually form and join exclusivist, extremist, and even terrorist groups. As mentioned previously, before Zahran was expelled, the CIG and the Islamic Centre in Kattankudy had already started to influence him and the fledgling Thowheed core, including Naufer Moulavi. Naufer was Zahran's senior and mentor and deeply influenced him. Both would go on to join a Thowheed fraternity, coming together to change the landscape of Kattankudy and later Sri Lanka.

To gain organizational control, the very first organization Naufer and Zahran attempted to infiltrate was the Islamic Centre, which was a local Salafi-Wahhabi institution established by Abu Bakr Falahi. Abu Bakr was a graduate of Madrasah Falah, the same Arabic college where Zahran and Naufer studied and reportedly had business interests in Saudi Arabia. After Abu Bakr's death in 2000, land was bought a few years later in 2004 and, in 2005, the Centre established the Jamaat Thowheed mosque.

In the second half of 2005, Zahran and Naufer rallied against the leadership of the Islamic Centre and questioned their teachings. 'Brainwashed by Naufer, the mastermind, the young Zahran openly said, "What you are preaching is not [Thowheed]"'.[115] In an interview discussing Zahran, Mohammad Mohilar, secretary

---

[114] V Shoba, 'Sri Lanka: The Hunt Widens', *Open*, May 2, 2019, https://www.openthemagazine.com/article/dispatch/sri-lanka-the-hunt-widens.

[115] Shoba, 'Sri Lanka: The Hunt Widens'.

of the Islamic Centre, said, '[Zahran] was a good social worker but lacked maturity. I thought of him as a brother and advised him to study more, but he didn't want any guidance. For instance, we are all for gradually banning *seedhanam* [dowry, often given in the form of a house when a girl gets married] but he said you must outlaw it overnight, otherwise you are not true Muslims. He took the route of instant fame. Once, when we gave him a chance to speak for fourteen minutes at a *jumma*, he went on for an hour-and-a-half and that was the end of our association.'[116]

This was but one example of Zahran's extremist and divisive beliefs. After being radicalized by the Salafi-Wahhabi organizations, Zahran wanted an immediate revolution—not a gradual evolution. He took radicalization to another level.

Co-creating Daarul Adhar

After Zahran was expelled from Falah Madrasah and removed from the Islamic Centre, the Salafi-Wahhabi network was reportedly reluctant to support him openly, though it was said that many still supported him discreetly. Amid impediments and challenges, Zahran eventually found an opportunity. A Salafi-Wahhabi madrasah, Ibnu Masood Arabic College in Hettipola under Moulavi Nasurudin, offered him a placement. Although Zahran did not graduate as a moulavi from the college, he was given the honorific title, Moulavi Zahran al Masoodi.

As for his plans with Naufer, after failing to infiltrate the Islamic Centre, Zahran and Naufer—student and teacher—sought to build their own Salafi-Wahhabi organization in Kattankudy to further harness support for the ideology. To operationalize this, Naufer founded Daarul Adhar ad Da'iyyah with Zahran. Led by Naufer, Daarul Adhar emerged as one of the most active

116 Shoba, 'Sri Lanka: The Hunt Widens'.

Salafi-Wahhabi organizations in the township. Although they did not openly call for attacks against Sufis, their doctrine reportedly called for subduing local and traditional Islam and replacing it with Thowheed ideology. Zahran started working for the organization in 2007. Under Naufer's guidance, he developed his mastery of Arabic, understanding of the Middle East, and use of the internet, especially social media.

Apart from Zahran, other Jamiathul Falah students also joined Daarul Adhar. These included Taufiq Moulavi, who would later go on to head the NTJ, and Niyaz, a journalist, who would help build the organization's media and communication activities, especially its short message service. Their organization was said to have focused on addressing social issues such as drug abuse, corporal punishment, and sexual harassment from an Islamic perspective. Zahran would also go on to establish the Daarul Adhar Jumma School. The school, which promoted Salafi-Wahhabism, was believed to have gradually and incrementally politicized and radicalized the children attending it. Zahran was dedicated and played an active role in the organization from 2007–2009, eventually gaining a place on its management committee.

After the LTTE war ended, jihad groups in the eastern province converged in Kattankudy for rest and recuperation.[117] At the convening, Zahran, who identified himself as 'Moulavi M.C. Zahran, the Propaganda Secretary of the Thowheed group in Kattankudy', said, 'We are not at all responsible for any incidents. Our members who number around 2,000 practice true Islam. We strongly oppose those who resort to un-Islamic practices.'[118] In his own words, he also firmly declared, 'There have been all forms of allegations against us. They say we got funds from west

[117] Asif Fuard (defence analyst and strategic communications specialist), interview by author, June 24, 2022.

[118] Kamalendran, Fuard, and Kariyawasam, 'Unholy tension in Lanka's Muslim East'.

Asia. They say we have weapons and are a militant group. We strongly deny these allegations.'[119] Just like the others, Zahran also believed that there was no other correct form of Islam. The Thowheed doctrine was so deeply ingrained in them that some believed it was the only way forward. Those deeply influenced by the doctrine were said to have been intolerant of local and traditional Islam. Perhaps it was this fire in them that would turn some into exclusivists and extremists, willing to use terror and violence to spread their ideology beyond Kattankudy. In other words, they were set on a path of war.

From the jihad hub of Kattankudy, the ideology spread island-wide, reportedly calling Sufis infidels or kafirs, apostates or *murthad*. Zahran would later use these same words to demonize his enemies on the eve of the Easter attacks.[120] Radicalization spread from the east, west, and south of Sri Lanka resulting in clashes between followers of Thowheed and Sufi ideologies and, later, Muslims and non-Muslims. As threat of Salafi-Wahhabism continued to spread, Zahran received an opportunity to preach at a mosque in Japan from January to March 2009 on what he claimed to be a three-month lecture tour.

After his return, the relationship between Zahran and the others at Daarul Adhar deteriorated. This was reportedly due to envy and because the credibility of his accomplishments in Japan was questioned. This included his giving lectures in Urdu, even though the others at Daarul Adhar knew 'he did not know Urdu'.[121] It was said that 'While other members of management worked as a team, Zahran wanted to speak for himself.' There was an incident of him misquoting Islamic scripture too.

---

[119] Kamalendran, Fuard, and Kariyawasam, 'Unholy tension in Lanka's Muslim East'.

[120] Fuard, interview.

[121] Izzadeen and Shahnawaz, 'Lightning, thunder and a blast'.

'Upset with his habits, the mosque prohibited him from giving speeches for three months in 2009. He never returned.'[122] They had a permanent falling out.

End of War

Zahran was twenty-three years old when the Sri Lankan war ended in May 2009. The government would go on to partially disarm the jihad groups, but militant Muslims were said to have covertly stashed a few dozen weapons.

The Salafi-Wahhabi groups in Kattankudy, forming the core of the jihad ideology, continued their agenda discreetly. The turbulent life of Kattankudy Muslims, including Zahran's, created a tumultuous relationship with Sufis and other communities, such as the Tamils, Sinhalese, Christians, Hindus, and Buddhists.

After Zahran clashed with the leaders of Daarul Adhar, the relations between him and Naufer remained strained. From Qatar, Naufer even argued via social media with Zahran—creating further discord. When Zahran left the organization in September 2009, he had already developed an affinity with the jihadists such as Milhan, who worked with Police Faiz and Niyaz, both of whom he met during his time with Daarul Adhar. Both would later become Zahran's associates.

Tamil Nadu Strain of Wahhabism

In late 2009, Zahran started to work as a preacher with the SLTJ, the TNTJ's sister Islamist organization that 'seeks and spreads Islamic knowledge in its purest form', and the ACTJ, which

---

[122] Shalini Ojha, 'Sri Lanka blasts: Brothers, father of mastermind killed in gunbattle', *NewsBytes*, April 28, 2019, https://www.newsbytesapp.com/news/world/sri-lanka-blasts-kin-of-mastermind-killed/story.

reportedly began to have links to the IS in 2014.[123] Zahran served both the Kattankudy branch and Colombo headquarters of the SLTJ and was in touch with the ACTJ's leader Wazni Nizar.[124]

Although Zahran never joined the ACTJ or SLTJ formally, he often delivered sermons at their events. A popular preacher, he built a following within the Thowheed fraternity. The three sects he rejected were Sufi, Tabligh, and Shia. Although he challenged and debated their leaders, Zahran never addressed their events.

As much as Zahran influenced the Thowheed fraternity, the Thowheed organizations also influenced Zahran. Though they often broke off, the ideologies of the TNTJ in Tamil Nadu and the ACTJ, SLTJ, CTJ, and NTJ in Sri Lanka were almost identical; the differences were insignificant, and they mostly clashed over leadership and personality issues. Influenced by these groups, Zahran would later form the Kattankudy Thowheed Jamaat (KTJ), the predecessor to the NTJ while Abdul Razik broke away from the SLTJ and formed Ceylon Thowheed Jamaat. With the plethora of groups, the Thowheed brand of Islam spread especially in Muslim enclaves in the western and eastern provinces.

Zahran's Thowheed Organizations

As seen thus far, Zahran's views were growing increasingly radical and extreme, which caused him to be at loggerheads with the SLTJ. As such, and as mentioned previously, Zahran would strike out on his own, forming his own organization called the KTJ in 2011. Having built a reputation as a fiery orator, Zahran already had a following and staff on hand. 'Hence, Zaini Moulavi, Taufiq Moulavi, Safi Moulavi, and a few others left Daarul Adhar with

---

[123] IANS, 'Mystery shrouds Sri Lankan group behind carnage', *Business Standard*, April 23, 2019, https://www.business-standard.com/article/news-ians/mystery-shrouds-sri-lankan-group-behind-carnage-119042301027_1.html.

[124] Hadiya, interview, January 20, 2020; Hadiya, interview, January 27, 2020.

Zahran Moulavi,' said an insider who did not wish to be identified. This group remained close with Zahran even when he formed the KTJ, after his stint at the SLTJ.

Zahran rented a place in front of his house, which was in Fisheries Road, New Kattankudy, to convene his organization. To listen to his sermons, Zahran's followers came to a small shed, a makeshift mosque, that he named the KTJ. Followers were registered as members, and they discussed and contributed funds to purchase land to build an actual mosque. With what was said to be financial support from the Thowheed fraternity, KTJ aggressively promoted Wahhabi ideology and reportedly countered local and traditional Islam.

Later, to mobilize his following outside Kattankudy, Zahran would rename the KTJ to NTJ, effectively founding this new organization in 2012. Headquartered in Kattankudy, the NTJ received funding from overseas. Zahran propagated foreign ideologies inimical to Sri Lanka and he used the organization to both radicalize and identify those willing to support the IS.

The NTJ preachers included his brother, Zaini, a qualified cleric, and Shafi, an unqualified one. Zahran's senior and former mentor, Naufer did not join the NTJ. The future head of the IS Sri Lanka's military wing, Milhan, was also working in Qatar at the time. Naufer said, 'When I went to have meals at a restaurant called Lakbima, I got to know Milhan from Kattankudy who was working in the building construction field. In that moment, I talked with him about the situation in Sri Lanka. We discussed issues that have been aroused between Daarul Adhar and NTJ.'[125] It may be worth noting that Sri Lankan intelligence's coverage of radical groups was still at an early stage here and would develop proficiency over time. However, perhaps if Sri Lanka had readily established a foreign intelligence service, it may have understood the rising tide of religious extremism. It may have, in turn,

[125] Statement by Naufer to the police, shared with author, October 19, 2020.

better monitored its local manifestations and disrupted these developments much earlier.

Zahran's Environment

Zahran's social environment, which profoundly influenced his beliefs, was the product of an inter-generational cultural and political radicalization of Muslims. The Muslim community was fragmented, with factions ranging from Sufism, syncretic Islam, to Tabligh Jamaat, conservative Islam, and Thowheed Jamaat, a political ideology. Influenced by their own milieus, Zahran and Naufer took this ideology to another level—the Islamic caliphate.

The Kattankudy landscape—from the mosques to the palm trees—is said to mirror the Gulf. This was likely due to the influence of foreign, particularly Arab, ideologies penetrating the township. The transformation was also evident in the culture and how the townspeople dressed. For instance, among Zahran's maternal relatives, his grandmother continued to wear the *saree*, which was the traditional attire of Sri Lankan Muslims. On the other hand, his mother, Sameema, began wearing a niqab to cover her face after joining Tabligh Jamaat, which she then stopped using after joining Thowheed Jamaat. Eventually, in Zahran's parental family, the women in sarees started wearing black *abayas*. Meanwhile, Zahran, who used to wear a *sarong* like his father, would also begin wearing ankle-length black trousers with plain white or light long-sleeved shirts with slippers.

With the Arabization and Islamization of Kattankudy, the hijab and *thob* reportedly started replacing the saree and the sarong. To create a 'pure' Islamic society, Zahran enlisted Muslim youth driven by extremist Wahhabism and Jamaat-e-Islami ideologies. Harnessing the support of a half a dozen organizations in Kattankudy, he started to raise awareness and enforce discipline. Learning from others, Zahran built the vanguard; the pioneers that would show the way to others.

Marriage and Married Life

As has been established, Naufer was Zahran's mentor. With cavernous eyes and a baritone voice, Naufer was said to have mesmerized his disciples. After he married from Kekunagolla in Kurunegala, they would often come over to visit him—and Zahran was no exception. During one such visit in 2005, a nineteen-year-old Zahran saw Hadiya for the first time. Hadiya, who was ten at the time, had gone to the mosque in Kekunagolla to study the Quran.[126]

Zahran did not waste time and, the very next day, asked Naufer about her, to which Naufer replied she was his 'wife's eldest sister's daughter'. With her parents in Kekunagolla, Hadiya lived with her three elder brothers, sister, and a younger brother. Zahran reportedly proposed to her immediately but was asked by her parents to wait until she completed her General Certificate of Education, Advanced Levels, at the Kekunagolla National School, a well-known Muslim school in Kurunegala District.

Zahran did not forget Hadiya. He waited patiently for four years and, during this period, started to build a network by preaching and propagating the Salafi-Wahhabi ideology. Meanwhile, Hadiya studied until grade nine, after which her grandfather said she could get married as her education was sufficient and she was at 'attaining age'.[127] This was reinforced by Hadiya, who said that, according to Islam, '[u]sually when a girl attains age at 12–14, they are permitted to marry.'[128] Hadiya liked studying, but her marriage ended her education. Nevertheless, she was said to have looked forward to what her married life would bring—unaware of the carnage that was to follow her and her family's lives in the coming time.

---

[126] Hadiya, interview, January 20, 2020; Hadiya, interview, January 27, 2020.

[127] Hadiya, interview, January 20, 2020; Hadiya, interview, January 27, 2020.

[128] Hadiya, interview, January 20, 2020; Hadiya, interview, January 27, 2020.

After Zahran returned from Japan in 2009, a dispute at Daarul Adhar arose. This continued between Naufer, who wanted to stay, and Zahran, who left. A month before the marriage in September 2009, Zahran fell out with Naufer. Though Naufer had said he would attend the wedding, their dispute further intensified and, ultimately, Naufer cut things off with Zahran for good. Zahran and Hadiya married in Kattankudy on 16 October 2009. The wedding was held in Zahran's cousin Fawmiya's house and was attended by family and relatives—excluding Naufer.

Zahran's Married Life

Hadiya lived with Zahran in his parental home in Kattankudy for three months. In addition to his parents, Zahran's brothers and sisters were in the house too. For every month Hadiya spent in Kattankudy, she spent 2–3 weeks with her parents in Kekunagolla. As both the families were Salafi-Wahhabis, there were reportedly no ideological disputes.

Zahran's activities with his organizations and, eventually, the IS would keep both Zahran and Hadiya busy in the years following their marriage. They eventually moved to Zahran's rented house at Fisheries Road and, a few years later, Hadiya would give birth to a daughter on 7 July 2015.

Later, in April 2016, Hashtoon from Ottamawadi in Valachchinai would visit the NTJ mosque to meet Zahran. Shortly after, Hadiya would meet Sara, Hashtoon's wife who had converted from Hinduism to Islam. They became close friends over time. The internet-savvy Hashtoon and Sara would become Zahran and Hadiya's most trusted associates and invaluable assets to build the NTJ profile and support the NTJ operations.

Apart from a house that Zahran built in Kekunagolla, throughout his life with Hadiya, they lived on rented properties and relocated frequently after Zahran became a fugitive.

The Drift

After Zahran married Hadiya, Zahran and Naufer grew even further apart. After Zahran was expelled from Daarul Adhar, there was no contact and communication between him and Naufer from 2009–2016. While Zahran established the NTJ in Kattankudy in 2012, Naufer guided Daarul Adhar from Qatar and the dispute between both organizations persisted.

In parallel to the NTJ, Daarul Adhar grew. Niyaz managed Daarul Adhar's Zajil News, where he helped with propagating the Salafi-Wahhabi ideology. 'Niyaz lived in another world', said an intelligence officer who monitored the news service but did not wish to be identified.[129] When there was a dispute over the mosque in Dambulla, he reportedly amplified the incident to create a conflict. He portrayed the discord as if there was killing between the two communities. In other words, he sensationalized events.

After summoning him, then-Major Prabath Bulathwatte, a military intelligence officer in Batticaloa, would tell him, 'Do not write falsehoods.'[130] Niyaz was told that what he wrote would create emotions of hate and anger. Ideologically motivated, and believing he was doing God's work, Niyaz laid low for a few days and started his campaign once again to spread Salafi-Wahhabism with even more aggression. When Muslim youth committed to defending Muslim towns and villages from the LTTE drifted towards radicalization, the Sri Lankan military intelligence officers brought them in for guidance and counselling and recovery of firearms to pre-empt their drift towards extremism.

Rise of the NTJ

As mentioned in preceding sections, Zahran's NTJ was run by four clerics—Zahran himself, Taufiq, Shafi, and Zaini—who left

[129] Interview by author with an intelligence officer in the eastern province, Sri Lanka, June 27, 2021.

[130] Interview with an intelligence officer in the eastern province.

Daarul Adhar with Zahran to form the organization. To build a network in the country, Zahran moved to Kekunagolla, where Hadiya's family lived. He built a following in Mawanella, which was about two hours from Kekunagolla. The Thowheed mosques were the ideal hubs for spreading the Salafi-Wahhabi ideology. As such, he moved to other locations in the same district of Kegalle to preach and reach out to the youth. He also travelled to neighboring villages and towns in Ganethanna, even going as far as Nuwara Eliya and Nawalapitiya in the Kandy district to spread the ideology.

Zahran likely saw himself as a reformer, dedicating his life to purifying Islam and cleansing Muslim society. He focused on sharia, Tarbiya, and Aquida. Tarbiya, which covered individuals and groups, meant development and the training—especially of children—in terms of physical, educational, moral, and spiritual needs. Aquida meant Islamic creed or belief.

Zahran often travelled a day or two from Kattankudy. When Zahran travelled, Hadiya was left with either her parents or Zahran's parents. In Ganethenna, where they lived for 6–7 months, Hadiya became pregnant again. Hadiya relocated to Kekunagolla to give birth to their son, who was born on 30 October 2011. Afterwards, they relocated to New Kattankudy and lived on Fisheries Road near Shafi Moulavi's house. Shafi Moulavi was an electrician who doubled as Zahran's cook and driver.

With the support of family, friends, and followers, Zahran would go on to create the NTJ. Zahran put together a *sittuwa*—a traditional fund-raising practice where the pooled funds would eventually be paid back over time to contributors. He collected money, and with additional funds from friends, purchased a three-wheeler. To raise more funds, Zahran worked consistently; both as a preacher and briefly as a three-wheeler driver for other schoolchildren. In 2013, with funds from one of his followers, Haja, Zahran also purchased a motor bike, which he used from 2013–2017. To win public support, the NTJ also engaged in social work. They donated blood, cleaned schools, and provided food and other services to people affected by floods. In addition to contributing *zakat*, NTJ members provided Rs. 5,000–10,000 for social services.

Zahran had a windfall in 2013 when he found a financier to support the NTJ. This was Haja Najmuddin, from Singapore and one of Zahran's few overseas followers. Influenced by the IS, Haja believed that if he gave money to Zahran, he would be spared from his obligation to fight in Syria. Haja would visit Zahran for three days in 2015 where the latter was said to have convinced the former that there were many different ways to please Allah. To help build the mosque, Haja returned to Sri Lanka in 2016 and donated Rs. 50,000 to Zahran. With these funds, Zahran paid Rs. 100,000 for land in New Kattankudy to start building the NTJ mosque in October 2016.

Haja's agent in Colombo, Kumar, also provided Rs. 5 million in stages to Zahran, who purchased cement and iron for the mosque's construction. Once built, the mosque would eventually generate funds to support Zahran and his fraternity. More than that, Zahran's standing in the eyes of his peers, community, and followers grew. Using the funds from Haja, Zahran also purchased land in Palamunai amounting to Rs. 2.5 million.

Zahran's Entry to Politics

In the last two decades, the Thowheed fraternity in Kattankudy emerged as a powerful political force. The political leaders would not have been able to neglect this emerging reality and likely formed political relations with Thowheed entities. The most aggressive group was Zahran's NTJ. Referring to Sri Lankan Muslim politician, M.L.A.M. Hizbullah, Zahran's wife Hadiya claimed that 'Hizbullah brought Zahran to politics—he was unknown and relied on his influence.'[131] Although this is Hadiya's perspective and may not be

[131] Hadiya, interview, January 20, 2020; Hadiya, interview, January 27, 2020.

the reality, it is worth noting that it was not just Hizbullah but also other political leaders who had met with Zahran.

For instance, a mainstream Muslim politician from Kattankudy, Shibly Farooq, worked with a range of parties including the People's Alliance and the Sri Lanka Muslim Congress. After Shibly Farooq won the eastern province's provincial council election in 2012, he reportedly declared at a political meeting in Palamunai that he did not support murthad or those who left Islam. A Sufi leader who did not wish to be identified said, 'He is a Tabligh Jamaat who worked with the Thowheed sects after 2012 to win votes.' Another resident of Kattankudy added, 'Very clever, Muslim politicians played with all communities and sects to win votes.'[132]

In the lead-up to the general election in 2015, it was said that neither Zahran nor Hadiya voted in the election. Hadiya was not a registered voter in Kattankudy and Zahran did not believe in the electoral system. Nonetheless, perhaps to gain political advantage of the electoral process in 2014, Thowheed groups in Kattankudy met with Economics Development Deputy Minister M.L.A.M. Hizbullah, who represented the Mahinda-Rajapaksa-led United People's Freedom Alliance (UPFA), As Sheikh A.L. Mumthaz Madani, and Urban Council Chairman S.H.M. Asfar. The Thowheed groups who were present included Daarul Adhar, Darul Manar, the SLTJ, Islamic Centre, the CIG, Majid al Kuba, and the NTJ, which Zahran represented. Hizbullah had appointed a Sufi called M.I.M. Jaseem as Urban Council Vice Chairman in Kattankudy, to which the Thowheed representatives reportedly said, 'According to Islam, you cannot politically or personally help [m]urthad organizations… Do not betray Islam. We will give you the votes.' Hizbullah was initially said to have been non-committal but, likely due to pressure, eventually conceded and would 'consider their request'.

The NTJ also took this opportunity and announced in a letter that they would support the candidate that would sign

---

[132] Interview by author with a prominent lawyer in Kattankudy, Sri Lanka, February 1, 2023.

an agreement with the NTJ not to support murthad. National Front for Good Governance Chairman M.M. Abdur Rahman, Sri Lanka Muslim Congress representative Shibly Farooq, and UPFA representative Hizbullah were said to have met the group individually at the NTJ mosque. Representing the NTJ were Zaini, Zahran, their sister's husband Niyaz alias auto Niyaz, and Taufiq. The NTJ announcement was as follows:

Why did NTJ make a political pact with Muslim politicians?

Dear Islamic Brothers and Sisters! Assalamu Alaikum Warahmatullah. This time sixteen major political parties and thirty independent groups are contesting the parliamentary elections on behalf of the Batticaloa district. You are well aware that in the Batticaloa district with five MPs, 388 people are vying for power, in which Muslim politicians are also active. Last [(3 August 2015 and 4 August 2015)] the National [Thowheed] Jamaat entered into a historic agreement with Muslim politicians with the aim of disciplining Muslim politicians and introducing a new order in the political stream.

What is the contract for?

Most politicians do not listen to advice. They have the power to control it and to achieve what they set out to do. They are going to the parliament by the vote of the people and are doing politics to get comfortable without doing the politics of rights. They sell out society when they get the chance. There is no order in our society to discipline them and impose reasonable restrictions. No religious organization controls politicians when election time comes. In other words, the da'awa organizations have no control plan. We see the religious movements, which have to boldly agree to call politicians and say, 'We will vote for you only if you are bound by the unselfish conditions we impose, otherwise we will go to the field against you.'

We prepared and sent it to the Muslim politicians contesting in this district. Among the politicians who visited the terms of the agreement were:

Brother M.S. Shafi Salih, on behalf of the Sri Lanka Muslim Congress Party.

Brother M.F.M. Shibly Farooq, on behalf of the [UPFA].

Brother M.L.A.M. Hizbullah, on behalf of the United National Party.

Brother A.L.M. Ruby, on behalf of the National Council for Good Governance.

Brother M.M. Abdur Rahman sent a letter of consent to make the agreement.

Therefore, the National [Thowheed] Jamaat entered into a political agreement with them.

Can we make pacts with political traitors in the past?

Contracts can be made with anyone. Throughout the history of Islam, the Messenger of Allah [(peace be upon him)] made frequent agreements with the Jews and the apostates.

If the other party breaks the contract, they will not re-contract. The deal we have made is not an election-time opportunistic deal. What has happened in the past is that if someone offers to sign, saying, 'Then I will do the right thing and see the field against me if I break the agreement,' he cannot be sidelined and make a deal with other politicians alone. We are well aware that our pact will not be enforced by hypocritical politicians for long. If any politician violates the agreement made with him, the agreement with him will be automatically cancelled. We will never re-contract with him after that.

Who do you vote for if you agree with everyone?

We have appointed a 'Monitoring Committee' to monitor the political activities of politicians after the signing of the agreement. Insha'Allah we will campaign to support those who go beyond the limits of the contract if the politicians are acting in violation of the terms of the contract. If everyone keeps the agreement, we will campaign 'Vote for whoever you want'.

There is no other method to eradicate evil politics except this trap.

This is the deal we made!

1. *They should not forget the goal and act for politics in this condition. Topics covered include:*
   - A. *[They] should completely avoid firecracker culture.*
   - B. *During election periods, they should abandon the practice of post-election processions.*
   - C. *When they go on an election campaign or share an election victory, they must get rid of the 'culture they carry on the skins of their supporters'.*
   - D. *They should restrict the playing of songs mixed with music in their election campaign advertisements or campaign platforms.*
   - E. *Abandon false praise of individuals and false praise of parties and movements.*
   - F. *They should use the slogan 'no one should cast fake votes' in their election campaign.*
   - G. *Do not make baseless accusations against other politicians or political parties. If you make an allegation, you should come forward to prove it with appropriate evidence.*
   - H. *It is necessary to consult with the NTJ Ulama as they consult with other Ulama when carrying out development projects related to the goal.*
   - I. *They should not openly or covertly provide financial support or political power support to the religious practices of Advaitis, Shias, grave worshipers, etc. who have left Islam.*
   - J. *They should not participate in the religious activities of Advaitis, Shias, grave worshipers who have converted from Islam.*
   - K. *When they take part in public events, they are completely prohibited from participating in other religious rituals, offering salutations, bowing hands, lighting ruthu lamps, prostrating at the feet of leaders, garlanding idols, offering khailagu to women, dancing, singing, and musical performances in violation of Islamic law should be avoided.*

2. *They should not take up the culture of violence for the sake of politics.*

   The contents of this clause are as follows:

   A. *Do not attack other politicians or their supporters in any way.*
   B. *Do not damage the belongings of alternative politicians, including their offices, banners and houses, or the belongings of their supporters.*

3. *There should be a need for transparency in the educational and health development projects they undertake.*

   The contents of this clause are as follows:

   A. *The 'Technical Research Report' should be published in their development plans.*
   B. *All matters relating to tenders in development shall be public.*
   C. *If constructive criticisms are leveled at their development and political activities, they should be responded to in a timely manner.*
   D. *A departmental committee should be appointed as supervisors while carrying out developments. The NTJ should also be included in that group.*
   E. *The departmental monitoring committee should be appointed at least 100 days after the election.*
   F. *The appointed committee should meet with them at least once every six months to give them an opportunity to discuss the benefits of the town.*
   G. *When the political party they belong to takes a wrong decision, they should immediately explain to the NTJ about it and inform the people.*

4. *When the shrines of Muslims or temples of other minorities are attacked, it is appropriate to issue stern condemnations in a timely manner.*

   Go to the scene on time and tell the government the truth and be the one to call the government.

5. *Racist opposition to clothing that reflects the culture of Muslims. They should try to take action by issuing timely denials without keeping their mouths shut while releasing.*

6. *When the life, property, and livelihood of Muslims are threatened, the people should pressurize the government to provide them, due protection.*

7. *They should focus on the reform of Muslim private law and give a strong voice as NTJ strives for it.*

8. *When racists argue that 'Sri Lankan Muslims do not have a long history', they should not remain silent and issue a statement against it.*

9. *If anyone connects the Muslims of this country with terrorist movements, they should issue a proper denial without keeping their mouths shut.*

10. *It should be insisted that, the duty of the government to interfere with the rights of a minority community in religious matters is not a democratic right or freedom of expression. Rather, it is a 'law and order problem.'*

11. *They should create an environment through democratic means of struggle so that if there is a 'law and order problem' in our society, the government should take notice of it.*

12. *The politicians must provide their full cooporation to the Bar Association when they fight against the 'law and order problems' in their community.*

13. *As the NTJ carries out the task of internationalizing the problem of Muslims in this country, they must work with us to confront obstacles posed by the government or racists.*

14. *When the NTJ holds discussions among the religions, you must provide full cooperation.*

15. *When there are problems faced by the muslim society, it has to be brought to the notice of the officers in due time.*
Also the seriousness of the problem must be informed to the civil, social leaders and to the foreign embassies, specially the embassies of the Arabic countries.

16. *If the racists provide wrong information about Islam and the history of Muslims, and if the NTJ is oposing that, then you must provide full support to us.'*

17. *If abuses of power by government officials are brought to their notice, they should take appropriate action.*

18. *You have to work in front line, regarding solving the problems of muslims, regarding land and resettlement.*
In that, the guidelines of NTJ and the civil social groups must be considered.

19. *Once you gain authority, you must make a public promise to, confirm that you will not engage in fraudulent activities.*

20. *When the government authorities are in the process of misusing authority and if it is brought to your concern, you must take due action.*

21. *If the contract is to be made with us and the contract is to be entered into with a separate party, the second contract they make must not be in breach of the first agreement made with us.*

22. *After entering into an agreement with us, the agreement they enter into with other political parties, congregations or individuals should be made public.*

23. *You must publicly declare your contract with us.*

Dear brothers!
These are our terms of contract.

Our support is for whoever maintains these rules. Alhamdulillah if all politicians follow these rules, they are all worthy of ruling power. But selfish people don't like it.

Insha'Allah we will see.

Abdur Rahman, Shibly Farooq, and Hizbullah reportedly signed the agreement with the NTJ, vowing not to support Sufi organizations and that no music would be played on the election stage. Rahman and Farooq joined forces and contested under the SLMC against Hizbullah. Although Hizbullah was defeated in the 2015 general elections, he was appointed to the parliament as a member under the UPFA national seat. In retaliation, Hizbullah's supporters were said to have arrived near the NTJ mosque, where the congregation was praying at the time, and lit firecrackers. Afterwards, a group assaulted Rilwan, who suffered a head injury and was rushed to Batticaloa general hospital, where he recuperated for 5–6 days. Apart from NTJ followers and relatives, Rilwan was also reportedly visited by Farooq, Rauf Hakeem, and a few other politicians. Zahran believed that such acts of violence should be met with the same level of brutality, and spearheaded the fight against the Sufis from that point onwards.

As extremism occasionally surged in ethnic and religious communities, the intelligence community constantly worked with law enforcement to curb their activities. It was also believed that some politicians allegedly exploited religious and ethnic sentiments to advance their narrow personal and party interests. During this time, there were very few officers with the understanding and knowledge to tackle religious extremism. The Yahapalana government had witnessed intelligence officers investigated, indicted, and incarcerated. When the IS was seeded and entered a formative phase, then-Major Prabath Bulathwatte and Sergeant Khaleel, both subject matter specialists, were no longer operational. While then-Major Prabath Bulathwatte was reportedly transferred out in 2013 and imprisoned in February 2017, Corporal Khaleel was imprisoned in January 2016. They were eventually released from custody, but human rights activists alleged they engaged in extra-judicial atrocities.

With their arrests, the intelligence capacity to monitor threat personalities and networks closely depleted. With disruptions in the security and intelligence community, Zahran and Naufer were given ample cover to progress with their activities; they saw to it that they would build the Sri Lankan branch of one of the most powerful terrorist movements in the world.

Seeding a State within a State

The IS emerged in Sri Lanka after those exposed to al-Qaeda, IS, and other virulent ideologies overseas returned to the country. The most vulnerable to the IS ideology were Salafi-Wahhabi and Jamaat-e-Islami followers whose major hubs were in the east and west, with Kattankudy and Dematagoda as the centres, respectively.[133] One such person who brought the IS ideology back home with him was Jameel.

---

[133] Andreas Johansson, 'Who are Sri Lanka's Muslims?', *The Conversation*, April 22, 2019, https://theconversation.com/who-are-sri-lankas-muslims-115825.

Radicalized in the UK and Australia, Jameel created an IS support group together with Imaad and Umair upon returning to Colombo. They met, among others who travelled to fight in Syria, Nilam, the first Sri Lankan IS fighter to be killed in Syria in July 2015. To Nilam, Zahran was known as a Salafi-Wahhabi preacher and not an IS propagandist in the years 2014–2015. Before Nilam travelled to Syria in January 2015, Jameel said that he had identified Zahran as a potential Sri Lankan representative for the IS. According to the IS ideologue in Sri Lanka, Naufer, Nilam had been viewing videos produced by Zahran. Although Wahhabi and IS ideology were believed to have similar roots, Zahran only identified with the IS in late 2016. In fact, when the IS attacked Paris and Saint-Denis in France from 13–14 November 2015, NTJ joined other Thowheed and Muslim organizations in Sri Lanka in condemning the attack.[134]

Zahran's transformation and drift from exclusivism and extremism to terrorism and violence was gradual. As mentioned, his inclination to the IS ideology only started in the second half of 2016. His mindset was said to have been influenced by the IS' battlefield successes in Mosul and Raqqa, and the enduring influence of Naufer—whose own worldview was shaped during his stay in Qatar, where he built the single largest Tamil website promoting the IS.

Zahran's Mentor

Naufer was already radicalized into exclusivism and extremism before he traveled to Qatar. Having been exposed to both Jamaat-e-Islami and Wahhabi ideologies in Sri Lanka, he was much more vulnerable to the IS' extremist beliefs. With the rise of the IS in 2014, he read widely on the organization and, after engaging in

[134] State Intelligence Service Sri Lanka, information on IS attack in France shared with author, 2015.

an internal struggle, eventually succumbed to its ideology. While in Qatar, Naufer spread his ideas online. By the time he returned to Sri Lanka, he was radicalized to tier-three, the highest level of radicalization.

Naufer lived in Qatar for ten years. Every year, from April 2008 to August 2017, he visited Sri Lanka for a month on vacation. He worked at Al-Mohomad law firm as an Arabic-English translator, earning a salary of QR 3,000 and receiving an increment from time to time up to QR 6,500.[135] He also earned extra monthly income of QR 1,200 by providing school transportation services to an Oman teacher and a child. While in Qatar, Naufer engaged in proselytism at 'Al-Fanar', a government institute conducting fifteen religious programmes on Fridays.

A year before leaving Qatar in 2016, Naufer was asked on social media about his opinion on the IS. As a high-profile online preacher and teacher, he was compelled to study the IS deeply. Though he could not find any books or videos explaining the ideology, he did find two books written against the IS. After a comparative study, Naufer came to a decision that the IS was wrong due to three main factors:

1. IS killed a Jordanian airman/pilot by burning him alive;
2. IS attacked Saudi Arabia, the land of the holy mosques Mecca and Medina; and
3. IS killed many Muslims.

Naufer said, 'After reading those books and analyzing facts one by one, I realized I did not have enough facts to come to a clear decision about the IS. Hence, I decided to explore further. I prepared a report with six sections against IS, and I published it on Facebook. I would like to say specially that I am the one who

[135] Statement by Naufer to the police.

posted in Tamil very first report against the IS. I did not stop there; I explored even further.'[136]

Dynamic and ideologically active, Naufer 'participated in three discussion programmes with Najeem from Kattankudy, who worked at Zajil Media institute, and Fahathin Valachchena who were both in Qatar during that time'.[137] Initially, critical of the IS, Naufer researched, debated, and opined on the following:

1. IS burning a Jordanian airman/pilot alive; and
2. A Muslim couple publishing sexual behavior on social media/internet.

After the discussion, Naufer said, 'I rejected my previous stance that ISIS is wrong, and I accepted the fact that ISIS is correct. I change my previous opinion. I joined the opinion that ISIS is correct.'

Naufer said, 'I accepted that ISIS is correct due to three reasons:

1. The IS clarified why they burnt the airman/pilot alive—and that was because the air attacks conducted by the pilot in an IS-controlled area killed thousands of civilians.
2. American military camps established in Saudi Arabia launched bombing operations and killed thousands of innocent Muslim civilians in Iraq and Syria. Saudi Arabia provided facilities to launch these attacks to the American forces.
3. Killing Muslims who give information to security forces is correct and justified.'[138]

---

[136] Naufer, interview, March 15, 2020.

[137] Naufer, interview, March 15, 2020.

[138] Naufer, interview, March 15, 2020.

Because of these reasons, Naufer was motivated to join the IS. In his own words, Naufer described the process: 'First, I have participated in the lecture conducted at Madampe Islahiya Arabic School under Sri Lanka Jamaat-e-Islami by [Moulavi] Hajjul Akbar on "Priority for IS" and lecture conducted by Husein [Moulavi] on "Democracy is Wrong". Second, the lecture "Co-existence is prohibited for Muslims" motivated me to accept that ISIS is correct and hence, I joined ISIS. Third, Sri Lanka's Buddhist extremist's activities against Muslims and their religious activities were not controlled by the government and those planned activities against Muslims since 2015.'[139]

As such, with increasing radicalization, Naufer moved from Jamaat-e-Islami, to Salafi-Wahhabi, and eventually to the IS. After turning into an IS sympathizer, supporter, and finally operator, Naufer experienced a significant change in his life. He said, 'I went to Qatar and stayed in my boarding till February 2015. I had to change the office and hence, could not stay in the boarding place for the rest of the year. Hence, I stayed with Fahath and Najeem who were journalists of Zaajil Institute. However, I could stay in my boarding place again in 2016. I came to Sri Lanka in 2017 after resigning from the job.'[140]

Moreover, the conflict between Naufer and Zahran, which persisted for years, eventually ebbed away in early July 2016. They began to communicate with each other again and even met during one of Naufer's visits in 2016. During one such visit in 'August or October 2016', Naufer met with Zahran and shared documents and videos outlining why he believed the IS was a legitimate Islamic movement. Naufer said, 'I realized that Zahran and I had the same ideology.'[141]

---

[139] Naufer, interview, March 15, 2020.

[140] Statement by Naufer to the police.

[141] Naufer, interview, March 15, 2020.

It was said that Hadiya caught Zahran watching the graphic IS videos provided by Naufer, which included beheadings and gun fights. This turned into a curt exchange of words between the two; an upset Hadiya worried that their children would see the videos.[142] Zahran was careful from that point on in Hadiya's presence, only reading IS content and literature in front of her and choosing to view the videos and photos with his followers instead.

Later, in 2016, when Zahran planned to promote the IS ideal in Kattankudy and elsewhere in Sri Lanka, their community of clerics was said to have met at the town's cultural hall to discuss their opposition against the IS. However, two of the most powerful Thowheed organizations in Kattankudy—the NTJ and Daarul Adhar—reportedly opposed this anti-IS meeting. Perhaps unbeknownst to others, these two organizations had already begun supporting the IS covertly and overtly—and Zahran and Naufer were at the helm of it.

Naufer-Zahran Dynamic

After Naufer returned permanently to Sri Lanka in August 2017, an opportunity to restore the relationship between the Naufer's and Zahran's families arose when the former attended Hadiya's elder brother's wedding. Hadiya and Zahran travelled from Kattankudy to Kekunagolla. When Naufer met Zahran again, he was said to have known that Zahran had publicly announced that the IS was a 'righteous' organization, and that Muslims should support it. When Naufer visited the house of his wife's older sister on 10 August 2017, Zahran was hiding there as he was wanted by the police. After setting aside past resentments, Zahran and Naufer discussed the IS at Hadiya's parental home. In the presence of Naufer's wife and their son, Naufer invited Zahran and Hadiya to break fast at his home—a show of goodwill, demonstration of forgiveness, and mending of their broken friendship.

---

[142] Naufer, interview, March 15, 2020.

Like Zahran, Naufer previously opposed the IS. Operating out of Doha in Qatar, Naufer built the most influential Tamil-language website propagating Salafi-Wahhabism. When he followed the political ideology of Islamism, he reworked his existing site to promote the IS alongside Salafi-Wahhabism. Within the global Tamil community, including Tamil Nadu, no one else ran a thorough online resource promoting the IS like Naufer. It was 'his lifetime's work' and was the 'single largest' site promoting the IS in Tamil'.[143] Zahran followed in Naufer's footsteps and built multiple platforms promoting Salafi-Wahhabism and, thereafter, the IS ideology.

The radicalization trajectories of Zahran and his mentor Naufer were almost identical. Like Naufer, Zahran's drift towards the IS was gradual. Zahran gravitated from Tabligh Jamaat to Salafi-Wahhabism and then to the IS. As a Salafi-Wahhabi, he reportedly verbally attacked the Sufis but as an IS follower, he was relentless and advocated open confrontation. In the lead-up to March 2017, Zahran had fully embraced the IS ideology. He may have still been with the NTJ then, but he was already ideologically with the IS.

Preaching Poison

As we know by now, Zahran emerged as one of the most popular preachers in Kattankudy during his time. Although local and traditional Muslims reportedly called him 'vulgar' and 'aggressive', he was also a crowd-puller, an entertainer, and an engaging speaker. According to Samanthurai Pradeshiya Sabha Chairman A.M. Mohammad Noushad, judicious Muslims tended to avoid Thowheed groups, with some reportedly calling them '*veralaattis*, [literally, finger-twitchers, for their practice of repeatedly raising the index finger during prayer]'.[144] However, many Muslims also came to listen to Zahran's speeches for entertainment, with some

143 Naufer, interview, January 18, 2020.

144 Shoba, 'Sri Lanka: The Hunt Widens'.

eventually being radicalized. Zahran's radicalization unfolded in phases: in phase one, Zahran verbally attacked Sufi Muslims, calling them apostates or murthad and the Sri Lankan government infidels or kafirs. In phase two, Zahran would physically attack both Sufi Muslims and non-Muslims. The third phase was, at the time, still underway. Zahran was a man of his word; he had promised a bloodbath but though he was eager to make true on his declaration, the conditions for his plan were not yet right.

Meanwhile, the NTJ mosque served as a secret enclave with lectures delivered in dark rooms. Zahran wanted to build up forces. Thus, with his direction, young minds were harnessed by Zaini Moulavi and Shafi Moulavi, who spearheaded recruitment and were supported by Taufiq Moulavi—turning them into religious extremists. The recruits were reportedly also made to watch IS video clips of attacks on mosques, rapes on women, and children dying in conflict zones, after which the indoctrination session was followed by a physical training session. An NTJ leader, Army Mohideen, put them on a swim-only approach to training starting from mid-2016 through March 2017. Nearly 90 per cent of NTJ followers were below thirty. About 300 were handpicked from 1,000 followers. At its peak, the NTJ's strength was estimated to be between 2,000–3,000 members. Although Zahran would have to keep a low profile in March 2017, these clandestine activities in the NTJ mosque continued.

At this point, Zahran had become much more radicalized by the IS ideology than ever. Having built his popularity by confronting the Sufi community and reportedly ridiculing its leaders, Zahran took things up a notch. He started to openly advocate 'jihad' against traditional Muslims, and, later, against non-Muslims. In physical and online spaces, Zahran publicly reiterated that the IS was a righteous organization and once again called on Muslims to support it.

Zahran was on the march to spread his poisonous ideology in Sufi spaces within Kattankudy and beyond. To him, it was his God-given mission. Zahran planned to deliver a sermon at Aliyar Junction, a Sufi stronghold where he believed drug addicts roamed. Discussing Zahran's increasingly extremist views and actions, Zahran's sister, Mathaniya, said he 'started to claim that his own interpretation of Islam was the only true faith. He was offensive about other religions, as well as moderate Muslims and Sufis. He would [even] call Sufis drug addicts and smokers.'[145] the NTJ had reportedly applied for permission from the police to hold Zahran's meeting-sermon at Aliyar Junction. As per the usual protocol, police officers were to be dispatched at the event. Usually, there would be at least 4–5 policemen at the designated venue by 4.30 p.m. or 5 p.m.—but it was said that this was not the case on that fateful day.

Aliyar Junction, Turning Point?

Zahran and the NTJ's meeting-sermon was held at Aliyar Junction on 10 March 2017. Zahran's followers were said to have meticulously prepared to defend it if attacked by the Sufis. By this time, the Sufis had repeatedly suffered from Wahhabi incursions and had apparently decided to fight back. Contrary to claims that NTJ followers attacked first, it was said that Sufi protestors actually dealt the first blow. The Sufis reportedly threw stones and firecrackers, to which Zahran's followers allegedly retaliated by brutally beating Sufi protestors with poles, cutting them with swords, and stabbing them with *kris* knives. By the time the police arrived at 6.30 p.m., there were plenty of casualties on both sides. Despite this, the Sufis were said to have lodged a report to formally accuse the NTJ. Zahran fled to avoid arrest while nine

[145] Arun Janardhanan, 'He learnt religion from wrong people, happy he's dead: Lanka bomber's sister', *Lankaweb,* April 27, 2019, https://www.lankaweb.com/news/items/2019/04/27/he-learnt-religion-from-wrong-people-happy-hes-dead-lanka-bombers-sister/.

of his members were charged and eight were remanded to judicial custody for eight months.

That night, Zahran never returned to his home in Kattankudy. A worried Hadiya repeatedly called him to no avail. Hadiya reportedly sought help from her brother, Ansar, and, together with her children, relocated from Kattankudy to her parents' home in Kekunagolla. Unbeknownst to Hadiya, Zahran had fled Kattankudy to escape the possibility of imprisonment, choosing to go underground and keep a low profile to avoid detection.

A little over a month later, it was said that Zahran appeared unannounced in Kekunagolla to meet Hadiya and his children. After which, he would pay them frequent albeit brief visits, sometimes extending these visits when it seemed there were no active efforts by the police to hunt him down. Apart from the Rs. 10,000 provided by Zahran for the household and children's expenses, Hadiya's elder brothers would also help provide for Hadiya and the children during this time. In between his visits, Zahran was unreachable, and this would be the family's setup until 19 February 2019.

Zahran, the Fugitive

The NTJ core—Zahran, Rilwan, Gafoor, and close associates Safi Moulavi and Taufiq Moulavi—went into hiding the night of the Aliyar Junction incident. Taufiq would eventually leave the organization. Rilwan remained with Zahran while Shafi and Gafoor performed most of Zahran's daily public functions. Shafi and, later, Gafoor also attended to Zahran's daily needs from cooking, household maintenance, driving, and shopping. Hashtoon would attend to Zahran's communications needs and would join the group later in 2018 to set up a studio, operating it for Zahran to produce his propaganda.

After fleeing Kattankudy in March 2017, Zahran and his team relocated frequently between houses that were either rented out or opened to them. These included:

1. The house of a registrar of marriages in Oluvil, Ampara, who hosted Zahran and did not report him and his team to the government.
2. Shafi Moulavi's house in Anuradhapura, where Zahran and his team stayed until April 2017.
3. Shafi Moulavi's ancestral house in Ikirigollewa.
4. Ariyan's residence in Kuliyapitiya, where three other associates also stayed.
5. Sanasdeen's house in Ethnugahakotuwa, which was also in Kuliyapitiya.
6. A safehouse in New Kattankudy that was rented by Zahran's mother for 40–42 days during Ramadan in May 2017. Hadiya and the children would meet Zahran here.
7. A safehouse within the Palavi area in Puttalam, which was rented by Shafi.
8. A safehouse along Niwasa Thiha Road, which was rented for twenty-five days between May to June 2017. Zahran was joined by Hashtoon, Rilwan, and Milhan. Hashtoon helped Zahran make videos to propagate his message.
9. A safehouse in Walpoladeniya, Mawanella, which was rented for fifteen days in June 2017. This was arranged by Abdi Nana, a hotelier and NTJ member who would eventually join the IS. Zahran was joined by Hashtoon and Rilwan, who assisted him with his daily needs to build his underground organization.

It was believed that the Cassim family lived in anxiety after the Aliyar Junction incident. While Zahran and Rilwan were on the run, Zaini and their father Cassim were incarcerated in Batticaloa prison. Although Zahran could not visit them, Hadiya did, prior to briefly reuniting with Zahran at the safehouse in New Kattankudy.

While on the run, it was said that Zahran read widely on the IS, especially how its leaders in Iraq and Syria survived and developed their ideology to fight back the regime. From Wahhabism, his foundational ideology, he moved a step beyond and actively promoted the idea of the caliphate. During the first year of going underground, Zahran invested his time crafting and propagating the ideology. An avid user of social media, Zahran explained his ideology both in articles and videos that he produced, thus continuing to advance Islamist supremacy.

Building a base of operations was vital to create a following, so Zahran embarked on preaching, propaganda, and proselytizing operations. Later, Hadiya would find out that Zahran had even created a Telegram channel in October 2017 to deliver sermons promoting the IS, and relied on Hashtoon for secure communication. Zahran would also provide Hadiya a dedicated phone with Telegram prepared by Hashtoon.[146]

At one point, Zahran wanted to travel to Iraq and Syria, the same way Nilam and Ishaq did in 2014 and 2015. However, because there was an arrest warrant out for him, Zahran knew that doing so was risky and near impossible. After the Aliyar Junction incident, Zahran was said to have developed a deep-seated anger against the police, politicians, and clerics. He reportedly did not hesitate to express his sentiments and sought to build public support against them.

Isolated from communities, Zahran became even more exclusivist and narrow-minded. He aimed to create the conditions to establish an IS branch in Sri Lanka. Zahran was said to have believed in an Islamic leader governing Sri Lanka according to the tenets of Islamic law. In defending sharia's implementation in Sri Lanka, Zahran told Hadiya, 'If a person robs, his hand will be amputated, and if a person [commits] adultery, that person should be stoned.' Zahran reportedly did not believe in the electoral system; he rejected democracy.[147]

---

[146] Hadiya, interview, January 20, 2020; Hadiya, interview, January 27, 2020.

[147] Hadiya, interview, January 20, 2020; Hadiya, interview, January 27, 2020.

When Zahran fled, the NTJ was run by its president, Yusuf Mohammad Toufeeq, and treasurer, Moiuddin Bawa Ahmed Faisar. Toufeeq released public statements by the NTJ dated 29 December 2017 and 31 August 2018, claiming the organization had 'severed ties with Zahran and Zaini'.[148] However, it was said that the government believed Toufeeq maintained clandestine links with Zahran and the transfer of responsibility was done to keep the institution intact.

The De Facto Headquarters - Katupotha Area

Naufer aligned himself with Zahran immediately after he returned to Sri Lanka to help build an IS branch there. Before Zahran and Naufer's joint efforts, it was said that no one else had resolved to establish an IS branch in Sri Lanka and contact the IS central about it. As the IS Sri Lanka branch's emergent leader and deputy leader, Zahran and Naufer reportedly approached the NTJ and Daarul Adhar, both Salafi-Wahhabi groups, and discreetly enlisted their support to build the organization in Sri Lanka.

After Zahran lost Kattankudy as the centre of operations in March 2017, he reportedly turned Kekunagolla into a backup base. Operating clandestinely from Katupotha in Kurunegala, Zahran would officially appoint Naufer as the IS Sri Lanka branch's deputy and ideological leader. Zahran and Naufer pledged allegiance to Abu Bakr al-Baghdadi in Hadiya's family mosque in Kekunagolla in September 2017.

Naufer pledged allegiance to Zahran only after the decision that the IS was 'correct'—or, simply put, once they reached an affirmative consensus on the IS ideology. According to Naufer, they 'got to meet and talk several times in the lead-up to and after,' before Naufer 'gave [his] consent to join [the IS]'. After doing so, Naufer said he 'appointed Zaini [Moulavi] and Safi

[148] Shoba, 'Sri Lanka: The Hunt Widens'.

[Moulavi] for propaganda work'. Although they were reportedly not yet acknowledged by or in direct contact with the IS central leadership, Zahran and Naufer already laid the groundwork and had begun establishing the Sri Lankan branch. Thus, from the beginning, there was significant autonomy on how the branch was built and how Zahran and Naufer operated it.

To start, Naufer and Zahran had to build the organization's ideology and operational capability. The ideologue and designated deputy leader, Naufer, was regarded as a high-ranking member alongside others who held key appointments such as Milhan, the head of the military wing. Milhan was said to have been central to building the IS Sri Lanka branch. He was a highly motivated killer, trained personally by Police Faiz, and had fought against the LTTE. As the group's quartermaster, he, Zahran, and Naufer formed the core of organization and its decision-making body.

Formation of a Consultation Council

Before the IS central establishes an IS branch or province, it would have to adhere to the following protocol, which they developed:

1. First, was to raise the awareness of the Muslim community.
2. Second, was to consult among leaders and elders of Islamic movements.
3. Next, a leader had to be selected.
4. Afterwards, disparate organizations would have to be merged and consolidated before starting to operate.
5. Finally, it was only after a significant attack that the IS leadership in Iraq and Syria would declare or claim the operating theatre, *wilayat*, or IS province.

Zahran was not a consensus maker. It was said that he lacked political maturity and believed so strongly in his own leadership that he was reportedly disinclined to or perhaps less assured about unifying different groups and leaderships. Nonetheless, he still consulted and brought together Sadiq's group in Mawanella, the central province, Jameel's group in the western province, and his own group in the eastern province. Once Zahran received the support of all three distinct entities, he merged them to establish the IS branch in Sri Lanka.

After putting together a *majlis shura*, or consultation council, Zahran set his sights on creating an IS province proper by waging war. Zahran's thoughts and actions may have been consistent with the IS ideology, but it was reportedly at variance with many Sri Lankan Muslims, including his wife, Hadiya. It would take much convincing for other Sri Lankan Muslims to follow Zahran and adhere to the IS ideology. Thus, to do so and communicate his views, Zahran, with Naufer and Hashtoon's assistance, created content for dissemination on various platforms.

Building Capacity and Legitimacy

It was said that Zahran wanted to ideologically prepare recruits before entrusting them with tasks or delegating assignments to them. As mentioned previously, the first crucial step in recruitment and radicalization was to raise awareness about the IS. The ideology from threat entities such as the IS reportedly had limited traction in Sri Lanka at the time despite isolated incidents of violence against Muslims, such as the Dharga and Digana riots. Propaganda to indoctrinate and groom potential recruits had to be produced first for the IS Sri Lanka branch to move forward with its plans and ideals.

At the same time, Zahran enlisted Naufer's expertise and experience to build organizational capacity and institutional legitimacy. According to Naufer, for one of his first tasks, Zahran 'gave [him] an Arabic book published by ISIS to translate into Tamil. Its Tamil name [was] *Thambikkei Kotipadei*.'[149] After this, and prior to filming their pledge of allegiance to the caliph, Naufer was also said to have prepared their oath's script in Arabic. According to him, 'The meaning of the oath was "The leader of God's trustee, Abu Bakr al-Baghdadi's orders with likeminded or without likeminded, easily or hard, given the priority for others than myself, I listen and obey! Until the God's displeasure, should not conflict with those who are responsible among us, with the blessing of God, everything will start! Allah is great, Allah is great, Allah is great!"'[150]

In September 2017, Zahran selected the ideal for him and his ten-member team to film their pledge of allegiance to the caliph, Abu Bakr al-Baghdadi—in the rich grasslands of Ikirigollewa. They brought a black IS flag with them. With the flag in the backdrop, the Sri Lankan extremists pledged their oath of allegiance in an isolated patch of the forest.

A few days after this, Zahran was reportedly informed that 'the video had been sent to responsible figures of [the IS] . . . and they [had] accepted to establish [IS] in Sri Lanka officially'.[151] According to Naufer, Zahran was given 'an audio tape of a conversation sent by Nilam's family to confirm [this]. Along with [it], Nilam's family had sent the syllabus to propagate and teach [IS] norms and principles in Sri Lanka. It was brought to [them] by [a contact] in Colombo.' Although Naufer did not name who this person was, the intermediary was believed to have been Jameel. The recording purportedly sent by the IS to Zahran appointing him as Sri Lanka's representative was treasured by Zahran and

[149] Statement by Naufer to the police.

[150] Naufer, interview, January 18, 2020.

[151] Naufer, interview, January 18, 2020.

it was said he often played it to selected family, friends, and followers too.

Joining the IS

During Ramadan in 2018, two dozen Muslims, including those in Colombo, were said to have discreetly joined Zahran. A few even left their organizations and would go on to pledge allegiance to the IS proper. Zahran reportedly claimed he was responsible for all IS activities in Sri Lanka and created the impression that he reported to Abu Bakr al-Baghdadi himself. After Zahran's new followers affirmed they would conduct themselves according to the IS' code, Zahran administered the oath of allegiance to Abu Bakr al-Baghdadi. He reminded his followers they were no longer under the jurisdiction of Sri Lanka—thus, they did not need to honor the Sri Lankan law, its criminal justice, and prison system.

Zahran also took unprecedented steps to further influence and shape the thinking of his rank-and-file. For instance, to build more support for his membership, Zahran, together with Zaini and Naufer decided to train the group's women—in other words, the wives, mothers, and daughters of current and potential fighters. In July 2018, Zahran invited the women to join a three-day training course in Kattankudy. Reportedly, Zahran also attempted to win his wife and the supposed 'First Lady' of the IS Sri Lanka branch, Hadiya, over ideologically by including her in the programme. However, it was said that Hadiya declined the invitation and did not participate or attend, even with Sara's persuasion.

The women's training course was held from 25–27 July 2018 and was conducted by Naufer, Zahran, and Zaini. During the training, IS' clerics discussed how women should conduct themselves according to the practices of the organization and the IS ideology. After the women's understanding, sympathy, and support for the IS grew, their husbands, sons, and fathers were also said to have served the group with less resistance.

Indoctrinating the Fighters

With his mastery of indoctrination, Zahran was then said to have tasked Naufer with developing a curriculum that covered Islamic politics, the IS, the history of Nabi's lifestyle, Islamic beliefs, and contemporary Islamic countries, among other topics. Naufer reportedly wrote a three-part modular curriculum with core subjects categorized into primary, secondary, and tertiary. Later, Zahran told Naufer that ten IS followers in Colombo 'that followed Nilam's classes' when he was in Sri Lanka had requested to join their group. According to Naufer, 'nine [of them]—Arkam, Ihsan, Ahamed, Umayir, Imath and few others—first came and clarified their doubt about [IS] with us.' After which, '[t]hey [consented] to accept [Zahran's] leadership and work with him. [The] organization [that these new recruits were from was said to have been] "Millathu Ibrahim" [or JMI]'.[152]

Later, Zahran, Milhan, and Naufer would meet the rest of the IS Sri Lanka branch's Colombo supporters at a sports-club-owned conference hall in Malvana. It was said that '[o]n that day, [the Colombo supporters] were educated and recruited to the organization. [Apart from the] previous nine members [who were the IS Sri Lanka branch's new recruits], new people—Ilaf, Ilham, and others—[participated in] the [meeting-workshop].'

After JMI's IS training programme, Zahran aspired and endeavored to spread the IS ideology nationwide. Zahran reportedly hosted training and orientation programmes in late 2017 and throughout 2018, particularly in Nuwara Eliya and Hambantota. Zahran and Naufer conducted indoctrination sessions, Milhan and Sadiq conducted weapons training, and Hashtoon conducted training in secure communication and explosives. At the end of each workshop, it was said that participants would pledge—in Arabic—to support the supposed caliph of the IS. The workshops

[152] Statement by Naufer to the police.

reportedly produced a cadre of 200 recruits, who would choose whether they wanted to be a fighter or a suicide attacker. Some of them would go on to play key roles in the lead-up and execution of the Easter Sunday attacks.

Indoctrination and Training Sessions

Aruppola, Kandy

The IS trained its rank-and-file in a rented premise in 2018. Zahran personally provided leadership and conducted lectures with Naufer.

Blackpool, Nuwara Eliya

The IS trained its rank-and-file in a rented premise in 2018. Zahran likewise personally provided leadership and conducted the lectures with Naufer.

Thakshila Lodge, Shanthipura, Nuwara Eliya

Training for rank-and-file was conducted in a rented premise in 2018. Just like before, Zahran personally provided leadership and conducted the lectures with Naufer. The participants and instructors, led by Zahran, arrived at the venue in four vans. Throughout the duration of the training, it was said that only one person was seen leaving the premises while everyone remained congregated in the lodge. This apparently caused suspicion since the venue was in a tourist area, which meant visitors would typically be seen walking around.

During a session on 5 May 2018, the police reportedly visited the lodge after receiving a tip from a neighbor, D.T. Ilesinghe. The police were said to have found cannabis that did not belong to the group. Rs 1 million and jewelry were found with Zahran too. Although they searched the premises, it was said that they were not thorough enough and failed to make any further discoveries. Milhan himself was armed with two weapons and was ready to fire if they were detected. As soon as the police left, Zahran cancelled the training and instructors and participants dispersed. Although Nuwara Eliya was no longer used for training after the incident, Zahran persisted in shifting training venues to the deep south.

Sippikulama, Hambantota

The IS trained its rank-and-file in a rented premise in 2018. Zahran personally provided leadership and conducted lectures with Naufer.

Palamunai, Kattankudy, Batticaloa

The IS conducted training for women in a rented premise in July 2018. The two-storied guest houses that were rented were on the road to the beach in Palamunai. The session reportedly focused on the role of Muslim women, especially how they should support their husbands to wage jihad. The event was coordinated by Rauf Nana, who was close to Zahran and was said to have lived near him in Kattankudy. Like previous sessions, Zahran personally provided leadership and conducted the lectures with Naufer, Milhan, and Shafi Moulavi. The training participants were Zahran's sisters, Hindaya and Mathaniya, and Zahran's mother. The wives of Milhan, Sadiq, Azath, Gafoor Mama, Rilwan, and Zaini also participated. At the end of the session, the participants pledged allegiance to the IS.

Mawanella

Other than the safehouses, classes were also conducted in rural areas away from the public. For instance, Sadiq and Sahid conducted classes in Mawanella in sparsely populated locations.

Reportedly, a trained IS member was entrusted with deploying a drone from Karabalakurukanpiti Road, Kattankudy and systematically mapping out the entire town. The IS maintained a safehouse there, which was owned by Riyazath, an NTJ member who trained in Nuwara Eliya and later formally joined the IS. Before his injury, it was said that Rilwan used the aforementioned property to test a drone. It was reported that the SIS recovered both the drone and its chip in the Samanthurai safehouse. According to the Sri Lanka Air Force UAV expert that examined the recovered drone, 'the commercially available drone [could] fly 1.5 km visual range. It [could] also fly on an autonomous flight on a preprogrammed GPS route. Although it was used for videography, it [could] be modified to carry a payload of 200 g of explosives.'[153]

IS Madrasah

Training the next generation of IS moulavis was a necessary, long-term investment. Thus, Zahran advised Naufer to recreate the Kulliyathu Muvahdeen Arabic Madrasah, which had originally been shut down in Kattankudy after the Aliyar Junction incident. The first IS madrasah was therefore reportedly established in Kekunagolla by Naufer on the upper floors of his home.

The Arabic madrasah was to start with three students who had completed their Advanced Levels examination. After which, it was said that they planned to enlist more students and formally establish the madrasah by 2018. The Ibrahim brothers reportedly funded the madrasah, which was information Zahran kept under wraps. Zahran was said to have claimed all the funds provided would be used to develop and operate the madrasah. To groom second-generation leaders, Naufer housed Wakar, Jaizeel, and Altaf from an Arabic madrasah in Kattankudy and Mueeth,

[153] Interview by author with a Sri Lanka Air Force UAV expert, December 5, 2020.

Sajith, Wafeer, and Shiraf. The madrasah was eventually registered with the DMRCA, which reportedly did not have an inspection regime, at least at the time. At Zahran's request, the madrasah would be moved to the upper floor of Luluar Ammar mosque in Kottapitiya a few months later.

The principal of the madrasah was Naseer, who resided in Hettipola and was a teacher at Ibnu Masood Arabic College, where Zahran had studied. The madrasah's teachers were Naufer and Mathaseer Moulavi from Kekunagolla. Both sharia and Arabic were taught. It was said that when the madrasah's teachers were brought in for questioning by the intelligence in August 2018, Zahran appointed Mawanella-based Sajith Moulavi from Naleemiya to teach in their stead.

Building the State

The IS Sri Lanka branch needed logistical capacity to move forward with its activities. Thus, Jameel, who was a highly resourceful operator, recruited and enlisted the steadfast support of the Ibrahim brothers—Ilham and Inshaf—for the IS. It was said that Ilham lived with his parents, siblings, and wife in a mansion opposite Jameel's brother Hakeem's home. After assessing Ilham's value to their group, Jameel approached him strategically. He built a friendship with Ilham first and, through him, motivated his wife and brother to join the IS Sri Lanka branch too. Unbeknownst to Ilham, he purportedly functioned as an access agent for Jameel to gain financial and human resources—including bombers—both within and outside the family. Jameel radicalized and recruited them to kill and die by sharing violent and radical videos and texts as well as passages and verses distorting religious scriptures.

The Ibrahims' family wealth would be the main financial and logistical support pillar to build the IS. It was believed that they capacitated Zahran to function effectively and efficiently especially when he went underground. For example, with their funds, Zahran managed to procure a fleet of vehicles that would help build the state and advance its operational agenda. Apart from this, the Ibrahim brothers also reportedly funded several of Zahran's safehouses in the eastern, northwestern, central, and western provinces. It was believed that this allowed Zahran to continue covert operations and plan the branch's organization. To further build the organization's capacity to produce state-of-the-art IS propaganda materials, accounts mentioned that Hashtoon also built and operated a studio in the Negombo safehouses for Zahran to record videos. The series of payments from the Ibrahim brothers was substantial. As the last payment, Inshaf was said to have paid Zahran, through Ilham, Rs. 34 million from Colossus (Pvt) Ltd company's safe on 17 April 2019.[154]

Explosives Lab and Test

While the safehouse in Negombo hosted Zahran's studio, another safehouse in Malwana was rented by the IS from 22 March 2018 –1 January 2019 to manufacture bombs. According to accounts, the safehouse was occupied by Zahran, Hashtoon, Rilwan, and Shafi. It was also visited by the IS' most trusted functionaries—Milhan, Sajith Moulavi, and Gafoor. Although Zahran moved from place to place to meet associates, this safehouse in Malwana was said to have been his primary place of stay.

After the explosives were manufactured, accounts stated that Rilwan attempted to transport them to Ariyampathy in the Kattankudy police area on the night of 26 August 2018 to test them. However, it was said that they exploded prematurely on a culvert in Ollikulam—severely injuring Rilwan. Zahran, who was in the midst of running an IS training programme, was said to have been distraught when he was informed of his brother's injury. Since the explosion badly disfigured and nearly

[154] Interview by author with a police investigator, March 2022.

killed Rilwan, this demonstrated that the IS was successful in its explosives manufacturing project. After treatment at the National Hospital in Colombo, Rilwan was discharged from the hospital and transported to the IS safehouse in Malwana. Gafoor served as Zahran's driver and looked after Rilwan for two months.

After nearly losing his brother, Zahran reportedly made the important decision to transfer the explosives manufacturing project from Rilwan to Hashtoon. After closely watching Rilwan's experiment, Hashtoon was believed to have had deep reservations. It was presumed that, to Hashtoon, who researched and applied science, Rilwan was not a professional. He shared his views with Zahran without offending Rilwan who, until his injury, presented himself as the branch's explosives expert. However, Rilwan was just a goldsmith and was said to have lacked Hashtoon's sophistication as an amateur scientist with a laser-focus mind. Unlike Rilwan, Hashtoon read widely and constantly studied texts on explosives found online which were presumably beyond Rilwan's education and intellect.

Acquisition of Firearms

After a failed first transaction where they received defunct weapons, Zahran mounted the IS' first military operation in Sri Lanka to acquire firearms. From a property owned by Gafoor, IS members from the NTJ planned to attack a guard post in Vavunathivu in east Sri Lanka on 30 November 2018.

A policeman on duty was reportedly shot and killed at point-blank range. The other policeman, who was sleeping, was stabbed to death. The attack was said to have been led by Milhan and his team under Zahran's instructions. Besides Milhan and Gafoor, the other assassins were Abdul Manaz Mohommadu Firdaus alias Firdaus and Hasma Mohideen Mohommadu Imran alias Imran. After the successful attack, the team met with Zahran and gave him the firearms, and it was believed that Milhan and

Zahran's confidence grew. With the tempo of the IS operations peaking, Zahran continued on.

IS Regions

According to accounts, Zahran appointed three IS regional leaders to the eastern province, western province, and in the central highlands. Jamaat-e-Islami youth leader, Sadiq was appointed to lead the IS in the central highlands of Sri Lanka in 2018. Along with other Jamaat-e-Islami youth, who formed the SLISM, Sadiq had been radicalized for over half a decade. It was said that he had even travelled to Syria in 2014 to receive weapons training from an al-Qaeda affiliated group known as Jamaat Khattab.

The IS developed two approaches in recruiting its rank-and-file. It was said that, unlike many Thowheed recruits, most Jamaat-e-Islami recruits were educated. SLISM and JMI members that joined the IS were radicalized online. While most SLISM members were from the centre of the island, most JMI members were from the western province. In contrast, Thowheed recruits, mostly from the NTJ, were family, relatives, and friends. Nearly 90 per cent were reportedly from Kattankudy and most were poorly educated. A considerable percentage looked after cows or were three-wheeler drivers.

It was believed that Sadiq and Shahid infiltrated SLISM's Youth Development Programme (YDP) and Human Resource Development programme (HRDP) to recruit educated youth. During the YDP and HRDP training, it was said that the youth were organized into teams of 10–15 and assessed for their thinking and commitment—in other words, Aqida, Ibada, and Akhlaq. Aqida meant creed, Ibada was servitude, and Akhlaq was morality. Accounts stated that they encouraged students to speak to determine if they could be developed further. These programmes were conducted discreetly, purportedly away from the official purview of mosques.

The best and most committed were said to have been identified and handpicked to enlist in the Follow Up Programme, which featured lectures from key IS officials. Sadiq, Shahid, and their father Ibrahim, and other scholars explained the religious concepts creating a deep commitment. Ironically, most Muslims directly affected by the Dharga and Digana riots reportedly did not join or support the IS. However, Zahran, Naufer, and others presumably harnessed other events to create a narrative that would let them radicalize and recruit. Both Zahran and Naufer analysed the global situation. They showed videos of attacks on mosques, rapes on women, and children dying in conflict zones overseas. To radicalize, the recruits were presented jihad or holy war as the only solution to discrimination. They were exposed to IS videos and *jihad nasheeds* or holy war songs to motivate them. When they were primed, their recruiters asked who were willing to join. Thereafter, accounts said that they would be sent for the IS course to bring their mind to suicide level. After radicalizing the Jamaat-e-Islami recruits, Sadiq was chosen by Zahran to provide weapon training to the IS trainees.

In the lead-up to Easter Sunday attacks, Buddhist, Hindu, and Christian statues were reportedly vandalized in the central highlands between 23–27 December 2018.[155] Muslim leaders immediately gathered to assist the police to uncover and capture perpetrators. The acts of vandalism were later revealed to have been done by Jamaat-e-Islami youth, who identified Sadiq and Shahid as the directing figures for the attack. In total, the police arrested nineteen Jamaat-e-Islami youth from 26–27 December. Sadiq, who led the vandalism, and his brother, Shahid, fled and, with Zahran's assistance, went underground following this incident.

---

[155] Michael Safi, '"Mawanella was the start": Sri Lankan town reels from bombing links', *The Guardian*, April 26, 2019, https://www.theguardian.com/world/2019/apr/26/mawanella-was-the-start-small-sri-lankan-town-reels-from-bombing-links.

Training Infrastructure

The IS Sri Lanka branch built a vast infrastructure throughout the country to prepare for attacks and support their efforts to advance the vision and mission of the IS. It was said that the entire support network, all Zahran's followers, believed they were 'fighters of God'. To build a robust organizational infrastructure, they invested in two types of properties—safehouses and land.

The safehouses were reportedly used for hiding, storing weapons, and manufacturing explosives. They were also used for conducting rehearsals in neighboring properties for testing explosives. In addition to mounting operations to surveil potential and intended targets, the safehouses were said to have been used as staging pads for striking targets too. While most of them were under the control of the IS, others were apparently homes of supporters and sympathizers. The IS also established camps for conducting indoctrination and training sessions to radicalize and prepare both suicide and non-suicide attackers. Most properties were rented while a few properties were leased or purchased. The IS had a vision; they rented and purchased properties with a purposeful strategy and a plan.

To fight the Sri Lankan state and other communities, Zahran envisioned recruiting and creating an island-wide IS infrastructure. Zahran meticulously planned three phases of training with the IS leadership: starting with two days of indoctrination, three months of physical training, and finally six months of weapons training. He rented or purchased three properties to build training facilities, reportedly naming them after what was believed to be Islamic and Muslim history. He meticulously implemented phase one and was likely preparing for phases two and three when he was detected and disrupted by the CID.

The capture of the training camp in Wanathavilluwa, the seizing of explosive precursors, and the narrow escape from arrest were the biggest blows to Zahran, the IS, and their followers. It was said to have been a huge setback for the organization, which had just entered an operational phase.

Zahran Identified

The investigations into Wanathavilluwa demonstrated the scale, magnitude, and intensity of the IS' threat. When Wanathavilluwa was raided by the CID, police, military, and intelligence were present. The intelligence and investigations revealed that Zahran was the central figure. At that point, it could have been possible that had the NSC—the highest body in Sri Lanka responsible for securing the state—acted, Zahran may have been caught and the Easter Sunday attack possibly curbed in time.

After Zahran went underground in March 2017, it was said that authorities did not seem to be aggressively looking for him. During this time, Zahran was actively travelling throughout the country, even between Kattankudy for IS work and Kekunagolla to visit family. In Kattankudy, Zahran reportedly conducted lectures, including the dedicated training programme for the IS wives and other family members. It was also said that Zahran met his deputy Naufer in Kekunagolla. It was believed that all these movements could have possibly and easily been tracked with human and technical intelligence.

Zahran was wanted by the authorities but, as mentioned, was apparently not actively hunted down by them. According to accounts, nearly 350 reports were submitted to the NSC, Defence Secretary, CNI, IGP, and other relevant officials on Zahran, the IS, and Muslim radicalization from January 2015–April 2019. Despite this, it seemed that the Yahapalana government did not adequately prioritize mitigating national security threats. In contrast to government authorities allegedly operating at a snail's pace, Zahran was said to have operated at maximum speed, maximizing the situation to supplement his agenda.

IS Fragments

To ensure their security, Zahran was reportedly determined to compartmentalize the activities of the IS. He created two teams—one led by him and another by his deputy Naufer. After which, Zahran instructed a house be rented in Enderamulla for Naufer and his team.

According to accounts, the 'Enderamulla House', as it was known to its occupants, was occupied from 21 February 2018–21 April 2019 by Naufer, Saajith Moulavi, Gafoor, Sadiq, his wife Sahidha, and their son. Zahran was said to have briefly joined Naufer and the others for a time too. The madrasah final year students Wakar, Jaizeel, and Altaf, who were personally taught by Naufer, also lived in the safehouse from February to April 2019.

In March 2019, a struggle for leadership reportedly emerged between Zahran and Naufer when Zahran started to operate separately without, as Naufer alleged, consulting the members of the majlis shura in the decision-making process. To resolve the dispute, it was said that Zahran visited and discussed the allegations raised against him. On 5 April 2019, IS members met at their safehouse in Wattala to debate Zahran's leadership. Naufer, Milhan, Saajith Moulavi, Sadiq, Shahid, and Gafoor reportedly challenged Zahran, leading to a group split. Zahran was followed by Ilham, Mubarak, Riskan, Rilwan, Hashtoon, Sanasdeen, and others Sadiq, Shahid, Sajith, Gafoor and others followed Naufer.[156] After the separation, the IS' majlis shura fragmented. One team joined Zahran, while another joined Naufer, thus creating two consultative committees.

Until the separation, the occupants of the house were said to have been the apex leaders and key members. Zahran left behind

---

[156] Mohamed Anwar Mohamed Riskan, interview by author, Colombo, Sri Lanka, March 2020.

a significant following in the safehouse including relatives Naufer and Gafoor. Following the split, it was believed that Naufer's followers were aware Zahran and his followers would carry out the Easter Sunday attacks. Despite a series of blows, likely Zahran wanted his legacy to continue. To him, striking on Easter Sunday must have been the highest priority. Those who remained aligned with Zahran were all said to be active participants in the planning, preparation, and execution stages of the attack.

The Farewell

After days of meticulous planning, painstaking preparation, and frequent trips between safehouses to avoid detection, it was time. The IS attackers had to part from their loved ones to carry out the strike.

Zahran's wife Hadiya and their children reportedly left Lucky Plaza at 2.30 p.m. on 19 April 2019 for the Panadura safehouse—where Zahran and the others were—to say their final goodbyes. Refaz, an NTJ turned IS member, drove the van where Hadiya and the children were, accompanied by Sara and Feroza. According to accounts, Zahran instructed a dividing screen to be placed along the wall before the three women entered the safehouse. While the two children ran towards Zahran, the three women rushed directly to the room. Hadiya, Sara, and Feroza briefly met their respective husbands who were preparing for their suicide mission; they would not meet again.

According to accounts, Zahran entrusted Rilwan, the newly designated leader of the IS, to relocate his family and the wives of the would-be suicide bombers to the east. It was said that Zahran also entrusted his brother with funds to carry out the second wave of attacks in his stead. Bidding farewell and handing Rs. 35,000 to his wife, Zahran's final words to Hadiya were said to have been, 'If I die, please do idda . . . If I do not die, I will return to you.'[157] After which, Hadiya and her children left with Rilwan, Sara and Feroza left for Sainthamaruthu, while Zahran and the other suicide bombers spent their final night in the Panadura safehouse.

Eastern Infrastructure

As mentioned above, Zahran relocated his family and other operatives to the network of IS safehouses in the eastern province before the Easter Sunday attacks. Three days prior to the bombings, family members were reportedly instructed to switch off their phones. On 18 April, Zahran's extended family—including parents, siblings, their spouses, and children—relocated from Batticaloa to Ampara. The only exception was Zahran's oldest sister Mathaniya, her husband, and child. Mathaniya's husband, Mohammed Riyaz, a small-time three-wheel spare parts dealer and humanitarian worker, was said to have opposed his brother-in-law's extremism and this caused a disconnect in their relationship since 2017. Though it may be interesting to note that, according to investigators, Mathaniya maintained links with her brother and was said to have participated in an IS training programme for women before.

With his second-tier leaders ready to run the branch, the safehouses in the eastern province were created to stage the second wave of attacks. Just like the infrastructure in the western province, Zahran reportedly instructed the IS Batticaloa leader Mohamed Niyaz to rent or buy a series of properties and vehicles, the former for hiding or storage and the latter for transport.

Meanwhile, the IS breakaway faction led by Naufer was said to have relocated the IS madrasah to a newly rented safehouse in Nintavur in April 2019. This was believed to be the only safehouse in the east under Naufer. It would be used to establish its mosque

[157] Hadiya, interview, January 20, 2020; Hadiya, interview, January 27, 2020.

and house three of its members—Wakar, Jaizeel, and Altaf, who were being groomed as second-generation leaders by Naufer. Naufer's faction remained in the east until their arrest by the police. It was said that the SIS had no knowledge of this safehouse since a breakaway group operated it. The CID reportedly investigated it only after Gafoor was arrested.

Planning for Second Wave

According to accounts, IS Ampara leader Kalmunai Siyam—who was highly influenced by Zahran's preachings—worked with IS Batticaloa leader Niyaz to create and build the IS infrastructure in Ampara district. Apart from static infrastructure, the IS reportedly rented and purchased vehicles to enhance its capacity for mobility. These included two new vans—a registered and an unregistered Suzuki Avery—purchased by Niyaz.

Prior to his death, Zahran was said to have planned ahead for the second wave of attacks. On the eve of the Easter attack, another lorry transported goods—for the organization's remaining members to use—from the Panadura safehouse to Sainthamaruthu. Items reportedly included 'a freezer, printers, washing machine, red bucket, van seat, five rigifoam boxes, and five empty bags' as well as eight long, black robes worn by the Easter attack suicide bombers for their final video. The robes, worn before they mounted the attack, were preserved, and relocated to the east at Zahran's request; to be worn by the next set of attackers participating in the second wave. The robes and headgear would later be recovered by authorities.

Zahran apparently also instructed that additional safehouses be rented to prepare for the second wave of attacks. This included a safehouse with storage facilities in Samanthurai, which was rented by Niyaz and used as a warehouse to store explosives from 18–26 April 2019, as well as another safehouse with storage facilities at Nintavur. This Nintavur safehouse, which was separate from and unrelated to Naufer's, was rented by the IS Ampara leader Siyam presumably to hide IS members and family. This was where Zahran's entire remaining family (except for Mathaniya), Hashtoon's widow Sara, and Azath's widow Feroza would be relocated amid the attacks.

Based on information provided by the SIS, the warehouse in Samanthurai was raided on 26 April 2019. Meanwhile, the Addalaichena safehouse, where Zaini and his family as well as Sara and Feroza had been staying after relocating from the Nintavur safehouse, was raided on 25 April 2019. According to information from the SIS, the pertinent individuals evaded arrest as they were not at the site during the raid. Nevertheless, the SIS recovered Zaini's birth and marriage certificates, Azath's hard-drive, and a one-and-a-half-hour video by the IS Sri Lanka branch. Other important paraphernalia recovered by authorities across different safehouses were phones, pen drives, hard discs, and laptops, which contained critical information.

Life Without Zahran

Hadiya said, 'I did not like to wear white.'[158] This was in reference to the mourning custom idda, which Hadiya was made to observe with the other women in the branch. When Hadiya's son asked his mother and aunt why they were wearing white and his question went unanswered, he apparently said, 'I want to speak to father.'[159] Hadiya spoke to Rilwan who then comforted the boy and reportedly told him that his '[f]ather [was] abroad. His phone [was] broken. He [would] get a new phone and call [him].'[160]

On D-day, news of the attack informed the occupants of the safehouse, and it was said that many of them were pleased. Most believed that Zahran and his team had reached heaven. However,

158 Hadiya, interview, January 20, 2020; Hadiya, interview, January 27, 2020.

159 Hadiya, interview, January 20, 2020; Hadiya, interview, January 27, 2020.

160 Hadiya, interview, January 20, 2020; Hadiya, interview, January 27, 2020.

Hadiya was apparently sceptical. 'I cried; I did not eat for two days.'[161] When asked why, Hadiya admitted, 'I did not think it [was] good.'[162] According to accounts, from 21–22 April, Hadiya contemplated what happened—and what was likely to follow. She did not eat. She was in a state of deep mental anguish, and it was said no one could bring her comfort or manage her state of agitation.

In the meantime, the IS plan was to move from temporary or renting to permanent accommodation—in other words, buying property. On the evening of 25 April 2019, Rilwan was said to have instructed Hadiya to see a house near Oluvil bridge. 'Zaini gave Rs. 1.9 million to me and said to write the house in the name of Feroza.'[163]

Final Battle

After the Easter attack, Zahran's entire family, Sara, and Feroza were housed in Sainthamaruthu. On 26 April 2019, it was reported that seventeen of them died in a mass suicide. Zahran's wife Hadiya and her daughter Rubeiniya were injured and were the only survivors of the incident.

Prior to this, the occupants had reportedly come under scrutiny when neighbours found out they were from Kattankudy. A week after the group took residence, neighbours apparently turned suspicious when they were seen continuously moving boxes of goods into the house—including a large stock of household goods and groceries. It was said that the stream of people going in and out and boxes filing in and out of the house throughout the day led to an exchange between Niyaz and the property owner. The conversation was believed to have further aroused suspicion, so much so that the owner decided to inform the local mosque.

---

161 Hadiya, interview, January 20, 2020; Hadiya, interview, January 27, 2020.

162 Hadiya, interview, January 20, 2020; Hadiya, interview, January 27, 2020.

163 Hadiya, interview, January 20, 2020; Hadiya, interview, January 27, 2020.

After visiting the mosque, the owner returned with four elders and the local administrator, known as *grama sevaka.* It was said that designated member-guardians in the group were armed with explosives and a firearm to protect the house occupants. Niyaz, who answered the door, appeared to have panicked and pointed his gun at the official. 'If it is money you want, here, take as much as you want and leave us alone to do the work of God,' was what he supposedly said, flinging Rs. 5,000 currency notes at the official, according to a source privy to the investigation.[164]

According to accounts, the police and the armed forces responded after a traffic police constable and a police sergeant were tipped by three Muslim citizens who suspected and reported that terrorists had established a presence in their town.[165]

When the neighbours surrounded the house, Niyaz, who was entrusted to protect the family, reportedly came out armed with a T-56 and began firing to disperse the crowd. By this time, however, the military and the police had apparently been tipped off and already surrounded the safehouse. In the ensuing gun fight, Niyaz was said to have been shot in the neck and bled to death. While this happened, Rilwan reportedly filmed a final message before directing the mass suicide.

From about 7.30 p.m., three bombs exploded. A video would later emerge on jihadist networks showing a disfigured Rilwan and two other men inside the house claiming that the 'movement' would not stop even if they were destroyed.

Mass Suicide

It was believed that the occupants committed mass suicide to prevent capture and because they believed that doing so would

[164] Shoba, 'Sri Lanka: The Hunt Widens'.

[165] Staff Writer, 'Police officers and informers get cash gifts for exposing terrorist safehouse', *Newsfirst Sri Lanka*, May 3, 2019, https://www.newsfirst.lk/2019/05/03/police-officers-and-informers-get-cash-gifts-for-exposing-terrorist-safe-house/.

allow them to enter heaven. Except his wife and daughter, the rest of Zahran's family and the widows of his associates reportedly perished. The names of the deceased are listed below:

1. Zahran's father, Hayathu Mohammed Hashim alias Hayathu Mohammed Cassim (fifty-five years old)
2. Zahran's mother, Abdul Cader Sitti Sameema (fifty-one years old)
3. Zahran's younger brother, Mohamed Hashim Mohamed Zaini alias Sinna Moulawi (thirty-one years old)
4. Zaini's wife, Adam Lebbe Fathima Aafrin (twenty-four years) old
5. Zaini's son, Umar (five years old)
6. Zaini's daughter, Hamama (three years old)
7. Zahran's youngest brother, Mohamed Hashim Mohamed Rilwan (twenty-nine years old)
8. Rilwan's wife, Mohamadu Nashath Fathima Nafna (twenty-six years old)
9. Rilwan's son, Maruwan Sahid (nine years old)
10. Rilwan's daughter, M.R. Mihra (four years old)
11. Zahran's youngest sister, who was eight months pregnant, Mohamed Cassim Hindaya alias Yaseera (twenty-one years old)
12. Hindaya's husband, M.I.M. Risath (twenty-three years old)
13. Hindaya's daughter, Rudeina (one-and-a-half years old)
14. Zahran's son, Wasith (eight years old)
15. Azath's wife Abdul Raheem Feroza (twenty-six years old)
16. Hashtoon's wife, Mahendran Pulasthini alias Sara Jasmine (twenty-three years old)

To avoid the mass suicide, Zahran's wife, Hadiya, who was twenty-four at the time, and their daughter, Rubeiniya, left for the washroom. According to Hadiya, their son, Wasith, stood with the bombers and was killed in the explosion. Hadiya said that despite her efforts to take Wasith with her, away from the mass suicide group, she failed.[166] She claimed that Wasith had identified himself with the adult men and insisted on being a part of the ceremony to reach heaven to join his father.[167] After the explosion, Hadiya and Rubeiniya were reportedly found in a room next to the living room, where the mass suicide took place. The mother and daughter were said to have been severely burnt and injured from the bomb blasts. Military personnel rescued them from the safehouse, administered first aid, and took them to be treated.

According to accounts, Mathaniya, the only relative of Zahran's who was not at the safehouse, could only identify Niyaz as all the other bodies were mutilated. Referring to Zahran, Mathaniya said, 'He lost God because he learnt the hadiths from the wrong people, and he learnt to kill people instead. I should say that I am happy that he is no more.'[168]

Unspeakable Dark History

Will history remember Zahran as the Muslim Prabhakaran? Just like Prabhakaran and Wijeweera, will those studying these events succumb to compartmentalizing this surge of religious extremism as another terrorist incident? Will it fall prey to being an overlooked part of the nation's religious trajectory, lost to momentary spectacle and nothing more? There is an apparent, palpable fear of history mis-chronicling Zahran as another remorseless killer whose intentions and true influences are lost to those relishing in its disastrous aftermath.

As an exclusivist, extremist, and terrorist, Zahran inflicted misery on Sri Lankan citizens and foreigners alike. By manipulating

166 Hadiya, interview, January 20, 2020; Hadiya, interview, January 27, 2020.

167 Hadiya, interview, January 20, 2020; Hadiya, interview, January 27, 2020.

168 Janardhanan, 'He learnt religion from wrong people'.

scriptures, he inflicted pain and suffering on the Muslim community. He disrupted goodwill and damaged cordial intra- and inter-Muslim relations built over a millennium. With the rise of Islamophobia, it was believed that Zahran's Easter massacre created a living hell for the Muslim community.

Zahran was seen by himself and his followers as a reformer. It seemed apparent that he wanted to be at the forefront when Islam revived, emerging in a certain political and religious context. With Sufism ossifying, a percentage of Muslims reportedly saw the rise of Arab Islam as an Islamic renaissance. Believing that Salafi-Wahhabism was the righteous ideology, Zahran followed it to the fullest. As an exclusivist, he shunned other ideas and ideologies. Once he moved from exclusivism to extremism, he took his faith to the extreme. Riding the wave of revival and renaissance, Zahran was believed to have been impervious to the tenets of Islam that cautioned against extremism.

Zahran's Shadow Lurks

Zahran has been killed but his shadow evidently lurks. The ideological virus replicates the threat, multiplies to spread, and mutates to survive. Although Zahran committed suicide, his ideology endures. As long as the ideology of hatred against traditional Muslims and other faiths persists, it is likely that Sri Lanka will suffer from other copycat fanatics. Dismantling the ideological foundation is the apex challenge. Much of the government's response thus far seems to have been catching terrorists after an attack. Perhaps it is time to focus on actively curbing such individuals before the terror is unleashed.

Directed by the charismatic preacher Zahran, the suicide attackers of the IS Sri Lanka branch were groomed to sacrifice their lives. They were indoctrinated to believe it was their religious duty. They believed it was a sin to associate with non-Muslims and that their loyalty was to Muslims only. With steadfast radicalization, they were convinced that they were receiving messages from God or Allah to fight His enemies. With enhanced devotion to Him, they demonized their enemies even more. With heightened extremism, they entered a trance willing to kill and die for God. For acting at His behest, they believed that they would be rewarded in heaven as martyrs; the fruits of their deliverance in the shape of divine glory and vengeance—but the truth of their terror reveals a far more sinister reality.

Author in conversation with Naufar Moulavi—Islamic State ideologue
Source: Dinithi Dharmapala Photographer

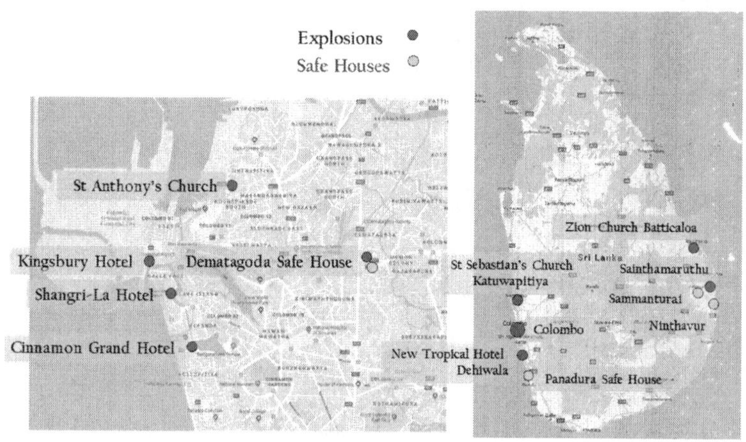

Locations of Explosions and Safe Houses
Source: SDIG Latiff, STF

Scenes from the mass suicide in Sainthamaruthu
Source: STF

'We will kill every man, woman, child, Shia, Sunni, Zoroastrian, Kurd, and Christian.'

—Nilam's Facebook Post, 3 July 2015

Chapter 3

The Colombo Team of the IS Sri Lanka Branch

The Game-Changer

It was believed that the Easter Sunday attacks resulted from a catastrophic union of Muslim extremists in the eastern and the western provinces of Sri Lanka. The harsh and untoward nature of Muslim extremists was not limited to the purportedly and relatively poor, devout Muslims of the east; they also supposedly wielded their influence among the educated and wealthy Muslims in Colombo. This combustion of various social groups tethered by the string of wayward extremism gave way to a calamitous outburst of ideological radicalization. To completely understand how this branch of Islamism reacted to Sri Lanka's socio-political climate and how this doctrine incentivized such a magnitude of unyielding chaos, the methodical polluting of true Islamic theology must be observed.

It is also believed that the two politico-religious actors—the extremist Salafi-Wahhabi and Jamaat-e-Islami streams—introduced to Sri Lanka from the Middle East and the subcontinent likely converged to heighten the threat. These two debilitating extremist ideologies presumably wedged divisions within Islamic society, and between Muslim and non-

Muslim communities. Such community divisions were thought to have acted as the catalyst for attacks on Sri Lanka and IS attacks across the globe. Though perceived as not as lethal as the IS doctrine introduced to Sri Lanka from the battlefields of Iraq and Syria, extremist Salafi-Wahhabi and Jamaat-e-Islami ideologies reportedly still politicized and radicalized a number of Muslims to embrace a higher-order threat.

Salafism, or more colloquially referred to as the Salafi-Wahhabi movement, is often classified by revisionists as a reformed branch of the parent Sunni doctrine. Founded upon the core principle of 'pious predecessors', this niche interpretation of Islam is said to bring forth the recycling of prophet Muhammed's traditional practices and calls upon a return to its nineteenth-century roots. Albeit containing various parallels to the latter, Jamaat-e-Islami is an entirely independent doctrine of Islam, one founded in British India and centric on a trifecta of beliefs—monotheism, the concept of prophethood, and the concept of life after death. Therefore, assimilating both ideologies into the socio-political framework of pre-attack Colombo, it may be imperative to see how these respective influences embrace their dualism by supplementing each other's agenda and occasionally hindering the movement's success.

It was said that the IS functionaries had a large pool of recruits to help establish a province of the caliphate in Sri Lanka, which had a large non-Muslim population. Sri Lankan Muslims indoctrinated by Salafi-Wahhabi and Jamaat-e-Islami ideologies reportedly provided the recruits and support for the founding of the IS Sri Lanka branch. The IS ideology harnessed the well-established ideological and operational infrastructures of extremist Salafi-Wahhabism and Jamaat-e-Islami rooted in Sri Lanka. These two foreign ideologies that were said to be challenging and supplanting Sufism had influenced and shaped a minute segment of a generation of Sri Lankan Muslims, especially the youth. Sufism is said to encompass a philosophy that vitalizes the mystical facets of Islam, specifically arranging the religion's mystical practices to conduct an inward expedition in search of God, shunning materialism.

As a community, Sri Lankan Muslims were said to have initially opposed these waves of political Islam promoted under the guise of pristine and pure Islam. Unlike local and traditional Islam, which was believed to value moderation, toleration, and coexistence, extremist Salafi-Wahhabism and Jamaat-e-Islami ideologies primed a slice of the Muslim community. This radical segment appeared to embrace the IS ideal of using extreme means to promote Islam, Islamic law, and Islamic supremacy. After infiltrating the ACJU, the main clerical body, Salafi-Wahhabism and Jamaat-e-Islami ideologies became well entrenched throughout the island. Thus, a significant Muslim segment presumably fell to the compulsions of what was said to be Gulf-funding and pressures of Arab and other foreign preachers.

It was believed that Muslims lived peacefully for centuries in Sri Lanka until political Islam shattered the glass—leaving long-term scars between the communities. Clashes and tensions followed, from Kattankudy in the east to Beruwala in the west. After the radical Salafi-Wahhabism and Jamaat-e-Islami infiltrated the Sri Lankan Muslim community, its 1,400-year heritage was purportedly eroded. The fissures created by radicalization likely paved the way for the IS to effectively drive Muslim extremism in Sri Lanka to another level of communal disharmony and violence.

The Context

Sri Lankan Muslims live throughout the country, but their stronghold is believed to be in the eastern province of Sri Lanka. In the east, both in Batticaloa and Ampara, Muslim culture was sustained and preserved until Sri Lanka became an open economy.

As professional traders, it was said that they migrated to the western province and flourished. But foreign ideologies crept and consumed a niche segment of the diaspora. It was said that radical and violent Islam took root in Kattankudy in Batticaloa, and Sainthamaruthu in Ampara, which were the supposed Muslim enclaves of the east.

As discussed, the Easter Sunday massacre was led by a group of extremist Salafi-Wahhabi Muslims from the eastern province. Although NTJ leader Zahran Hashim, who choreographed the attack, hailed from Kattankudy, most of the other attackers lived in the western province. The recruits were Jamaat-e-Islami with a sizable presence in western and central provinces. Just as the extremist Salafi-Wahhabis were said to have provided recruits for the NTJ, Jamaat-e-Islami reportedly provided recruits for the JMI, a highly secretive IS support group in the Colombo metropolis. Known as the Colombo team, the JMI formed the vanguard that staged the Easter Sunday attack.

As a coordinated effort to form the IS Sri Lanka branch, its support groups, the NTJ and JMI, provided ideological, financial, and material support. While Jameel's JMI in the western province provided six of the nine suicide terrorists and immense resources, Zahran's NTJ in the eastern province provided only two suicide terrorists and meagre resources. While many contributed to the Easter attack ideologically and operationally, it was believed that none contributed as much as the Colombo team.

Background

The IS was a vicious by-product of global developments that the international community allegedly failed to foresee. It was an event that neither Sri Lanka's political leaders nor its security and intelligence community reportedly followed up on and combatted. As mentioned previously, it did not seem like the government acted decisively, even with nearly 350 intelligence reports about the threat of religious extremism. The highest decision-making body, the NSC, was said to have overlooked a surging threat to the nation. Global and regional security—including the Sri Lankan threat landscape—was supposedly shaped by four pivotal events that preceded the creation of the IS:

1. The al-Qaeda's 9/11 attack on America's iconic landmarks;
2. The US invasion of Afghanistan and Iraq;
3. The deteriorating security situation in Afghanistan, Iraq, and Syria; and
4. The radicalization of a segment of Muslims worldwide due to rising global political oppression and the subsequent harnessing of ideology by extremist leaders to tackle their disempowerment.

After its formation on 11 April 2013, ISIS was rebranded as the IS and a caliphate was proclaimed on 29 June 2014. The self-proclaimed IS caliph, Abu Bakr al-Baghdadi, reportedly galvanized global Muslim support. After its conquest of a third of Syria and 40 per cent of Iraq, caliphate ideology was said to have influenced fringes of Muslim youth—including in Sri Lanka—to believe in the IS ideal. Likewise, foreign radical and violent preachers, primarily based in Britain and Australia, likely shaped a segment of migrant Sri Lankan Muslim students or workers to embrace hateful ideologies. Some believed that the harsh aftermath of the conflict between the LTTE and the security forces also led to a gaping hole that further disconnected the Sri Lankan public and government alike from its diaspora.

It was believed that most local and traditional Muslims in Sri Lanka did not fall for these ideologies of conquest and revenge. Through retrospective analysis and thorough archival research, it is said that almost no Sufis in Sri Lanka likely joined the IS—whether at its centre in Iraq and Syria or its Sri Lankan branch.

Sufism practised for millennia was apparently perceived as an antidote against exclusivism and extremism. The steppingstone to joining the IS of Sri Lanka were said to have been those primed by Jamaat-e-Islami and Thowheed Jamaat.

In a country where 90 per cent of Sri Lankans are Buddhists, Hindus, and Christians, the two aforementioned Islamic movements reportedly advocated 'love' or 'Al Wala' for Muslims and 'hatred' or 'Wal Bara' against non-Muslims. The creeping radicalization debilitated a segment of Muslim youth and adults vulnerable to recruitment by an even deadlier force. According to accounts, starting in 2014, a handful of IS personalities that returned from overseas, planted ideological seeds that would evolve into clandestine networks and underground groups. Although the footprint was small, their recruiters allegedly mobilized Jamaat-e-Islami and Thowheed Jamaat followers to form IS support and functional groups. An outlier of the Sri Lankan Muslims was said to have abandoned their heritage and joined these Islamic movements. They remain a continuing threat to Sri Lanka's security and stability today.

Introduced to Sri Lanka after its independence, Jamaat-e-Islami, from the subcontinent, and Salafi-Wahhabism, from the Gulf, started to influence Sri Lankan Muslims. These allegedly deviant ideologies espoused separation and segregation. Muslim-non-Muslim division became pronounced and intermittent violence against mainstream Muslims and other religious denominations grew. Like Jamaat-e-Islami from Pakistan and India, Salafi-Wahhabism was an imported concept from Saudi Arabia, Qatar, and Kuwait.

It was said that Sri Lankans who embraced this politico-religious ideology became exclusivist, acutely promoting the belief that only this branch of theology was 'true', thus alienating individuals outside the community of practice and some extremists. The most zealous formed and followed a dozen Salafi-Wahhabi sects and named them Thowheed Jamaats.

They reportedly rejected Sri Lankan practices like rising for the national anthem and greeting 'Ayubowan' or 'May you live long'. Some leaders engrossed in ideology were alleged of overly practising the Thowheed doctrine as a service to receive Gulf and foreign funds. The danger to Muslims and non-Muslims came from such 'true believers' living in isolated pockets and religious enclaves. Exposed to foreign ideologies, they distanced themselves from the vibrant Sri Lankan culture and its communities.

Evolution of Threat

The genesis of the threat leading to the Easter Sunday attack can be traced back to the establishment of the IS in Sri Lanka. From the Middle East, the IS inspired an ecosystem worldwide, which included Sri Lanka. Sri Lankan followers—supporters and sympathizers of the group—reportedly emulated its best practice by committing mass murder against non-believers, particularly Christians and westerners. The threat's trajectory can be traced to Sri Lankan Muslim extremists across the island and abroad. With political Islam steadfastly replacing or challenging the 1,400-year-old Sri Lankan Muslim heritage, Muslim Sri Lankans became vulnerable to recruitment by radical and violent threat entities.

The bastion of Salafi-Wahhabism and Jamaat-e-Islam in the heart of Sri Lanka was believed to be the primary conception of radicalization. Thowheed and Jamaat-e-Islami strains of Islam grew in areas in Dematagoda and Colombo, which housed communities of Sri Lankan Muslims. The purportedly divisive ideology acted as a beltway to join al-Qaeda and the IS—the deadliest terrorist movements in the world.

Under the pretext of preaching pure and pristine Islam, the political ideologies of extremist Salafi-Wahhabism and Jamaat-e-Islami dressed as religion were said to have disrupted and damaged the social fabric of Sri Lanka. These ideologies separated Muslim sects from their own communities. They seemingly abandoned their identity as Sri Lankans, kept only to themselves and stopped socializing with 'non-believers', removed photos—including family photos—from their living spaces, and even changed how they looked or dressed. It was believed that many Muslims were not aware of the politicization, radicalization, and ideological exploitation that surrounded them. The radicalized Muslims likely perceived it as a revival of Islam instead.

Wherever Islam travelled, it shaped local cultures and, likewise, local traditions influenced Islam. With its interaction with Buddhism, Hinduism, and Christianity, Sri Lankan Islam was said to have been idyllic. Sri Lankan Islam and its Muslim heritage were believed to have been formed by embracing all religions and ethnicities. Local and traditional Islam reportedly identified all Sri Lankans as 'Eka Mawakage Daruwo' or the children of one mother.

With the influx of foreign forms of Islam, in effect politico-religious ideologies under the pretext of authentic Islam, Sri Lankan Muslims' peace with other religious communities eroded. The extremist Jamaat-e-Islami and Salafi-Wahhabi forms of Islam introduced to Sri Lanka appeared to reflect the political conflicts between the Hindus of India and Muslims of Pakistan, and the animosity between the Turks and Saudis. With globalization and enhanced interaction between Sri Lankans and foreigners, the face of Sri Lankan Islam began to change. With the shift in ideological alignment, idyllic Islam hitherto practiced by the Sri Lankan Muslims seemed to dissipate.

Muslim radicalization promoted reciprocal radicalization step-by-step. 'Cumulative extremism', by scholars Busher, Holbrook, and Macklin, references a mutualist enabling of radical and unorthodox thinking, particularly in the context of religious discourse and exchange.[169] As they began to appear non-Sri

[169] Joel Busher, Donald Holbrook, and Graham Macklin, 'How the "Internal Brakes" on Violent Escalation Work and Fail: Toward a Conceptual Framework for Understanding Intra-Group Processes of Restraint in Militant Groups',

Lankan, it was said that Sinhala and Tamil nationalism turned against Muslims. A few Sinhala Buddhist organizations that spread hatred and advocated violence against Muslims, their homes, businesses, and vehicles reportedly emerged. There appeared to be no policy coherence in dealing with these organizations, their leadership, and their followers. According to accounts, there seemed to be a false belief by national, political, and community leaders that decisive and concerted action against Sinhala radical and violent groups would impact the Sinhalese voter base. As such, there could likely have been a reluctance to act and take firm action to dismantle Sinhala groups such as BBS, Sihala Ravaya, and Mahason Balakaya. At the same time, the surging Muslim radicalization was said to have been ignored by national, political, and community leaders at their peril.

The growing Muslim-non-Muslim gulf, the separation between the communities, and the government's apparent neglect of security during the last four decades were believed to have opened the way for the Easter attack. The cascading exclusivist and extremist religious ideologies took root in Sri Lanka with enhanced contact between Sri Lankan Muslims and the outside world. With political Islam from conflict-torn countries starting to supplant the Sri Lankan Muslim heritage, the multi-religious fabric of Sri Lanka began to fragment. It was said that attitudes held by the international community, specifically agendas that pushed for western democratic principles, were often considered antithetical to the infringement on human rights and religious freedom facilitated by the local government. This communicative traffic between foreign diplomatic centres and Sri Lankan foreign policy networks may also have led to a growing vulnerability in maintaining national security networks. According to accounts, in some instances when the government attempted to act against radicalization, objections seemed to be raised by Muslim politicians

---

Studies in Conflict and Terrorism, (2021): 1–22, https://doi.org/10.1080/1057610X.2021.1872156.

allegedly receiving funds from Arab countries to promote their brand of Islam and rights activists allegedly receiving funds from western diplomatic missions to promote religious freedom.

The Antecedents

As with any colossal event of influential nature, an array of global shocks and regional events shaped the minds of Sri Lankans. Sri Lankan Muslims were not immune to the declaration of an Islamic caliphate in 2014. Seated behind their laptops and other electronic devices, thousands of al-Qaeda and IS propagandists harnessed the momentum. It is believed that, of the 1.6 billion Muslims worldwide, a tiny but significant fraction embraced the IS ideology. The constitutionally protected freedom of religion in western liberal democracies was believed to have created the environment for extremist preachers to maintain a direct physical and virtual presence. Many preachers, clerics, and pseudo-religious leaders communicated effectively in English and other languages to convince their listeners or followers to kill, maim, and injure non-Muslims or non-believers. These religious entrepreneurs engaged and enraged Muslims worldwide to successfully turn them to kill for Allah and Islam.

The IS brand of Islam was believed to have reached Sri Lanka in two principal ways. First, a sliver of Muslims, especially youth, in Sri Lanka were influenced online by the IS doctrine. Second, Sri Lankan Muslims studying or working overseas were exposed to al-Qaeda, the IS, and similar ideologies circulating in foreign nations.

Apart from being groomed by the likes of Naufer, who was radicalized in Qatar, Sri Lankan Muslim youth and students overseas were also reportedly radicalized by foreign pseudo-clerics who brought their mentors' ideologies to Sri Lanka. Some examples were British national Anjem Choudary, Bosnian-born Australian Harun Mehicevic, British national Mohammed Mizanur

Rahman alias Abu Baraa, Jamaican convert Abdullah Ibrahim al-Faisal, and Australian Musa Cerantonio, among others. To spread hate, they all exploited the freedoms of expression and religion enshrined in the constitutions of western liberal democracies. The presumed failure of key leaders to regulate extremist content online likely contributed to the internet becoming a resource base for extremists and their organizations too. For instance, although a US drone killed Anwar al-Awlaki, an American Yemeni al-Qaeda member, in 2011, his audio and video propaganda remained online, which could have played a part in radicalizing second-generation extremists.

Thus, sermons by these charismatic preachers continued to mobilize Sri Lankans overseas and at home. Their virulent ideologies calling to fight for Allah and Islam cascaded, radicalizing Sri Lankan hearts and minds through digital and physical spaces.

Five Phases of Confluence

It was believed that Sri Lankans living overseas—who were in touch with friends and family at home—transmitted ideology and funds to shape their countrymen's thinking. In addition to travelling to fight overseas in the 'holy wars' of Iraq, Syria, Afghanistan, and other theatres, the idea of creating, developing, and consolidating an IS branch in Sri Lanka was said to have originated in five distinct but interrelated cases. These were:

1. Expatriate Sri Lankans exposed to the ideologies of the IS, and its predecessor al-Qaeda, travelled to Sri Lanka to radicalize and recruit Sri Lankans. For instance, Ahmed Lukman Thalib, a Jamaat-e-Islami activist turned al-Qaeda facilitator who was visiting from Qatar and Australia, organized Jamaat-e-Islami student wing leader Sadiq from Mawanella to train with an al-Qaeda-associated group

in Syria. Upon his return, Sadiq reportedly switched allegiances from al-Qaeda to the IS and joined as a recruiter for the organization and an instructor for Zahran.

2. Naufer Moulavi radicalized Zahran. Naufer was raised in Kattankudy and studied at a Jamaat-e-Islami madrasah, Islahiya Arabic College, in Madampe in Sri Lanka. A childhood friend of Zahran and relative by marriage, Naufer left Sri Lanka and worked in the Gulf for a decade, where he was said to have embraced the IS ideology. On a visit from Qatar to Kattankudy, accounts stated that he provided Zahran with a pen drive full of IS content to radicalize him. After relocating from Qatar to Kekunagolla, where his wife lived, he joined Zahran to indoctrinate and groom Muslims in Sri Lanka with the IS ideology.
3. Mohamed Mushin Ishaq Ahamed reportedly facilitated the recruitment of Sri Lankans to travel to Iraq and Syria. Ishaq traveled to the UK after 9/11 and was radicalized as a student there. He apparently developed suspicions and prejudice against non-Muslims. Upon his return, Ishaq married Fathima Seenath Akbar from Colombo. Gainfully employed, Ishaq served a charity, Muslim Aid, while his wife worked in the humanities at the Open University in Nawala. In 2009, Ishaq left for Tanzania to join Islamic Help, another charity. Ishaq was said to have joined the IS on 13 August 2013 while on a humanitarian visit to Iraq and Syria. After entering Syria with his wife and five children, Ishaq recruited his Sri Lanka-based younger brother, Nilam. Nilam and his family of six children and pregnant wife joined the IS in January 2015. It was said that Ishaq's parents, sister-in-law, her two brothers, their families, and their domestic worker also relocated to Syria and Iraq.

4. Aroos, known as Abu Asia, led the Sri Lankan contingent in Iraq and Syria and acted as an intermediary between the IS and its Sri Lanka branch. Born on 19 December 1980 and raised in Balangoda, Aroos travelled to Australia for his education. In Australia, both Jameel and Aroos were said to have been radicalized at the al-Furqan centre in Melbourne. After Australia deported Aroos to Sri Lanka in 2013, he met Nilam and Jameel in Colombo and entered Syria on 12 November 2014. Aroos married Ishaq's eldest daughter Asma in March 2015. After Nilam left Sri Lanka and joined the IS, a US air strike killed him in Syria on 12 July 2015. Based in Syria until his death, Aroos was said to have assumed leadership of the Sri Lankan contingent in Iraq and Syria.
5. Jameel and Mohammed Imad Ibthisam Fakeer were reportedly exposed to extremist preachers at their universities in the UK and Australia. Determined to join the IS, the Sri Lankan Muslims travelled to Turkey to enter Iraq and Syria. While Jameel was unsuccessful, Imad was dissuaded by his mother, and he returned home with the family. More than the impact of families from Sri Lanka that travelled and remained in the IS theatre, Jameel and Imad, who returned from Turkey, the gateway to the theatre, were said to have had a profound impact on Sri Lanka. Imad built a Quran study group that evolved into an IS support entity. After Mohamed Umair Iqbal and Jameel infiltrated it, the entity turned operational. They mobilized Salafi-Wahhabi and Jamaat-e-Islami followers to grow the JMI—also known as the Colombo team. Thus, the most extreme elements of the network were co-opted by Jameel to join the IS Sri Lanka branch. JMI mastermind Jameel reportedly mediated between the IS' Sri Lanka contingent under Aroos and the IS Sri Lanka branch under Zahran.

Ideology Takes Root

A small but important segment of Sri Lankan Muslims enamored by Salafi-Wahhabism and Jamaat-e-Islami believed that they were a part of the Muslim renaissance. They allegedly wanted to destroy Sri Lankan Muslim materials and literary heritage—and they partially succeeded in it. The most virulent strain of Salafi-Wahhabism was said to have been introduced in Colombo, Sri Lanka, and Tamil Nadu by a Sri Lankan Muslim, Nizar Quwathi. He founded Jamaat ut Thowheed fi Seylani or the Thowheed Jamaat Republic of Sri Lanka in 1973. Nizar published *Wan Sudar*, a Tamil bulletin and magazine challenging traditional and local Islam. Nizar reportedly created the first Salafi-Wahhabi organization in Sri Lanka too, after JASM in Paragahadeniya.

According to Nizar's son, Wazni, Nizar visited Paragahadeniya where radical Sri Lankan Salafi-Wahhabis allegedly destroyed a Sufi saint's grave. In a country where every street was dotted with Buddhist, Christian, and Hindu images, Nizar's motto was said to have been 'anti-polytheism'. Praiseworthy aims for Muslims were, love and affection, truthfulness, fulfilling a promise, not violating trust, and fearing Allah alone and none else.[170] It was said that some Muslims went to the extent of taking 'Allah alone and none else' so literally that they did everything they could to destroy and get rid of other entities of worship, especially idols. Likewise, this intolerant segment of extremists would kill non-believers in the name of Allah, believing it was highly virtuous to do so.

After Nizar passed away in 1984, *Wan Sudar's* publication stopped. However, its back copies continued to inspire Muslims—including P.J., an Islamic preacher in Tamil Nadu. As discussed previously, after co-founding Tamil Nadu Muslim Munnetra Kazagham in 1995, P.J. founded the TNTJ on 16 May 2004. Claiming to preach true Islam to both Muslims and non-Muslims as per Quranic and Prophetic ways, he radicalized Muslims in

[170] Quran 49:9–15.

India and Sri Lanka until May 2018, when he was expelled from the TNTJ.

After visiting Sri Lanka many times, P.J. reportedly inspired the formation of the SLTJ, CTJ, and NTJ, and similar Salafi-Wahhabi organizations that separated Muslims from non-Muslims. P.J.'s influence was believed to have indelible and Thowheed Jamaat leaders—from Abdul Razik of the CTJ to Zahran of the NTJ—started to adopt his animated style. The key tenant was love for Muslims, hatred of non-Muslims, and the ultimate wish of spreading Islam by holy war or jihad.

Foreign Fighters and Families

The first batch of foreign terrorist fighters to migrate from Sri Lanka to Iraq and Syria was said to have precipitated a support network in Sri Lanka. While the operational vanguard travelled to the theatre, the resident support network grew far and wide. The most extreme of the bunch merged with Zahran's IS of Sri Lanka. It was said that the core of the operational vanguard in theatre and the support network at home was created through the union of two families driven by Salafi-Wahhabi and Jamaat-e-Islami ideologies. Jamaat-e-Islami and Salafi-Wahhabi families and followers predisposed to the IS ideology were reportedly recruited by Ishaq and Nilam to travel to Iraq and Syria. While a few other Sri Lankans living in Australia joined the contingent, most foreign fighters were produced by Mushin and Thajudeen families from central and western provinces.

Just as the LTTE continued to venerate its pioneer suicide terrorist 'Miller', the IS iconography recognized Sri Lankan pioneer Nilam after he was killed while fighting in Syria during a US-led coalition airstrike in July 2015.[171] Ishaq, who was

---

[171] Rohan Gunaratna. 'Defeating the Sea Tigers of LTTE', in *Global Responses to Maritime Violence: Cooperation and Collective Action*, ed. Paul Shemella (Redwood City: Stanford University Press, 2016), pp. 203–223.

the eldest, Ruwaizah, and Nilam, the youngest, hailed from Kurundugolla in Sri Lanka. After graduating from the prestigious Trinity College in Kandy, Nilam reportedly developed an interest in becoming a religious scholar. He studied Islam for 6–7 years at Darul Uloom Al Humaidiya Arabic College, a Tabligh Jamaat madrasah in Colombo. After graduating as a moulavi, he taught Islam in Kandy and taught at an international school. Nilam's drift towards extremism was said to have started when he joined Jamaat-e-Islami, which was a sect originating in India.

Reportedly regarded as the Asian version of the Middle Eastern Muslim Brotherhood, Jamaat-e-Islami invited Nilam to attend classes at their building in Dematagoda Road. Nilam would go on to marry Jhudi Thajudeen, who hailed from nearby Maligawatte in Maradana. After their marriage, they travelled to Pakistan where Nilam studied sharia at the International Islamic University of Pakistan. Jhudi, who was a former student of Ilma International, taught English to children in Pakistan. Upon his return from Pakistan, Nilam served as a visiting Urdu lecturer at the University of Colombo between the years 2011–2012.

Nilam was reportedly influenced by Jamaat-e-Islami founder, Abu A'la Maududi, who also promoted the idea of a caliphate and advocated jihad. He was said to have been influenced by the prophet to keep fit, and thus encouraged his students to engage in martial arts. After rigorous training, Nilam excelled as a martial artist and became a black belt third dan. Nilam participated in several tournaments, including the international tournament organized by the Japan Shotokan Karate Association at Sugathadasa Stadium in 2012. The host was Sensai Saldin, a Sri Lankan with five children, all black belts, whose family were followers of the Thowheed Jamaat. As founder and head coach, Saldin allegedly promoted Salafi-Wahhabism among his students, including the Sri Lanka Air Force.

With deepening Salafi-Wahhabi influence, Nilam crossed the sectorial barrier and joined the Thowheed Jamaat, which happened to be his wife Jhudi's denomination. In addition to his brother Ishaq, Nilam's parents—a notary and housewife—would also embrace Thowheed Jamaat. Apart from Nilam's father-in-law, Thajudeen, his wife's grandparents, Nizar and Ameena, also belonged to the Thowheed Jamaat fraternity in Colombo and its suburbs. In fact, Nizar was Nizar Quwathi—the founder of Thowheed Jamaat Republic of Sri Lanka.

After Nilam was appointed as principal at an international school located in the Hameedia Building, his family relocated to Galewela in the Matale district. Nilam taught English to seventy students, held martial arts classes in the evenings and served as principal from January 2013–December 2014. After December 2014, and in preparation for travel to Syria and Iraq, Nilam and his family left Galewela and relocated to Colombo, where he reportedly met with IS operators and supporters.

The first batch of Sri Lankans that travelled to Iraq and Syria included Jhudi's two brothers, who travelled through from Turkey, and Muhammad Thawsi's family. Before flying out with his family and extended family, it was said that they heeded Nilam and Ishaq's advice to keep their move to the theatre a secret only to those who had reservations about their decision or refused to travel. While Nilam falsely informed work colleagues and friends that he was going to Mecca on pilgrimage, Rawzia apparently told her family—particularly her mother Ameena—that they found work in Dubai. According to Wazni Nizar, when Ameena found out the truth, she 'fell ill'.[172]

Unlike Ishaq and Nilam, it was said that their sister Ruwaizah and her husband Yahiyah Nizzamdeen, who was a Tabligh Jamaat practitioner and *hafiz*, rejected Salafi-Wahhabism. Both

[172] Wazni Nizar (ACTJ leader), interview by author, February 7, 2022.

declined to travel to Iraq and Syria. Their son, Thaseen Ahmed, and daughter, Zainab Thajudeen, reportedly did not wish to go as well. According to Wazni Nizar, they believed the IS' way of fighting was not the 'Islamic way of jihad,' and added that 'Ishaq [had] sent money and brainwashed Nilam and Jhudi.'[173]

When Nilam and his family applied for a tourist visa at the Turkish Embassy in Colombo in December 2014, the entire family of ten was present—including 'his pregnant wife, six children between the ages of 5–10, and his parents', according to Turkish Ambassador Iskender Okyay.[174] However, Ambassador Iskender noted that Nilam was the only one with a proper visa. When applying for the visas, Nilam also claimed 'he was the general manager of a company named Minza Traders, [which was an importer] of textiles, leather, and cosmetics'.[175]

Thus, deception, an integral part of warfare, was very apparent in the IS playbook. Nilam practised the IS guideline to conceal travel and instructed others to follow suit. Unbeknownst to friends and relatives, Nilam and his family were heading to massacre in the name of fundamentalist religion and ideology.

Salafi-Wahhabism and Jamaat-e-Islami Bastion

Back home in Sri Lanka, the IS' footprint expanded. In memory of Thowheed Jamaat founder Nizar Quwathi, it was said that his son Wazni Nizar, family, relatives, and neighbors purchased a property along Dematagoda Road, where his followers established an Islamic Dawa Centre. The Islamic Dawa Centre changed its name to Masjid ul Thowheed and, eventually, a breakaway faction

---

[173] Nizar, interview.

[174] Sulochana Ramiah Mohan, 'How Nilam Took Turkey Visa to Join ISIS', *Ceylon Today*, July 26, 2015, https://publicpolicy.pepperdine.edu/newsroom/articles/dr-robert-lloyd-isis-ceylon-today-sri-lanka.htm.

[175] Mohan, 'How Nilam Took Turkey Visa'.

of the Thowheed Jamaat Republic of Sri Lanka called ACTJ would be created by Faiz Moulavi and Abu Sali Moulavi.

Radicalized to different degrees, members of the Muslim community reportedly began to provide support and recruits to fight western and other forces in Iraq and Syria. Starting with Dematagoda-Maradana, the Salafi-Wahhabi ideologies were said to have spread to Wellawatte-Dehiwala, Mattakuliya-Wellampitiya, and beyond. The Salafi-Wahhabi-centric mosques, madrasahs, and Muslim organizations would become bridgeheads. It was believed that a number of these Muslim institutions instilled the belief that Islam should be spread by conquest, and thus prepared adherents to commit violence against non-Muslims. During Nizar's lifetime, the Salafi-Wahhabi footprint was said to have expanded both in Sri Lanka and overseas—to Tamil Nadu and Singapore. After Nizar's demise, the ideology that he birthed in Sri Lanka would arguably kill a part of his own family and bring death and destruction to the community.

The Sri Lankan contingent in Iraq and Syria reportedly provided leadership, inspiration, and guidance to fledgling IS support and operational groups in Sri Lanka. Before his death in July 2015, Nilam and, subsequently, his elder brother, Ishaq, were said to have mentored Aroos, who would succeed Nilam and go on to marry Ishaq's daughter, Asmaa, in Syria. Accounts also stated that Nilam had seeded the nucleus of a support and operational group in Sri Lanka when he met with like-minded extremist Sri Lankan Muslims in Colombo in late 2014, just before he left Sri Lanka in January 2015.

During said dinner-meeting at his wife's ancestral residence, Nilam was said to have recruited friends and family. Although the meeting was originally organized to discuss plans to travel to Syria, it was believed that the gathering created a commitment to seeding an IS branch in Sri Lanka. Two of Nilam's guests then, Jameel and Imad, would travel to Turkey but return to create the

JMI in Sri Lanka together with Umeir Mohammed Iqbal or Abu Afiya. Another guest, Aroos, would also enter Iraq and Syria to lead the IS as Abu Asia. Jameel and Aroos, who knew each other in Australia and supported the IS, reportedly maintained their links until Aroos was killed in theatre. Jameel, as discussed thus far, would go on to become one of the nine suicide bombers of the Easter Sunday attack in 2019.

Returnees from Theatre

As seen in the section above, social and family ties strengthened the continuity of links between the Sri Lankan contingent in Iraq and Syria, and their followers in Sri Lanka. The same could be said when a Sri Lankan woman unintentionally fostered the link between the IS and a Sri Lankan Muslim youth group that would eventually become the JMI. This woman was Shabnam Minasha, a promising fashion designer and psychology student who was radicalized by her husband.

Together with her then-newly wedded husband, Imad, she was apparently duped into travelling to Iraq and Syria by the IS propaganda that was said to have offered 'opportunities' for Muslims worldwide. After hearing that the IS provided housing, food, schooling, and an allowance per family member, Shabnam and Imad reportedly decided to take the chance and explored how they could travel to the group's heartland. According to accounts, Shabnam introduced Imad to Ishaq Ahamed, her cousin Ameen Akbar Fathima Zeenath's husband, and Nilam's brother. According to Shabnam herself, she and Imad learned that Ishaq had joined the IS. Shabnam would also tell authorities that Ishaq travelled to Tanzania to work in a non-government organization (NGO) called Islamic Help. After which, '[h]e travelled to Syria on official duty to deliver aid and [decided to join] the IS [while he was there]'.[176]

---

[176] Sri Lanka Terrorism Investigations Department, debriefing of Shabnam Minasha shared with author, 2019.

It was said that Shabnam and Imad first contacted Ishaq on Twitter, then over the phone to seek his advice about travelling to the theatre. Ishaq reportedly connected Imad with his brother Nilam in Sri Lanka. Eventually, in 2014, Nilam would invite the couple to his wife Jhudi's house in Dematagoda for lunch to make plans for them to travel to Syria.

After much planning, Shabnam and Imad were able to make it to Iraq and Syria—but it was not what they expected. In Shabnam's own words, '[W]e flew into Turkey on 15 January 2015, along with Nilam's family and parents. Upon reaching Turkey, we were visited at the hotel by a member of the IS who had identified himself as Brother H. Brother H advised us to pack all belongings into one bag and that we would be driven to the Turkey-Syrian border. We would have to walk our way into Syria after being dropped at the border. On hearing details, we changed our minds and returned to Sri Lanka on 18 January 2015.'[177]

Upon their return, Shabnam said, 'Jameel telephoned my husband after six months. Jameel [reportedly] held extreme views and ideas even at this time.'[178] In 2016, accompanied by his parents, Jameel visited Shabnam's parent's house at Collinwood Place in Wellawatte. There, it was said that Shabnam's father reprimanded Jameel and did not let him in. After Jameel was 'chased out', Shabnam claimed that Imad did not tell her about his relationship or conversations with Jameel.[179] Unbeknownst to Shabnam, Jameel and Imad were already working together to build a support group for the IS. Both unsuccessful returnees were said to have endeavored to gather aspirants to serve the state and play a vital role in shaping Sri Lanka's threat landscape.

[177] Sri Lanka Terrorism Investigations Department, debriefing of Shabnam Minasha.

[178] Sri Lanka Terrorism Investigations Department, debriefing of Shabnam Minasha.

[179] Sri Lanka Terrorism Investigations Department, debriefing of Shabnam Minasha.

After Nilam died, Aroos, as Abu Asia or son of Asia, would take over the Sri Lankan contingent's leadership mantle. Jameel reportedly met and developed a lifelong friendship with Aroos in Melbourne and Colombo from 2013–2015. Thus, Jameel remained in contact with Aroos during the latter's stay in Syria from 2016–2019. Back at home, Imad networked, groomed, and raised the first local IS support group—JMI. Jameel would later introduce Zahran to the IS, financially empower his group, and later participate in the Easter attack.

IS' Ideological Foundation in Sri Lanka

Before the birth of the IS and its precursor al-Qaeda, fighting was mostly—and arguably—confined within conflict zones. Later, al-Qaeda's 9/11 and the IS' Easter Sunday attacks would show how the entire planet was now the operating theatre of threat groups; demonstrating that threats now spilled off the battlefield. It was believed that the IS could operate effectively beyond its borders because its directing figures understood the power of the Internet, especially social media. The battlefield and off-battlefield successes of al-Qaeda and the IS were said to have piqued interest worldwide, especially among curious and vulnerable Muslim youth who were more tech-savvy and likely to follow developments online. Those most susceptible were possibly swept away to support and join the fight.

To harness its momentum, IS recruiters and other 'predators' reportedly started radicalizing and recruiting. With the deepening influence of the IS propaganda, Jameel, a religious fanatic, was said to have set his sights on multiple networks of impressionable, English-speaking, and tech-savvy youth learning about Islam and the IS. They were said to be a resourceful group, mostly from educated and arguably wealthy families in Colombo and its immediate neighborhood. Operating on social media platforms in Sri Lanka and across the globe, a tiny but significant segment reportedly provided operational and moral support to seed and sustain the IS.

The most passionate in Sri Lanka would go on to form a group to study the Quran. Later, Jameel would reportedly bring them a copy of Abu Muhammad al-Maqdisi's book, *Millat Ibrahim*. Jameel named the Quran Study Group 'JMI'.

A Ramified Network

As discussed thus far, the Sri Lankan threat landscape changed dramatically when IS-directing figures harnessed the IS ideology into support and operational action. A globalized ideological force was developed by *Millat Ibrahim*'s author, Abu Muhammad al-Maqdisi, who was also the mentor of Abu Musab al-Zarqawi—the founder and father of the IS.

While in prison, Abu Muhammad, a Jordanian of Palestinian descent, was said to have radicalized Abu Musab. The world's leading radical and violent ideologue, Abu Muhammad's book has been recognized as 'an important source of inspiration for the global jihadist movement, including the al-Qaeda branch in Iraq led after the US-led invasion in 2003'.[180] Exploiting Muslim suffering believed to have been caused by western intervention, the al-Qaeda branch in Iraq would later birth the world's most powerful threat movements—the IS and its breakaway rival, Hay'at Tahrir al-Sham, the largest al-Qaeda entity.

It was believed that the ideological foundation of these movements drew from *Millat Ibrahim*, which translated to 'the religion of Abraham', a reference in the Quran to Abraham as a role model in faith due to his obedience to God's word and disavowal of idolatry. The organization Millat Ibrahim was said to have been established in Europe in December 2011 and its

[180] Jean-Charles Brisard and Damien Martinez, *Zarqawi: The New Face of Al-Qaeda*, (Cambridge: Polity, 2005).

followers travelled from Austria, Belgium, Denmark, France, and the UK to Iraq and Syria to serve the IS. Like most Salafi-Wahhabi groups, it was said that Millat Ibrahim built loyalty and adherence or *wala* to divine law and struggle against unbelief by renouncing infidel legislation or *bara*, including democracy.

Presented as true religion, Millat Ibrahim followers reportedly regarded secular state leaders as apostates. Although many countries banned Millat Ibrahim, the group allegedly continued spreading propaganda, radicalizing and recruiting from existing networks. Operating from the UK before and after his imprisonment for supporting the IS, Anjem Choudary was said to have promoted the doctrine and created a robust following worldwide. Communicating effectively in English, Anjem Choudary, the co-leader of Al-Muhajiroun, a breakaway faction of Hizb ut-Tahrir, also promoted Millat Ibrahim, mobilising Muslims to join the IS. Although Hizb ut-Tahrir did not explicitly advocate violence, it may have created the social tent to radicalize Muslims and promoted the idea of the caliphate. In Sri Lanka, Jameel, a disciple of Anjem Choudary, established a branch of the ramified network of Millat Ibrahim by infiltrating the Quran Study Group in Sri Lanka.

It was said that Jameel already had a readymade following when he started to radicalize Sri Lankan Muslim youth. This was thanks to Aadhil Ameez, who had reportedly radicalized and created an online community of IS supporters. The online activities spearheaded by Aadhil started in 2013 and peaked in 2014. The accessible and far-reaching nature of these online groups, especially on social media, likely enabled the propagandists to reach a wider audience.

In other words, the virtual footprint of the IS created by Aadhil in Sri Lanka was co-opted by Jameel, who was an effective operator. He was said to have harnessed the fruits of Aadhil's efforts to politicize, radicalize, and mobilise a section of youth. Catering to the pre-existing cultural and ethnic divisions that marked Sri Lanka's social landscape, the amalgamations of approaches and these two ideologies were believed to have enabled a more intricate intersection of Islamic society within the domestic sphere to be canvassed.

Who is Aadhil AX?

The ideological foundation for creating an IS branch in Sri Lanka was believed to have been seeded through online propaganda in 2013 by an eighteen-year-old Sri Lankan Muslim called Aadhil Ameez. Aadhil, who was from Dharga town in Aluthgama, was said to have been regarded the main driver of the IS digital community. After being influenced by ISIS, he reportedly turned from a sympathiser into a supporter. He operated virtually, and later physically, to recruit and radicalize Muslims to support the IS. Although many attribute the Dharga riots to radicalizing Aadhil, he was said to have already been active online even before the religious clashes. Though his drive and commitment to espouse the IS may have also been fuelled by said riots and the proclamation of the caliphate exercising jurisdiction over Muslims worldwide, which happened in succession in June 2014.

With the battlefield successes in Iraq and Syria throughout 2013, the IS ideology had apparently and effectively appealed to a tiny segment of Sri Lankan youth. Although the IS deviated from Islamic theology, a number of English-speaking youth and teenagers from Colombo reportedly got swept up in its highly articulate propaganda campaign, which would culminate in the Easter Sunday attack.

Aadhil, operating under the name Aadhil AX, was at the heart of community initiatives such as 'Did You Know', where he published content on the IS, the war in Syria, the history of world terrorism, and the like. He also worked with groups radicalized males and females across the world, sharing their experiences across global regions. Aadhil AX radicalized not only Sri Lankans but foreigners as well. This included the twenty-six-year-old Sheikh Azhar ul Islam, alias Shaykh azhar ul Islam, alias AsGazi_S6, and alias Fb Aseem India. Referring to Sheikh Azhar ul Islam as A-1, the charge sheet of the NIA said:

> *A-1 used to browse, search, and read Jihadi speeches on the internet and terrorists' quotes for self-radicalization. A-1 posted quotes on Facebook and Twitter and got self-radicalized by online contents of speeches of Islamic scholars of [IS] including but not limited to Anjem [Choudary], Abu Barra @ Mizanur Rahman, Abu Haleema, Abu Rumaysah and Abu Izzadeen, and Musa Jibril. A-1 was in contact with the [IS] operatives, active on Twitter including Abu Dujan, Karen Aishia, Marayam Khalil, Marayam Obaid, Lone Wolf, Kashmiri witness and Jannah Deen. Other contacts [were] Marayam Khalil from Australia or America, Karen Aishia from the Philippines Abu Dujan, who distributed online books in English related to [IS], Marayem Obaid [unknown person]; Jammah Deen, an Australian girl; Kashmiri witness, an unknown resident of Kashmir, and Lone Wolf, username Zia Bhat. A-1 had obtained the [IS]-related incriminating material online from Aadhil AX (internet identity) and his Facebook and Twitter pages namely Aadhil AX and 'Did You Know?'. 'Did You Know?' [was] a page both on Twitter and Facebook founded by Aadhil AX, who posts information about the past wars of Islam, and the history of the commanders of Islamic forces.*[181]

With his mastery of the virtual landscape, Aadhil AX created digital platforms to heighten interest and engage and empower followers. It was said that he successfully manipulated both Sri Lankans and Indians to travel to the Iraqi-Syrian theatre using

---

[181] National Investigation Agency, Ministry of Home Affairs, Government of India, *Final Report (U/S 173 (2) Cr PC) Before the Hon'ble Special Court NIA, New Delhi*, July 25, 2016, https://www.satp.org/Docs/Document/1032.pdf.

social media and communication platforms like Facebook, Twitter, Pinterest, and WhatsApp. On his blog, his profile points to another blog site titled, 'We Are Coming To Establish Khilafah Across The Muslim World', which was last active in 2013. Those who could not travel were advised by him to remain in their home countries and advance the IS agenda. Unlike the marginalized Muslims of Europe, many Muslims in Colombo that turned from secular to radical were believed to have been affluent. Thus, they were likely more willing to risk their families, funds, and even die for their cause. While the IS partnered with regional terrorist groups to extend its reach, Aadhil partnered with the IS. He created a global fallback network as an immediate response to when the physical caliphate crumbled in Syria.

The Light Series

Of the many propaganda materials shared or introduced by Aadhil, a number of Sri Lankan youth and teenagers were radicalized, in particular, by a documentary video series on YouTube titled 'Light Series'. The video series was first posted in 2010 by the channel EnterTheTruth Productions, and its last post was in 2018. It was believed that it aimed to contextualize the events for Muslim masses. In 2013, it gained prominence on social media for its simple yet effective method of explaining current events and supposed religious realities.

The series covered events from the fall of the Ottoman Empire to the 9/11 attack, and the rise of the caliphate. It was likely watched by all current and would-be members of the JMI and may have radicalized the Colombo team members to become extreme too. It was said that the series legitimized al-Qaeda and the IS to build support for exclusivist and extremist ideologies. When exposed to such ideologies, followers' worldviews, events, and internal understanding of history would likely become distorted—and may push them to succumb to the ideology.

Step-by-Step Radicalization

The Muslim youth idealising the IS and enlisting with its support groups—including the JMI—were likely, and often, shaped by their 'environment, family, and friends', as affirmed by then-JMI member Hamaaz. The radicalization by family and friends was seen as a key driver—as was the case of St Anthony's Church bomber, Muaath, whose Salafi-Wahhabi parentage could have made him susceptible to Jameel and Zahran's influence. Like many of the other suicide bombers, Muaath was also driven by online propaganda, particularly Aadhil's.

In contrast to Salafi-Wahhabi and Jamaat-e-Islami Muslims, local and traditional or Sufi Muslims may not have been as vulnerable to radical ideologies, especially since they seemed more open to diversity and multiculturalism. Unlike Sufis, who often interacted with non-Muslims, it was believed that IS recruiters could radicalize Muslims from political sects such as Jamaat-e-Islami and Salafi-Wahhabism with less effort. Muslims from these sects reportedly kept to themselves much more, which could create a dangerous brand of exclusivism that would prove detrimental to the country's security and harmony. It was said that those religiously, culturally, and politically radicalized resisted integration into the larger Sri Lankan culture and looked abroad for their community of practice instead—more notably, towards the Gulf.

The Furnace of Radicalization

It was said that the IS' battlefield victories from 2013 onwards likely fooled many youths into believing it was 'real' Islam in action. One such group of English-conversant youth living in Sri Lankan's western province began conducting meetings to discuss the IS' ideology and develop a deeper understanding of it. Since they were internet-savvy, their main source of knowledge, understanding, and guidance was reportedly the internet. In addition to radicalizing others online, it was also said that the group learned Islam from hate preachers. Though it was comforting for some parents that their children were learning about their faith, they were unaware that these were not the teachings of religion. The furnace of IS radicalization was burning for their children instead.

As discussed, an online community of supporters—mostly from Colombo—emerged shortly after the IS ideology began rapidly cascading in 2014. The name given by the IS Sri Lanka branch, led by Zahran and originating in the east, to the followers of the IS in the western province was said to be the 'Colombo Team'. The IS reportedly relied on this team for human and material resources. It may also be worth noting that, according to accounts, Colombo Muslims were believed to look down on eastern Muslims for various reasons, which could stem from status and culture. However, because they had to work together, the IS ideology essentially bridged these disparate groups.

In the metropolis of Colombo, religious extremism spread in the physical and cyberspace. Dematagoda, Maradana, and Dehiwala were presumed nerve centres of this. As discussed previously, propaganda—mainly through social media platforms—radicalized segments of the Muslim community especially the youth, which, along with their recruitment, drove the extremist threat in the country. They reportedly engaged in continuous religious debates raising awareness within themselves and the community. Although physically living in Sri Lanka, a tiny group of youth glued to their laptops and phones were more influenced by developments in Iraq and Syria. They likely watched with anger the intervention of US-led western forces in Iraq and the suffering of the Iraqi people. They possibly wanted to help the Muslims under threat and support the formation of groups fighting against the western forces. The most committed of the youth were said to wish they could travel to Syria and join the IS proper.

Access to Radicalize and Recruit

The IS ideology spread through an intricate network comprising friends and colleagues, family and relatives, worshippers of mosques run by sects, and mentors and their disciples. Those indoctrinated likely believed that they were the most committed to Islam and were carrying out the work of Allah. In reality, they had embraced a vicious political ideology that was spreading under the guise of religious fervour. With this ideological virus spreading between and among personal networks, a domino effect was created that would turn a chunk of the Muslim community into a terror-seeking, indoctrinated unit of destruction.

Umair Iqbal and Imad, who led the JMI, spearheaded radicalization and recruitment within the organization. After this, identifying and recruiting JMI followers into the IS Sri Lanka branch became Jameel's priority. It was said that Jameel also accessed the network of his brother, Hakeem, to engage and radicalize his friends and their sons. In hindsight, it might not even be a stretch to say that Easter Sunday attack was only made financially and materially possible with Jameel recruiting Ilham and Inshaf, whose family owned the company Ishana, the largest exporter of Sri Lankan spices.

Jameel's radicalization started with Ilham, who Jameel would also use as an agent of influence to recruit his wife, Fathima Jiffry and his brother, Inshaf. When Ilham visited his father's pepper spice cultivation in Matale in 2015, Jameel, Imad, and Amjad reportedly travelled with him to 'see the spices'—however, the only 'spice' they inspected was the level of funding that could be milked for their terror activities. After assessing their high-end resources, Jameel was said to have connected the Ibrahim sons to Zahran. Ilham and Inshaf would go on to provide the necessary funds and other resources to build the IS Sri Lanka branch and, later, execute the Easter attack.

As they became better friends, Jameel reportedly enlisted Ishana facilities and that of its affiliates to conduct radicalization classes and manufacture components for suicide vests. It was said to have been done gradually and constantly, with Jameel continuously assessing how comfortable the brothers were with these operations.

Ilham's brother Inshaf, who was conscious of operational security, was careful not to attend JMI events. In fact, according to Amjad, he only ever 'met Inshaf only in mosques', specifically Salafi-Wahhabi mosques patronized by the IS followers. Although he was radicalized alongside Ilham, it may be interesting to note that Inshaf was only successfully recruited by Ilham nearer to the Easter attack. Ultimately, Ilham was successful in radicalizing his brother, Inshaf, and his wife, Fathima Jiffry, as well.

Institutional Radicalization

According to accounts, most Sri Lankan Muslims practised their religion in moderation. However, with foreign ideologies, notably Jamaat-e-Islami and Salafi-Wahhabism, supplanting Sufism, it was said that the face of the religion changed in Sri Lanka. The lives of the IS followers reflected the contemporary wave of violence that stemmed from embracing fundamentalist religion to an extreme. For instance, Amjad shared the following details about his apparent religious devotion: 'I have been to Mecca to worship Allah in Saudi Arabia in the years 2012, 2015, 2016, 2017, and 2018. I went with all my family members in 2012. In 2015, I went to Mecca with my friend Abdullah Rashid of Maligawatte and his family. In 2016, my father and I went with Ansar, a gem merchant from Beruwala, and Imad, an aeronautical engineer from Wellawatte.'[182] Imad was a JMI

[182] Amjad (JMI member), interview by author, March 10, 2022.

member who had travelled with his wife, Shabnam, to Turkey with plans to enter Syria to join the IS. As mentioned previously, his return to Sri Lanka was catalysed by his parent's guidance and the ultimatum received by the IS to walk from Turkey to Syria.

What Sri Lanka experienced could be regarded as institutional radicalization, where political ideology—under the pretext of religion—was delivered through compromised educational and religious institutions. For example, the writings of Salafi-Wahhabi clerics such as Ibn Abdul Wahab and Jamaat-e-Islami clerics such as Abu A'la Maududi were reportedly integrated to the teacher guides. The first step of radicalization was thus believed to have been promoted by parents, schools, madrasahs, mosques, sects, and Islamic society at schools or universities.

The extreme religious ideology was allegedly preached in Salafi-Wahhabi-infiltrated international schools, madrasahs, and mosques, which were mostly run according to Thowheed principles. As Salafi-Wahhabis in ideology, JMI members purportedly believed it was a sin to worship at Sufi mosques. Thus, they worshipped at mosques managed by Thowheed personalities or organizations instead.

Moreover, since the JMI's inception at the madrasah on Prathibimbarama Road, it is interesting to note that many of their gatherings took place in the vicinity and premises of mosques, madrasahs, and other Islamic centres. To radicalize its recruits and reinforce the ideology of its followers, the JMI likely harnessed these Islamic centres of gathering for outreach and networking. These Salafi-Wahhabi centres were also believed to have been carefully selected or endorsed by JMI functionaries—notably its shadow leader Jameel.

The Shift and Gradual Infiltration

Social media served as an ideal platform for networking before meeting in the physical space. The IS and their supporters were said to have exploited a range of virtual platforms, most notably Facebook, to radicalize innocent Muslims into cold-blooded killers. Insaf Ifthikar played the role of skipper when lending the virtual 'olive branch' onto other pioneer IS supporters: Aadhil Ameez, Arkam Akham, Imad, Ihsan, Umair, Jameel, Amjad, Zawahir, and Khalid. Soon, it was said that Insaf Ifthikar revealed that the meetings transcended from the loose footing of virtual rendezvous to in-person congregations in Bambalapitiya, Colombo, where they discussed avenues of assistance to those willing to travel to Syria and to raise awareness of their plans among the Muslim community. This series of meetings would be the genesis of the group that would come to be named JMI.

Similarly, Sri Lankan Muslim youth exposed to the IS ideology online gradually clustered into cells in several locations too. The initial cells that converged to form the JMI network were reportedly in Maligawatte, Maradana, and Dehiwala. Followers of extremist Jamaat-e-Islami and Salafi-Wahhabi ideologies were said to have gathered to discuss the war in Syria and role of the IS. According to accounts, some participants provided intellectual inputs during these discussions while others offered resources and infrastructure that could help carry out their activities. Eventually, the Maradana and Dehiwala clusters would emerge as centres before gradually merging.

Later, Imad would introduce Jameel to the Muslim youth who gathered at Prathibimbarama Road in Dehiwala. With Jameel formally joining their group, the character of the so-called Quran study group initiated by Imad and led by Umair, transfigured and, as mentioned, would become the JMI as many know it today.

The Genesis of JMI

Until radical Salafi-Wahhabi and Jamaat-e-Islami ideologies allegedly caused friction among Sri Lankan Muslims, it was believed that Sri Lanka's Muslim community lived in complete camaraderie with other non-Muslim communities. However, a number of those who would move out of the Sri Lankan milieu would become vulnerable and, eventually, radicalized. As mentioned thus far, developments in Iraq and Syria after the US invasion seemed to galvanize a fringe of the Muslim youth worldwide. Sri Lankan Muslims were no exception to this surge of anti-western resentment and anger. After the US invasion, the coalition failed to provide necessities and it was said the public then turned against the occupation force. Iraq, and later Syria, suffered from a Shia-Sunni confrontation orchestrated by al-Qaeda in Iraq led by Abu Musab al Zarqawi, the founding father of the IS. The JMI members, like other supporters of the IS, reportedly blamed US-led interventions for the conflict.

Similarly, popular dictator Assad was said to have suppressed a western-backed popular uprising that was once again distorted by IS supporters. Referring to the former Iraqi dictator, then-JMI member Hamaaz claimed that 'Saddam was wrong, but he kept the Shia and Sunni peace.' Referring to the Syrian leader, Hamaaz added, 'A Shia, Assad, killed Sunni men and imprisoned Sunni women. IS freed prisoners. The IS was a hero in our eyes.' It may come as no surprise, then, that the caliphate's proclamation on 29 June 2014 would only motivate its supporters further.

With the indoctrination of youth, IS support groups formed in Sri Lanka. During its formative phase from 2014–2017, the IS supporters were said to have gathered at multiple venues, including in Colombo, where the IS directing figures, supporters, and sympathisers met at the Barista Restaurant. The IS propaganda was believed to have reached its peak in 2014–2015, when the women, wealth, and weapons of the IS reportedly enticed Sri Lankan youth. Based on the debriefings conducted by the CTID, CID, and other government agencies, the JMI drew from youth that gathered at the following venues during the aforementioned formative phase of recruitment and radicalization:

1. Centre for Islamic Studies, Rohini Road, Wellawatte
2. Pentagon Academy, Charles Place, Dehiwala
3. Masjidur Rahman Jumma Masjid, Ebenezer Place, Dehiwala
4. Madrasah at Prathibimbarama Road, Kalubowila

As planned, classes to promote the IS were reportedly held in 2014 and 2015 at the madrasah on Prathibimbarama Road, Dehiwala. According to accounts, these were attended by Imad, Inshaf Ifthikar, Amjad, Suaid, Arkam Akham, and others. Despite having no clerical qualifications, Umair was still instructed by Imad to teach the Quran, while Hadith, Seera, and Jameel introduced the IS' ideology. An adherent of Jamaat-e-Islami turned Salafi-Wahhabi, Umair may have been the group's first teacher but Jameel, a key proponent of the IS, was very likely recognized as the key influencer.

It was said that when Jameel came to the madrasah with Imad, the IS' activities in Syria and Iraq were among the key topics discussed. Later, the venue moved to Akham's house, where the IS followers were further indoctrinated. Eventually, they needed a bigger space to accommodate their growing numbers. In 2015, accounts said that Amjad suggested they move the sessions to his house in Maradana, where Umair would eventually conduct lectures on Thowheed. Afterwards, with Fahma Residential Apartments reportedly coming under the scrutiny of security and intelligence agencies, the gatherings moved back to Dehiwala and Wellawatte.

By uniting existing local milieus, a ramified network emerged. Muslim youth committed to the IS ideal came together to form the JMI, which would eventually become the pillar and support network of the IS Sri Lanka branch.

Geographic Clustering

The leadership and membership of the support groups that made up the JMI were organized into geographic clusters, and all of them were reportedly located in the western province. With the greatest number of followers in Dehiwala and its surroundings, Dehiwala emerged as the first meeting point. Since many of the roads in Dehiwala were interlinked, the meetings were said to take place along the by-lanes of Galle Road. As per first-hand accounts, JMI meetings and gatherings would often shift between venues based on the need for space and convenience too. Alternative venues used by the group, which were mostly homes of the JMI pioneers, allegedly included:

1. The madrasah along Prathibimbarama Road, which was used as a boarding house for Moulavi Abdul Razak to live and teach children in the afternoon.
2. Arkam Akham's residence along Quarry Road.
3. Fahma Residential Apartments at Ananda Mawatha where sessions were held on the rooftop in a building owned by Amjad and Suaid's parents.
4. Ahmed's residence along Galvihara Road.
5. Imad's parent's residence at Tissa Mawatha along Quarry Road.
6. Imad's in-laws' residence at Collinwood Place.
7. Jameel's residence at Lansiyawatte.

The JMI belt, both coastal and hinterland, expanded north to Negombo and south to Galle. However, it was said that its core remained in Colombo and in the city outskirts—Dehiwala and Wellampitiya. While JMI meetings began in the above-mentioned locations, its second phase led to six primary hubs in:

1. Dehiwala-Wellawatte where Umair, Arkam Akam, Shazni, Ahmed, and Ihsan lived.
2. Maligawatte where Zawahir and Khalid lived.
3. Mahawila Gardens, Dematagoda where Ilham and Inshaf lived.

4. Maradana where Amjad, Suaid, and Hamaaz lived.
5. Mattakuliya where Insaf Ifthikar, Muaath, and Infaz Inayathullah lived.
6. Wellampitiya where Jameel lived.

Founding Leaders and Members

The most significant members of the IS diaspora in Sri Lanka formed the JMI. Although they were Sri Lankan citizens, it was said that many spent time overseas working towards global jihad. JMI's digital platforms used for propagation, radicalization, cultivation, and recruitment were in English, which was believed to have allowed them to recruit more widely across different platforms. The JMI's founding leaders and members as well as those who participated in its formative phase reportedly came from a cross-section of society too, and include the following:

1. Imad - aircraft engineer.
2. Hamaaz - IT specialist with laptop repair expertise
3. Muaath - law graduate
4. Amjad - gemology student, accounts student, and food business
5. Ihsan - quantity surveyor
6. Ahmed - software engineer
7. Hilam - businessman
8. Jameel - manufacturing engineering
9. Khalid - food delivery
10. Inshaf Ifthikar - graphic designer and cashier

The diverse backgrounds of the JMI members made it seem like the JMI leadership and membership bridged and united the Muslim divide. It may also be interesting to note that middle-class teenagers and adults were almost all from the western province.

Unlike the typical Muslim population of businessmen and traders, most were reportedly professionals or aspiring professionals, with many proficient in technical, more logical subjects and fields of work. However, it was said that their knowledge of the humanities—philosophy, culture, and the arts—seemed to be lacking. Limited critical thinking could have led to them adopting a narrow worldview, which may have allowed Islamic supremacy—a view advocated by Jameel—to gain traction within the group.

Jameel, the Slithering Snake

In the wheel of radicalization and terror, the hub that connected the spokes was believed to be Jameel. Besides helping to keep the group's cogs turning, Jameel's well-educated and influential family background equipped him with the know-how to handle high-value personalities such as the Ibrahim family and the professionals that formed the core of the JMI following. Working in the shadows, Jameel's vast knowledge and understanding were believed to have been used when he built a system linking ideologues to financiers, and operators to experts.

Jameel was said to have dominated the lives of the JMI rank-and-file, and the transformation was evident in the lives he touched. For example, it was said that Muaath, who would become one of the Easter massacre's bombers, initially had no propensity for violence but Jameel brainwashed him—as he did to Ilham, Inshaf, and, by proxy, Ilham's wife, Fathima Jiffry. Jameel was also the one who linked Muaath to Zahran, who become an overwhelming influence on the former.

Muaath and Zahran reportedly saw the world from the same vantage point—they spoke the same language and were from similar backgrounds. Since Muaath and Zahran were from the east, they belonged to a common conservative eastern Muslim culture. Zahran, who was recognized as a charismatic preacher and a master indoctrinator, may have been able to influence Muaath, but it was Jameel who guided him, nurturing and sustaining the ideology and working through him to enlist other JMI members to join and expand the Easter attack suicide team.

According to Fathima Shifana, Jameel's wife, Jameel held 'extremist views on religion'—which, according to counterterrorism investigators, other suspects in custody confirmed.[183] In her debriefing, Fathima revealed that Jameel was a regular listener of Zahran's and Abu Bara's online sermons, and longed to relocate to a country with 'strict sharia', which he often fought for.[184] Jameel reportedly got into several debates and arguments with fellow Muslims including a Muslim lawyer who reprimanded him. In the face of warnings from authorities, he was said to have received guidance from relatives and threats from parents whose children he attempted to recruit. Despite these interventions, Jameel persisted and stayed true to his ideology.

As established thus far, Jameel operated as a contact point for recruitment and radicalization in the exclusivist space. He often left the house to meet 'his friends' and sometimes stayed over at their homes too.[185] He reportedly did not mention the names or whereabouts of these friends he visited to his wife. When asked, he simply reasoned that he was under surveillance and could be in trouble if his whereabouts were found out.[186]

Operating in the shadows, Jameel could be likened to a slithering snake that poisons clear waters with the IS' venom. Jameel would watch out for the most unsuspecting and susceptible individuals, waiting for the right time to strike. He approached

---

[183] Sri Lanka Terrorism Investigations Department, debriefing of Fathima Shifana shared with author, 2020.

[184] Sri Lanka Terrorism Investigations Department, debriefing of Fathima Shifana.

[185] Sri Lanka Terrorism Investigations Department, debriefing of Fathima Shifana.

[186] Sri Lanka Terrorism Investigations Department, debriefing of Fathima Shifana.

them to be radicalized and recruited when they were most vulnerable. Although he was reportedly narrow-minded and his thinking convoluted, the JMI members and followers perceived him as a powerful personality. A discreet networker constantly focusing on his prey, Jameel linked everyone and radicalized them to different degrees.

Facilitator to Operator: Jameel's Trajectory

After declaring a caliphate on 29 June 2014, the IS started to influence and reach out to Muslims worldwide. After Nilam's death in July 2015, Sri Lankan security and intelligence services, and investigative authorities reportedly started to pay attention to a new threat. This included Jameel, who would be interviewed by both the SIS and TID.

It was said that reports on Jameel did not only come from Sri Lankan authorities, but also from foreign counterparts, most notably the Australian intelligence in 2015. Apart from Jameel, a number of those radicalized at the al-Furqan Islamic Information Centre in Springvale South, Melbourne allegedly joined the IS. Although the Centre, which was led by Bosnian-born Sheikh Harun Mehicevic, would eventually close in 2016, it was believed that those who were radicalized had already turned into killing machines—and Jameel was one of them.

Back in Sri Lanka, Jameel worked clandestinely to avoid detection. According to accounts, Sri Lankan services the DMI and SIS worked with foreign counterparts to comb through the web to gather evidence against him, but, likely because he was so cautious, they could not find anything. Nevertheless, they eventually managed to identify his network and attempted to prevent its organization—which, in hindsight, may have been futile. After a debriefing with Jameel, the SIS' counterterrorism chief Mahil Dole even said, 'Jameel tried to convert me to the IS ideology.'[187]

Creating an IS Contingent in Sri Lanka

As mentioned before, it was believed that Sri Lankan Muslims lived relatively peacefully until political Islam reached Sri Lanka's shores. Many Muslims radicalized by the IS dreamt of travelling to Iraq and Syria and fighting for ideology. The drive to travel to the Iraqi-Syrian theatre reportedly persisted until the IS instructed them to remain and stage attacks in their own countries against non-Muslims, who were viewed as the enemies of Islam—and Jameel did exactly that.

As touched on previously, Jameel likely cultivated a friendship with Imad—who ran the Quran study group—to gain access to more potential recruits. After getting 'very close' to him, Jameel reportedly propagandized the group with Maqdisi's book *Millat Ibrahim*, turning it into the JMI. It was said that Jameel, who was skilled in religious manipulation, managed to build and leverage personal relationships to successfully engage and, eventually, radicalize the greatest number of JMI members.

Later, Jameel also recruited—directly and indirectly—the most members for the IS, after Zahran. Jameel's recruits included Ilham, Inshaf, Fathima Jiffry, Muaath, and Mubarak. As noted, Ilham and Inshaf would become the IS' primary financiers, personally funding Zahran, the group's activities, and the Easter Sunday attacks, where they were bombers. Besides this, Jameel was also reportedly in direct contact with Aroos, who had personally invited members of the JMI to travel to Syria and join the IS.

Jameel's house also became a meeting venue for the JMI membership and leadership. According to Fathima Shifana, Umair, Imad, Ahamed, Akham, Ilham, and Muaath visited Jameel's house

[187] Mahil Dole (SIS counterterrorism chief), interview by author, March 2022.

on three occasions in 2016. They reportedly met in the study room to discuss political Islam, the IS, and its publications, or to hold meetings where Umair and Imad gave hour-long lectures on the exegesis of the Quran. During these lectures or *tafsirs*, it was said that they elucidated, explained, interpreted, and provided commentary for understanding what they believed was God's will.

Planned Killings and Assassinations

With the JMI members embracing the IS ideology, many turned radical, violent, and reportedly engaged in militant behavior. When ranking targets for elimination, it was said that the JMI discussed the killing of Galagodaaththe Gnanasara Thero, leader of Sinhala nationalist group BBS. The BBS had been accused of fomenting violence against Muslims during the June 2014 riots in Kalutara district, where the BBS and Sihala Ravaya members were alleged to have chanted anti-Muslim slogans. The riots also resulted in 500 Muslim dwellings and businesses being attacked, over 100—mostly Muslim—people injured, and approximately 8,000—also majority Muslim—people temporarily displaced. It was said that Gnanasara claimed no involvement in these incidents. Nevertheless, for instigating violence against Muslims, Gnanasara was said to have been identified with Ashin Wirathu of Myanmar, whose advocacy of violence against the Rohingiya Muslims reportedly tarnished the image of Myanmar, Buddhism, Buddhist monks and Buddhists.[188]

Apart from Gnanasara and the BBS, accounts also stated that the JMI membership discussed the killing of Shia Muslims in Sri Lanka. Shia Muslims, mostly Bohras and Khojas, made up just a few thousand of the country's populace and largely lived in Colombo and Jaffna. It was said that the Colombo team discussed the use of weapons and explored gaining access to explosives to

---

[188] Hannah Beech, 'The Face of Buddhist Terror', *Time*, July 1, 2013, https://content.time.com/time/subscriber/article/0,33009,2146000,00.html.

attack the Shia Muslims. They allegedly also discussed a proposal to use paintball guns and commence military training in jungle areas to prepare for the attack.

Though these plans would not bear fruit, Sri Lankan authorities would reportedly still receive information that, at a meeting on 14 January 2016 at Ahamed's residence, the JMI discussed plans to assassinate Gnanasara. Although not validated, it was said that the DMI may have also received reports that the JMI member Shazni had access to a T-56 rifle.

JMI Infiltrating Charity Space

Just as the LTTE once exploited the notion of charity and charitable organizations for fundraising, procurement, and radicalization, the IS attempted to do the same.

On 14 May 2016, Sri Lanka suffered its worst natural disaster since the Boxing Day Tsunami of 2004. Torrential rain and floods forced over 350,000 people from their homes, and 125,000 houses as well as 300,000 small and medium businesses were damaged. Times of chaos, despair, and disaster were often the best opportunities for groups like the JMI to network and grow. Thus, the JMI seized the opportunity to potentially mobilize, exploit, and infiltrate the charity space.[189]

The Colombo team commenced their operations in the affected area of Wellampitiya, where Jameel lived. The most dedicated JMI rank-and-file were said to have provided humanitarian support for the affected. According to active JMI member, Amjad, '[w]hen the security forces came to help during the floods in 2016, [they] supported them through the Shabab organization at Maligakanda Road. Those who [played] football, as well as Jameel from Wellampitiya[,] helped.'[190] Apart from Jameel, it was said that two

[189] Interview by author with DMI staff, February 16, 2023.

[190] Amjad, interview, March 2022.

other would-be suicide bombers, Ilham and Muaath, participated too.[191] However, as was consistent with their ideology, Jameel and Ilham reportedly wanted to grant support exclusively to Muslims.

The JMI organized a flood relief operation where kitchen utensils, gas stoves, clothes, and dry rations were distributed. Among those who participated were Umair, Imad, Akham, Ahamed, Muaath, Inshaf Ifthikar, Amjad, Hamaaz, Jameel, and Ilham. Though the latter two had reservations about assisting non-Muslims, it was said that they nevertheless followed through and distributed the goods to those affected irrespective of ethnicity and religion. Hamaaz, who flew in from the UAE the previous day and joined the relief efforts, said, '[w]e [even] gave more relief items to non-Muslims.'[192] Since, statistically, there were more non-Muslims, and there seemed to be no discrimination in the charity space in Sri Lanka, this was, likely, indeed, the case.

It may be interesting to note that charity is codified in Islam, hence why Sri Lankan Muslim organizations, including the ACTJ, the ACJU, and others, participated in community outreach efforts during this time. In addition, the National Shoora Council, the ACJU, Colombo District Masjid Federation, Muslim Council of Sri Lanka, and other organizations jointly formed a Relief Coordinating Committee too.

Muslim charities in general assisted both Muslims and non-Muslims, and JMI members like Hamaaz were determined to do the same. However, more exclusivist members such as Jameel and Ilham had different views. This ideology and perception would gradually overwhelm and overtake some of the other JMI members. In the meantime, in a classic twist of striking two birds with one stone, Jameel, Ilham, and other more radical JMI followers assisted exclusively for the 'believers', while also building

---

191 Amjad, interview, March 2022.

192 Hamaaz (JMI member), interview by author, March 2021.

rapport with the Muslim community for future radicalization. With constant radicalization, the JMI would only become more extremist over time.

Foreign Links

As an organization, the JMI reportedly did not maintain formal operational links with like-minded entities overseas. As an individual, however, Jameel had links with the IS leaders, members, and supporters in Syria, UK, and Australia. The JMI followers, in their respective capacities, also built relations with the IS followers overseas.

For instance, Karen Aisha Hamidon, wife of Mohammad Jaafar Maguid, the slain head of Ansar al-Khilafah Philippines, was in contact with Sri Lankan IS followers, including Umair Iqbal Mohamed—one of the JMI's leaders. This was affirmed by JMI member Hamaaz, who claimed that another member, 'Insaf Ifthikar was [also] in touch with [the] Philippines family'. He added, 'Due to a visa issue in Qatar, they stayed in Sri Lanka [at] his house in Mattakkuliya.'[193] Interestingly, the DMI's identification of the IS Philippines female operator Karen Aisha and her contacts in Sri Lanka reportedly demonstrated links within a global network too. Apart from Indians, it was said that Karen Aisha 'also targeted Muslims in the US, UK, UAE, Argentina, Bangladesh, and Australia. She would target youth through groups which she named "Islam Q&A" and "Ummah Affairs"'. According to accounts, Karen was accurately identified by the DMI as a Bangsamoro Islamic Freedom Fighter, but she had graduated to join the IS. As per the DMI monitoring, it may also be worth noting that the IS women from the Philippines visited the JMI leaders in Sri Lanka too.

---

193 Hamaaz, interview.

During this time, a western intelligence service reportedly brought to the attention of their Sri Lankan counterpart the Facebook account belonging to Anak Sabeel, a foreign IS activist who maintained contact with Sri Lankan Muslims. Another Facebook account, 'Soldiers of Allah', was also said to have been brought to the attention of Sri Lankan intelligence.

The Caliphate's Province in Sri Lanka

During the second half of 2016, the IS activity in Sri Lanka reached a new high. Even before Zahran entered the scene, it was believed that Jameel already guided the IS support group JMI to create a wilayat or province of the caliphate. The declaration of a territorial province in Sri Lanka would have helped further the IS' ambitions of establishing a global caliphate. As of June 2016, there were twelve internal wilayats located in Syria, eleven in Iraq, and external wilayats in nine other countries. Since 1 July 2016, the IS or the 'State', as they called it, had declared provinces in Nigeria, Libya, Algeria, Egypt's Sinai Peninsula, Yemen, Saudi Arabia, the Caucasus, and the Afghanistan-Pakistan region too. The IS reportedly planned to expand further in line with its vision and mission of global expansion.

Determined to create a wilayat or territorial base for the IS in Sri Lanka, it was said that Jameel informed the JMI followers to convene at Vihara Maha Devi Park, or Victoria Park, in the heart of Colombo. Jameel claimed he had received instructions from the IS headquarters in Syria, after which the JMI membership discussed the necessary steps to create a wilayat. Then-JMI member Hamaaz was said to have recalled the presence of nearly a dozen members at the meeting, which included Khalid, Inshaf Ifthikar, Jameel, Imad, Umair, Ihsan, Amjad, and Zawahir.

A prerequisite to declaring a wilayat was to strengthen the JMI. As such, the group planned to step up its propaganda and recruit even more widely. To prepare for and establish the wilayat, the JMI planned to visit the northern province to recruit members, rent a house for meetings, distribute leaflets after the Jumma prayers, and convert non-Muslims—mainly Hindus—into Islam. IS propaganda leaflets that JMI intended to distribute included:

1. 'The Gravest Sin Shirk', dated 5 August 2016.
2. 'What Takes You Out of Islam—Nullifiers of Faith', dated 12 August 2016.
3. 'Enemies of Allah', dated 9 September 2016.

However, the distribution was subsequently terminated after members were reportedly taken into questioning by security and intelligence services, who had amplified their monitoring efforts on the group and received information about their meetings. Nonetheless, it was said that the JMI did not cease its activity and continued operations underground.

Bridging the East and West

Of all the *waleema* or wedding ceremonies the JMI members attended, the one with the greatest impact on the organization was government schoolteacher Husni Mubarak's, which was held in Ampara district, in the eastern province, on 14 October 2016.

A follower and supporter of both the NTJ and JMI, Husni was influenced by the IS with its rise in 2014. When the IS footprint gained traction in Sri Lanka, the young teacher was effectively radicalized. After the IS online community grew worldwide, including in Sri Lanka, IS content providers such as Aadhil Ameez became key nodes of radicalization. Husni was committed to the IS expansion, and was said to have translated articles published by Aadhil on 'Did You Know?' from English to Tamil, and attended a few JMI meetings during his travels to Colombo.

Husni first met Zahran and Rilwan of the NTJ on Facebook in 2014. According to accounts, he joined Zahran's seminars promoting Salafi-Wahhabi and later the IS ideation on Facebook before becoming radicalized. Since he was active online, Husni also joined the JMI WhatsApp group, where he would meet and befriend JMI followers such as Ahamed and Inshaf Ifthikar and would even visit their homes in Colombo. Husni thus networked with the IS support clusters across provinces. However, when he invited the JMI to celebrate his wedding, he would unintentionally bring together disparate groups with a common ideal—thus creating a devastating union of terror.

After the wedding ceremony, Akham recalled that Amjad, Zawahir, Ahamed, Jameel, Insaf Ifthikar, and Sashini met the 'influential scholar' Zahran at the NTJ office in Kattankudy. After that, they travelled to Kattankudy beach where it was said Zahran would learn that Jameel had links to the IS. This, and Jameel's access to resources in Colombo, likely prompted Zahran to forge a close relationship with the JMI.

Husni's wedding was therefore a decisive event that apparently brought together the western and eastern hubs of Muslim exclusivists and extremists. Institutionally, it was a merger of the NTJ and the JMI. Individually, it was Zahran and Jameel starting to work together; Zahran had a support base and Jameel had the links to the IS. The forging of relations between the JMI and NTJ would thus change the threat landscape forever.

Zahran's Visit to Colombo

To link up with the JMI, Zahran and his brother Rilwan visited them at their de facto headquarters—Amjad and Suaid's house at Maradana—in February 2016. Zahran brought a set of pen drives with him that contained IS videos and documents. He reportedly distributed the pen drives to other Muslim clerics in Colombo to further champion his extremist ideology.

After the JMI delegation met Zahran at Kattankudy during their visit to Husni's wedding, it was said that his preachings impacted their minds indelibly. A charismatic preacher, Zahran's sermons were believed to have been widely shared and followed by the JMI members. As such, Jameel felt that Zahran was the best choice to build and lead the IS in Sri Lanka—but this was apparently a decision that not all JMI followers agreed with.

Since there were diverse views within the JMI, Jameel reportedly took it upon himself to build support for Zahran. Eventually, Zahran would successfully radicalize a segment of the JMI members beyond the point of no return. Addressing him as 'Moulavi Zahran', these members followed his preachings eagerly and passionately. Over time, Zahran's grip on the Colombo team tightened.

The Ideological Trap

Zahran and Jameel functioned in a high-pressure environment. The countervailing forces included the parents of the youth targeted by Zahran and Jameel for radicalization and recruitment. After being alerted by the government, it was said that some parents realized that the IS, which was violent, extremist, and exclusivist, was not Islamic. But despite their efforts to dissuade their children from joining the IS support groups, it was reportedly too late. The power of ideology under the supposed guide of religion had already overwhelmed these youth; the lure of and their attraction to the IS ideology persisted.

However, there were a few fortunate individuals who reportedly broke off from the organization's tightening grip. For instance, it was said that Amjad, who had become depressed after losing Rs. 5.5 million in gem trading, moved away from the JMI in 2017 and focused on rebuilding himself. Meanwhile, Suaid, who was to be wed to would-be suicide bomber Muaath's sister, ultimately declined the marriage citing cultural clashes between eastern and western Islamic traditions. Suaid would likewise distance himself from the JMI after leaving for Malaysia on 19 July 2014 to study civil engineering. When he returned to Sri Lanka on 31 July 2018, after the JMI had split, he chose to join his father's construction business as a qualified civil engineer rather than join the IS Sri Lanka branch.

Both Amjad and his brother Suaid were a part of the JMI until challenges and opportunities in life severed their links with the group. Neither Amjad nor Suaid participated in the IS orientation or training. However, they were either friends or relatives with the JMI rank-and-file, and would reportedly continue to have contact with individual JMI members. Similarly, Hamaaz and others would eventually distance themselves from the Colombo team too before Zahran took the most ardent IS followers to a point of no return. The others, chained to the locks of ideological manifestation, would become remorseless killers; the new faces of terror that Sri Lanka, the region, and the world will likely confront in the future.

Zahran's Drift towards Violence

As discussed previously, Zahran went underground after the Aliyar Junction incident in March 2017. Once he became a fugitive, it was said that Zahran transformed from an instigator to a perpetrator of violence. With a much more sinister ideology of the IS taking root, Zahran drifted from preaching hatred to directly engaging in violence. To prime the rank-and-file to strike 'Allah's enemies', as the IS followers see non-believers, the virulent ideology was inculcated by orientation and training. To prepare the perpetrators, its directing figures disseminated the IS publications—including magazines and pamphlets.

Working with his close associates, Zahran also focused on building infrastructure and networks underground. Since his resources—both intellectual and material—were limited, he reportedly planned to develop and enlist existing and potential recruits, raising awareness through orientation and training. After talent spotting, he identified those who seemed most committed to serving Allah. To test their loyalty, discipline, and integrity, Zahran and his close associates assigned them tasks to complete before enlisting them to join the IS rank-and-file. Of the dozen training programmes conducted in Kattankudy, Nuwara Eliya, and Hambantota, the IS conducted one orientation programme in Malwana and one training programme in Aruppola for the Colombo team. Upon completing said trainings, a faction of the JMI was absorbed by the IS.

Not long after continuous discussions between Ilham, Jameel, and Zahran, the IS Sri Lanka branch was established too. It was said that the first step to building the organization and infrastructure was to create a human and material resource base to help enhance militant capability. Thus, in addition to approaching the JMI directly by co-opting its leadership, Zahran had also approached the JMI members individually to join the IS. After the orientation and training programmes, Zahran reportedly approached participants to find out who were willing to fight or participate in suicide attacks. According to accounts, Jameel, Muaath, and Milhan were the only ones who volunteered.

When Zahran fled the eastern province, he relocated to the north-western province, which was said to have provided him with significant access to two new theatres for radicalization and recruitment. Since his recruitment pool was limited in the east, Zahran sought to recruit Muslim youth living in the central and western provinces, particularly those from Salafi-Wahhabi and Jamaat-e-Islami organizations or beltway groups. These organizations, which were believed to have been staffed by radical Muslims, were said to have critically espoused Islamic law and radicalized the youth to implement sharia in Sri Lanka. While it was exceptionally difficult for the IS to recruit Sufi Muslims, the followers of Salafi-Wahhabi and Jamaat-e-Islami were vulnerable to recruitment and radicalization.

Eventually, with Zahran's IS ideology infiltrating the JMI, the Colombo team started to breakaway into two entities in March 2018. After an alleged ideological clash with the JMI leader, Umair, Jameel, who was its most fanatical member, reportedly broke off with his close associates. The breakaway faction consisting of the most radicalized and extremist JMI members, joined Jameel. In early 2018, the DMI reported that some members, such as Jameel, who were willing to kill and die, 'splintered from the JMI and joined a separate group'—this being Zahran's IS.

The orientation of the JMI factions differed both operationally and tactically. Some, especially members of the breakaway faction like Jameel, Muaath, Ilham, Fathima Jiffry, Mubarak, and Inshaf were willing to kill and die, mounting attacks on Sri Lankan soil. A relatively less violent JMI body emerged under Umair who, though apparently willing to fight in Iraq and Syria, did not seem as willing to mount attacks in Sri Lanka.

Original Plan Compromised

As discussed in previous chapters, in the lead-up to the bombings and after the IS base in Wanathavilluwa was detected by the security forces in January 2019, Zahran's original timeline to strike in August 2020 was compromised. The original plan—as visualised by Zahran, Naufer, Jameel, and other leaders of the IS Sri Lanka branch—was to strike throughout the island. Since he was personally angry with the Sinhala Buddhists at the time, Zahran's original island-wide plan reportedly coincided with the Kandy Esala Perahera in August 2020. However, with the government and authorities closing in on him, he decided to advance the attack to Easter Sunday in April 2019.

Zahran was presumably eager to advance the IS' foreign agenda by striking Christian and western targets. In contrast, Naufer was arguably more strategic; he wanted to build stronger capabilities by further radicalizing Muslim support base on the island to prepare for an attack of greater magnitude. The Zahran and Naufer timelines and targeting thus differed. While Zahran's vision was more global and was influenced by a foreign agenda, Naufer's seemed more indigenous and was influenced by a domestic agenda.[194]

Later, after the bombings, Naufer would reportedly reveal his disappointment over the outcome of the Easter attack. The security forces dismantled the IS infrastructure and placed restrictions on promotion of extremist Salafi-Wahhabi and Jamaat-e-Islami ideologies. Although Naufer admired Zahran, he noted, 'Zahran set back the IS agenda by 100 years.'[195] To Naufer, the Easter attack was likely a waste of resources as it did not achieve anything tangible and compromised prospects. Naufer wanted to strike in all the districts—an ideal that Zahran shared as well but was unable to do due to human resource constrains and an unfavourable environment.

IS Sri Lanka Splits Before Attack

In March 2019, the IS Sri Lanka branch split into two factions—one led by Naufer and the other led by Zahran. Both groups may have wanted to wreak havoc in Sri Lankan society but, unlike

---

[194] Dr Malkanthi Hettiarachchi (debriefer of the Easter Sunday detainees), interview by author, March 22, 2022.

[195] Dr Hettiarachchi, interview.

Naufer, who was not wanted by the government authorities, Zahran was on the run. Rather than be captured, Zahran wanted to strike and die as soon as possible. After the split, both factions commenced the enlistment of the JMI followers. However, reportedly none joined the Naufer's faction although he was the JMI's original theoretician. Meanwhile, the safehouses rented by Zahran housed the IS leadership and membership. They were also used to procure and manufacture explosives and prepared the mindset of the bombers to strike.

Final Plans and Changes

As an organization, the JMI gradually disintegrated as the IS developed. With Jameel and Ilham emerging as Zahran's trusted confidants and the IS' resource base, the JMI diminished in size, strength, and influence. Nevertheless, a segment of the JMI leadership and membership, as individuals, reportedly remained connected to Jameel who likewise continuously linked with and attempted to enlist from their ready pool of recruits. It was said that potential recruits from the JMI members were motivated to different degrees; not all wanted to kill and die, and among those who did, it seemed no one was as motivated as Zahran.

A month before the Easter attack, Zahran was determined to attack twenty targets. He only had nine attackers, and, desperate to enlist more, he reportedly reached out to radicalized Muslim youth from the JMI, including Khalid and Zawahir—JMI members he had identified as potential suicide attackers. Together with Inshaf Ifthikar, they were to join the group of potentially twenty bombers to carry out explosions at twenty separate locations.[196]

However, these plans would not come into fruition as, in their final surveillance mission in the lead-up to the attack, Khalid and

196 Dr Hettiarachchi, interview.

Zawahir would decide to withdraw and quit the group.[197] Inshaf Ifthikar would likewise withdraw from the operation at the last moment. When arrested by the CTID after the bombings, they would go on to identify the participants and those connected to the Easter attacks.

Jameel's End

As the shadow leader of the JMI, Jameel played a pivotal role in providing the purported link to the IS, which was essential for Zahran's legitimacy. After structuring the IS Sri Lanka branch by its ideology, organization, and rank-and-file, Jameel reportedly chose to sacrifice his life and family. A review of phone records showed that, on 18 April 2019, three days before the attack, Jameel's wife, Fathima Shifana, had been in contact with him. When interviewed by the CTID, Fathima said Jameel had informed her he would be going to Dematagoda to fulfil a family commitment and had even contacted her while he was away.

On D-day at the Taj Samudra, when Jameel's suicide vest malfunctioned, he was previously instructed to retreat from the hotel to a nearby mosque to rendezvous with an IS operator who was to receive bombers whose attacks were unsuccessful. Afterwards, Jameel was to relocate to the east where a second strike was being planned. After keeping the vest at the New Tropical Inn, Jameel visited the mosque.

However, because there was no one to receive him there, Jameel reportedly became disoriented and directionless. Rather than risk arrest inside the mosque, Jameel decided to walk out and wait. After this, he was said to have been approached by a three-wheel driver, a Muslim, Mohammed Thassim Mohammed Nilwan alias Siqqi, from the Pick Me taxi service. After watching

[197] Dr Hettiarachchi, interview.

the Easter Sunday explosions on television that morning, Siqqi had left the house to pick up passengers. It was reported that Siqqi 'had met the suicide bomber Jameel near the mosque at Ebenezer Place. He had stopped the taxi and asked Jameel if he [needed] a ride. Jameel had got into the taxi and travelled along the Ebenezer Place, turned left to Galle Road moving towards Colombo and turned to Allen Avenue and stopped at the New Tropical Inn. After dropping Jameel at the Inn, the driver drove to Ahmed Hotel on Galle Road to have lunch'.[198] When Jameel tried to fix the suicide vest at the Inn, the device detonated and killed him.

Aftermath of the Attack

The Easter Sunday attack was deemed a game changer in Sri Lankan security. It was believed to have disrupted Sri Lankan Muslim-non-Muslim relations and, later, Sri Lankan-Catholic community relations. It was said that no member of the Sri Lankan Muslim community openly sympathised with the IS. The scale of the carnage even surprised and shocked other IS followers and families. When their friends and family were arrested, they had a diversity of views.

'The Easter attack was against religion,' said Amjad adding, 'My father lost 10 kg and developed diabetes, depression, and tension. My mother is strong on the outside but weak inside.'[199] Referring to Hamaaz, Amjad continued, 'his mother fell ill and was admitted to hospital.'[200] While many other JMI members remained in custody, those who were released, such as Amjad, Suaid, and Hamaaz, reportedly went back to lead their lives. Most

---

198 Mohammed Thassim Mohammed Nilwan alias Siqqi (Pick me taxi service driver), interrogation by authorities shared with author, 2019.

199 Amjad (JMI member), interview by author, Sri Lanka, February 22, 2022.

200 Amjad, interview, February 22, 2022.

would eventually marry and build their own businesses, doing better over time.

Many JMI members, including those in custody, cooperated with authorities. Some, like Hamaaz, claimed and alleged that Muslim leaders—particularly Mufthi Rizwe, president of the Muslim clerical body ACJU—knew of the threat. According to Hamaaz, '[a]s a leader, Mufthi Rizwe should have done more.'[201] In particular, Hamaaz noted that, 'Mufthi Rizwe could have helped police to arrest Zahran. He should have informed every sect and mosques. He should have alerted them to the lectures given by Zahran and others who are extreme. For their safety, they may have not but if they [had done so], we could have saved the young.'[202]

Reeling from the horror of the Easter attack, the thinking of the JMI leadership and membership was said to have changed over time. It was believed that most if not all the JMI members sincerely regretted the tragedy of the Easter attack.[203] Although none legitimized the Easter attack, a few spoke of justice for Muslims overseas. Though, in Sri Lanka, likely very little could be done to fix the challenges they raised about in Iraq and Syria, Libya, Afghanistan, and in the Horn of Africa.

Some released JMI members had concerns, especially since they claimed security officers frequently visited them or their surrounding homes and businesses to inquire about them.[204] Most JMI members who were not involved reportedly did not wish to help those in custody or who were released.[205] It was said that they were either disinterested or voiced that it was a security

---

[201] Hamaaz (JMI member), interview by author, March 5, 2022.

[202] Hamaaz, interview, March 5, 2022.

[203] Amjad, interview, February 22, 2022.

[204] Amjad, interview, February 22, 2022.

[205] Amjad, interview, February 22, 2022.

risk.[206] With time, it was believed their regret and remorse of the perpetrators and family members over the Easter carnage dissipated.[207]

According to accounts, none of those involved in the attack subscribed to the conspiracy theory that it was staged by Sri Lankan intelligence or by a foreign government.[208] Like most others, they too knew the truth; Zahran was driven by the IS ideology—and religious extremism precipitated the Easter attack.

Rehabilitation Disrupted

Most arrested in the aftermath of the Easter attack, including the JMI followers, had been radicalized. After they were detained, they were assessed to determine their radicalization levels prior to being rehabilitated. At the early stage, members were said to have been exposed to motivational interviews to promote moderation, toleration, and coexistence. They were also provided literature to mitigate their resentment, anger, and hatred. However, further plans to introduce critical thinking, mathematics, philosophy, and religious knowledge classes were reportedly disrupted by Malcolm Cardinal Ranjith who allegedly opposed rehabilitation over punishment.

Efforts by Lalith Weeratunge, senior adviser to the President, and the Defence Secretary, General Kamal Gunaratna, to convince the Cardinal were said to have been unsuccessful. Thus, for four long years, the detainees were held without a rehabilitation programme, and many were released on bail. According to accounts, the Cardinal could not be convinced by anyone that future attacks were inevitable unless those radicalized men and women in custody or in the community were rehabilitated.

[206] Amjad, interview, February 22, 2022.

[207] Amjad, interview, February 22, 2022.

[208] Amjad, interview, February 22, 2022.

Although the Cardinal was respected for pre-empting an anti-Muslim riot immediately after the Easter Sunday attack, it was said that his belief in a conspiracy theory and seeming lack of a far-reaching leadership to implement rehabilitation reportedly disappointed many, including some of his hitherto admirers.

If radicalization is not countered with rehabilitation, terrorists released back to society may continue to:

1. pose a security threat;
2. join terrorist iconography; and
3. drive regeneration.

Keeping a detainee beyond the required period would likely be deemed counterproductive as the anger could transform into support for or result in the continued conduct of violence against the country. Government prisons ideally should be at the forefront of rehabilitation, but there were reportedly no active programmes for this, and, particularly, the reintegration of former terrorists.

Later, plans to promote inclusivity would seem to give out once more with a case in the Supreme Court filed against rehabilitation. With the stay order on rehabilitation, the Bureau of the Commissioner General of Rehabilitation's plans to mainstream the thinking and actions of detainees and inmates—classified as beneficiaries of the rehabilitation programme—were likewise disrupted. It may also be worth noting that the provision for rehabilitation was a gazette and not a part of the main law.

By disrupting rehabilitation, the window of unlearning and relearning of those who enabled and perpetrated the Easter attack is likely lost. To manage radicalization in custodial settings, it is imperative for governments to work with partners to develop and implement rehabilitation programmes. In crafting a full-spectrum response to secure nations from terrorism, upstream prevention and downstream rehabilitation are central pillars. The rehabilitation of terrorist operators and supporters can reduce violence and human suffering and promote harmony and healing. Not doing so could mean the opportunity for securing Sri Lanka is lost, and unless radicalization is reversed through rehabilitation, future attacks by terrorists and their supporters will continue to be a likely possibility.

Conclusion

Like a dark dye contaminating pure water, an extremist ideological doctrine had been infiltrating Sri Lanka's Muslim community. Reportedly stemming from radical teachings of extremist sects in Saudi Arabia, Salafi-Wahhabism was believed to have flown and settled in Sri Lanka through fundamentalist preachers, media, and widespread Islamist propaganda.

Of the nine suicide attackers on Easter Sunday, six were JMI followers. While four—Jameel, Ilham, Inshaf, Muaath—were JMI members, two—Fathima Jiffry and Mubarak—were JMI-connected personalities. The only non-JMI bombers to kill and die on Easter Sunday were Zahran, Hashtoon, and Azath. It was believed that Jameel empowered Zahran with legitimacy by creating the perception that he was chosen by the IS central to be the Sri Lankan Amir. Jameel was also believed to have capacitated Zahran by financing the Easter Sunday attack through the Ibrahim brothers. Apart from content provided by Jameel, literature by preachers such as Zahran, Abu Bara, Abu Hamza al-Masri, and Abu Musab al-Zarqawi created a tunnel vision in the group's followers. Though, at the very beginning, Jameel infected and steered the group, radicalization deepened with Zahran and Naufer training the JMI followers.

Sri Lankan Muslims were believed to have lived in relative harmony with other communities. Having shared a common heritage for over a millennium, many Sri Lankan Muslims were said to have rejected the IS' call to kill non-believers. As such, and because they were unwilling to kill and die, Zahran built a niche group that would provide him the ideologically committed and psychologically vulnerable recruits to advance the IS ideals and agenda—and Zahran succeeded.

Debris after the riots in Dharga Town 2014 - Anti -Muslim Riots in Sri Lanka in 2014 and 2018, one of the contributing factors towards Zahran's mayhem in 2019
Source: Ceylon Today Chief Librarian

Author in conversation with Hadiya
Source: Dinithi Dharmapala - Photographer

Milhan - head of the military wing, Islamic State, Sri Lanka
Source: Dinithi Dharmapala - Photographer

There is no compulsion in religion.[209]

—Quran

We will not allow [terrorists] to distort our peaceful religion. Today we are sending a strong message that we are working together to fight terrorism . . . Today we affirm that we will pursue terrorism until it is eradicated completely.[210]

—His Royal Highness Crown Prince
Mohammed bin Salman, 27 November 2017

---

[209] Quran 2:256.

[210] The Embassy of the Kingdom of Saudi Arabia Washington D.C., *Saudi Arabia and Counterterrorism*, March 4, 2019, https://www.saudiembassy.net/sites/default/files/SAUDI%20ARABIA%20AND%20COUNTERTERRORISM.pdf.

Chapter 4

Easter Sunday's Lessons and Reflections

A Recap of (Politico-Religious) Events

Perfect Target

To date, and as discussed thus far, the Easter Sunday massacre is considered one of the worst attacks mounted outside Iraq and Syria by the IS—the world's deadliest terrorist movement. In the blink of an eye, it changed Sri Lanka's future and decimated the nation's social harmony, economic prosperity, and already fragile political stability.

Apart from Sri Lanka's strategic geographical location, the political situation at the time was also deemed favourable due to internal political feuds waged by the President and Prime Minister. Sri Lanka ended a thirty-year war. In Churchillian style, the government that won the war was electorally defeated. The west reportedly disliked the Rajapaksa camp and preferred other political strategists instead.[211] It was said that the slogan of the new Yahapalana government in 2015 was not national security, but good governance. Since it purportedly appealed to the minorities

[211] James Crabtree, 'Lynton Crosby helps mastermind Sri Lanka election victory', *Australian Financial Review*, August 19, 2015, https://www.afr.com/world/lynton-crosby-helps-mastermind-sri-lanka-election-victory-20150819-gj2rbo.

for their votes, this administration seemed reluctant to raise radicalization and separatism. Such issues were allegedly swept under the carpet and seemingly overlooked by political leaders. Members of the intelligence community who raised these issues were said to have been frowned upon too. It seemed like everyone had to behave as if there was no threat.

Tragedy Strikes

It was believed that many Sri Lankans and government officials were reportedly unsuspecting or even complacent when the Easter Sunday attack took place. April marked all communities celebrating their festivities—including the Hindu and Sinhala New Year as well as Easter Sunday. The Yahapalana government, at the time, seemed to have their hands full with what seemed to be conflicts with the Mahinda Rajapaksa administration that had ended separatist terrorism.

While parading the good governance slogan, it was said that Yahapalana political leaders systematically dismantled the security and intelligence platform while its architect then, Brigadier Suresh Salley, was posted to Malaysia. Politicians were allegedly under pressure from the human rights fraternity, and were believed to have directed the police to arrest and imprison intelligence officers and question the assets and sources of the DMI. With political leaders directing the DMI to scale down its operations, the ground coverage of this main tactical intelligence service suffered. This included Operation Blind Eyes, the invaluable project mounted by the Directorate to discover the JMI network in the western province.

With no Intelligence Act to protect those mounting operations, DMI officers and other rankers that kept Zahran and his associates in the eastern province under watch were reportedly incarcerated. This included Sergeant Khaleel, an accomplished intelligence officer and himself a Muslim from the eastern province, who was said to have had a deep knowledge and understanding of Zahran and his associates. He was said to have been imprisoned with NTJ members and Zahran's family for five years, from 7 January 2016 until 11 January 2021.

Despite apparent political obstacles, accounts stated that the rank-and-file of the Sri Lankan intelligence community persisted. Having learnt from experience and trained by seasoned officers, they were goal-oriented—not rule-oriented. The community, led by the SIS and DMI, had developed considerable coverage on the IS, Muslim radicalization, and Zahran. They knew of almost all the Easter Sunday attackers but reportedly needed political patronage and legal support to keep the steadfast build-up of threats in check.

It was said that the sister services of the DMI were not as thorough as the DMI staff that had developed deep expertise and experience. For instance, although the SIS was also closely monitoring the NTJ and JMI, it was believed that their coverage was not as robust as the DMI, a service that had proven experience for developing ground intelligence. However, it was said that the elected government wanted the SIS to take over the intelligence functions of the DMI, which had originally been formed to fight the LTTE. Though the DMI excelled in ground collection and had developed comprehensive coverage of especially Sri Lanka's north and east, the SIS engaged in strategic analysis, assessment and forecast. Perhaps influenced by western liberal values and ideals, in some political leaders' eyes, domestic intelligence was solely within the SIS' purview. With the decline in the LTTE threat, they likely believed there was no need for the DMI to exist; in other words, they probably no longer saw a role for the DMI in maintaining internal security.

Political direction, guidance, and orientation reportedly shaped the security posture—creating an environment for security threats such as the IS to mount an unprecedented attack. To turn its vision into reality, the IS craftily co-opted directing figures, cunningly exploited the vulnerable, and harnessed instability in communities. Perhaps five decades of identity-based politics since the ethnicization of communities in 1956 also made radicalization a relatively easy feat for threat groups.

Political Climate

The political, defence, military, law enforcement authorities, and intelligence saw Zahran as an extremist. However, as mentioned several times thus far, it seemed like no adequate measures were taken to curb him and his group. Perhaps those who saw him as an imminent threat were also reluctant to act after seeing the fate of their colleagues who were marginalized, removed, or imprisoned. This may thus be why many repeatedly underestimated religious fundamentalism and Zahran's voracious appetite for it in the lead-up to the Easter attack.

The Sri Lankan security apparatus was believed to have been weakened after defeating the first insurgency and terrorist campaign of the early twenty-first century. It seemed that the national security apparatus—including its apex body, the NSC—did not foresee that Sri Lanka would suffer from an attack of the scale of April 2019. Had they known the magnitude and intensity of the attack, they would likely have acted immediately; calling for a press conference to inform the public and relevant establishments and institutions of the threat as well as deploying security forces in strength. Perhaps due to overconfidence or a sense of laxness following the LTTE's defeat, the NSC leadership and members may have unwittingly neglected threat intelligence and did not follow up on strengthening national security.

Ten years after the separatist conflict ended and its notorious suicide-mounting leader Velupillai Prabhakaran was killed on 18 May 2009, the curse of terrorism returned. The Easter bombings showed that, even with the most capable security force and intelligence community, a government is likely unable to protect its people unless political leaders pay close attention to security and create the right space for the relevant actors to carry out their duties—in this case, security, and intelligence services. The unforgettable dictum and lesson 'political climate determines security and stability' remains repeated and retold.

Muslim Leadership

As mentioned throughout the book, Sri Lanka's diverse religious communities typically lived harmoniously for over a millennia-and-a-half. Within the Muslim community, enlightened leaders set standards, regulated the religious space, and worked closely with the government, keeping religious fanaticism and fanatics under control. After the country opened in 1977, Islamisation, Arabisation, and Muslim identity politics reportedly emerged and were said to have been left unchecked, which inadvertently gave rise to incidents that likely affected Muslim-non-Muslim relations. These cracks were, in turn, exploited by threat entities like the IS to push forth their ideologies.

Successive governments and Muslim leadership may have neglected Muslim radicalization too. Unlike other countries that addressed Muslim radicalization swiftly and robustly through comprehensive community engagement and rehabilitation initiatives, the local government appeared reluctant to admit there were problems. It did not seem like the Sirisena administration nor the Rajapaksa governments possessed the sophistication—including the presence of specialists—necessary to adequately comprehend the gravity of the situation and manage the rise of religious intolerance. Although Muslim leaders reportedly alerted the government of radicalization, comprehensive measures were not employed to respond to the warnings.

At the defence ministry in November or December 2014, then Defence Secretary Gotabaya Rajapaksa reportedly raised the issue of increased radicalization with Mufti M.I.M. Rizwe, the ACJU president. As the president of the supreme body of Islamic theologians in Sri Lanka, the Mufti promised to address it, but it did not seem like adequate steps were immediately taken to do so. For instance, Muslim clerical leadership reportedly pledged to establish harmony centres in every district to promote moderation, tolerance, and coexistence. However, even after the attack, it was said that the ACJU had not yet kept its promise to engage the Muslim community and mainstream Islam. After the proscription of deviant Muslim groups, accounts stated that neither the government nor the ACJU seemed to play a significant role in their rehabilitation. Reportedly, the ACJU did not seem to counter the threats by some Salafi-Wahhabism or Jamaat-e-Islami followers to the Sri Lankan Muslim heritage even after the Easter attack.

Faith and Policy

Mainstreaming Islam

To stamp out fanaticism that had infiltrated Islam, it may be imperative for national and Muslim leaders worldwide to consider an overhaul and revamping of existing systems. This includes:

1. screening and registration procedures for local and foreign clerics;
2. blacklisting of hate preachers;
3. regular re-education and re-certification for existing clerics;
4. rehabilitation programmes for radical and violent clerics;
5. development of a comprehensive and holistic curriculum for student clerics, including possible audiences and counterterrorism dialogues with survivors of the radical Islamist sect;

6. regular reviews of key texts; and
7. banning texts that advocate violence—among many others.

Political and clerical leadership must work together to address faith issues of concern for all communities. Due to the infiltration of exclusivist and extremist ideologies, harmony hitherto enjoyed by the Sri Lankan Muslims and Sri Lankan society as a whole reportedly suffered. The Sri Lankan Muslim community fragmented, creating three milieus that allegedly competed, intermittently clashed, and sowed discord within and between religious communities.

To maintain harmonious living, the religious space, which is a sacred treasure, should be protected from such infiltrations. One such consideration is the establishment of a consultative process where Islam and other religions are mainstreamed. In Sri Lanka, such a mechanism does not exist yet but Singapore has an effective platform for doing this—the Presidential Council for Religious Harmony, where apex religious leaders meet periodically to resolve emerging conflicts or issues.[212]

A lack of adequate leadership and direction may cause religious issues to arise periodically, remain unresolved, and occasionally lead to violence. For instance, ultra-Sinhala nationalist groups such as the BBS, Sihala Ravaya, and Mahason Balakaya were said to have emerged when the government did not immediately address the grievances of the Sinhalese. However, condoning their presence and permitting their operations greatly harmed national unity. The ACJU, Waqf board, and other Muslim bodies entrusted to regulate the Islamic religious space should therefore

[212] Office of the President of the Republic of Singapore, *Appointment of Members to the Presidential Council for Religious Harmony*, September 15, 2020, https://www.istana.gov.sg/Newsroom/News-Releases/2020/09/15/Appointment-of-Members-to-the-Presidential-Council-for-Religious-Harmony.

rise to the occasion—alongside national leadership—with the advent of Muslim radicalization.

ACJU's Apparent Ambivalence

As the apex clerical body, the ACJU's primary responsibility is to protect and promote the Sri Lankan Muslim heritage. Unlike Sufism, which was the foundation of Sri Lankan Muslim heritage, Salafi-Wahhabism and Jamaat-e-Islami were said to have advocated or been founded on elements of exclusivism. However, the ACJU leaders seemed to overlook the infiltration of radical and violent Muslims within the Sri Lankan Muslim community. Eventually, radical Muslim leaders from deviant Salafi-Wahhabi groups reportedly took control of the ACJU and allegedly worked against the Sufi community.

After Mufti Rizwe assumed the presidency two years after the 9/11 attack in 2003, it was said that the ACJU started to shift away from Salafi-Wahhabism. However, some believed that Mufti Rizwe allegedly kept away from Kattankudy and the fighting between Salafi-Wahhabi and Sufi sects to avoid a direct confrontation with their groups. Even when some Salafi-Wahhabi groups were radicalizing Muslims in Kattankudy, the ACJU leaders were reportedly unable to protect the Muslim community. If they had, perhaps, not kept away from the developments in Kattankudy and responded to issues from the get-go, the Muslim-majority township may not have evolved into Sri Lanka's ground zero of terrorism.

As a religious minority living in a multi-religious country, it would be most recommended if the ACJU could work with the DMRCA to promote and/or protect local and traditional Islam. With an amazing resource of 6,000 Sri Lankan clerics island-wide, the ACJU leadership would be able to prime, direct, and mobilize clerics to build and work towards a harmonious country. After the Easter attack, ACJU General Secretary Sheikh M. Arkam Nooramith spoke of accrediting clerics by imparting religious knowledge and promoting *wasathiyah*, the concept of the middle path, enshrined in Islam. The aim was to train clerics to speak about the commonalities in faiths rather than highlight differences. These, among many other initiatives, should be spearheaded by the ACJU to build a healthy Muslim community.

Sri Lankan Muslim heritage would likely be the best antidote against exclusivist and extremist ideologies. Though there were reportedly discussions by Muslim leaders on reforming mosques and madrasahs and standardizing their sermons and curriculums, there has not been any further progress yet. Should these discussions bear fruit, sermons and curriculums can be approved by the ACJU, the Waqf board, and the DMRCA with the aim of promoting unity and religious harmony to prevent further attacks.

Restructuring or reforming religious leadership will be vital in implementing these measures successfully. Doing so can, in turn, close the credibility gap and trust deficit leading to greater acceptance by the community and government, eventually creating a body of competent leaders—secular intellectuals, professionals, and businessmen and women—to guide the Muslim community properly.

Dysfunctional Environment

It is largely believed that governments usually embrace extreme ends when it comes to response. In many cases, including the Easter Sunday attack, there would be non-reaction when there were no attacks, and complete overreaction when there were attacks. Both reactions create space and exacerbate radicalization. Such challenges require appropriate responses, including dedicated religious and secular bodies that frequently work together to prevent and counter ideology. Muslim religious, cultural, and political radicalization cannot be managed in the same way that ultra-Tamil nationalism was handled. Since comprehensive countermeasures are a work in progress, the government and other partners must continuously control divisive ideologies and promote unity to keep the threat from morphing into terrorism and political violence.

With the government change in January 2015, it was believed that the nation's pendulum swung from national security to reconciliation. Reconciliation is beneficial—but not without security. Former president Maithripala Sirisena, Foreign Minister Mangala Samaraweera and other Yahapalana leaders reportedly delisted the LTTE fronts. This was believed to have revived separatist activity in the north and east and overseas including in Geneva, where said fronts allegedly masqueraded as diaspora groups and lobbied western capitals with funds and votes culminating in a co-sponsored UN resolution against Sri Lanka. As discussed in previous chapters, it did not seem like the government took Muslim radicalization seriously even after Sri Lankan Muslims in Iraq and Syria were highlighted at the NSC.

Due to perceived inaction, the DMI reportedly decided to inform the nation through the parliament. The then-Justice Minister Wijeyadasa Rajapakshe, based on intelligence provided by then-DMI Brigadier Suresh Salley, highlighted the threat.[213] However, it was said that both Muslim and national leaders allegedly reacted with apparent denial and condemnation, likely ignorant of the ramifications or negligent of security.[214] Perhaps,

---

[213] 'Muslim Council objects to Wijeyadasa's statement on Lankans joining IS', *Ada Derana*, November 19, 2016, https://www.adaderana.lk/news/37908/muslim-council-objects-to-wijedasas-statement-on-lankans-joining-is.

[214] Shihar Aneez, 'Lanka says 32 "elite" Muslims have joined IS in Syria', *Reuters*, November 18, 2016, https://www.reuters.com/article/us-mideast-crisis-syria-sri-lanka-idUSKBN13D1EE.

to the then-Yahapalana government, national security was the previous government's brand. Thus, they may have downplayed such concerns. In turn, however, political leaders did not seem to take safety and security seriously, bureaucrats allegedly did not stand up to the political leaders, and civil servants and other officials were believed to have gone with the flow to survive.

A dysfunctional environment was reportedly created after Permanent Secretaries were appointed by politicians. They ensured the continuity of policies, procedures, and practices. They served the interests of nation and the masses, not the interests of their political masters. Perhaps if bureaucracy had not been imploded, there may have been continuity. However, with no machinery, an apparent lack of foresight, insufficient critical thinking, and seemingly personalized appointments, the quality of bureaucrats diminished. The purportedly weak political and governance apparatus has caused Sri Lanka to pay the price.

Investigative Findings

Fact-Finding Reports

The Easter Sunday attack had far-reaching impacts on Sri Lanka's public policy, particularly in the arena of national security. The attack and its aftermath reportedly compromised Sri Lanka's security framework, creating a sense of insecurity for all nationals and foreigners, investors, and tourists. It created multiple crises, driving the country to a seeming abyss. To deter, prevent, and counter-exclusivism and extremism, leading to terrorism and violence, four fact-finding bodies drafted reports and proposed wide and varied recommendations for relevant actors like the Sri Lankan government, private sector, and civil society to help restore national security in Sri Lanka. The four bodies and the full titles of their reports are listed below.

1. Report of the Special Board of Inquiry [SBI] Appointed to Inquire Into the Series of Incidents Related to the Explosions that Occurred at Several Places on the Island on 21 April 2019. (Not for public release.)
2. Sectoral Oversight Committee [SOC] on National Security Report of the Proposals for Formulation and Implementation of relevant laws required to ensure National Security that will eliminate New Terrorism and extremism by strengthening friendship among Races and Religions. (Available online.)
3. Report of the Select Committee of Parliament [PSC] to look into and report to Parliament on the Terrorist Attacks that took place in different places in Sri Lanka on 21 April 2019. (Available online.)
4. The Presidential Commission of Inquiry [PCoI] to Investigate and Inquire into and Report or Take Necessary Action on the Bomb Attacks on 21 April 2019. (Summary is publicly available.)

The reports were well crafted and adequately supported with evidence. Although three of the four were available for public consumption, their content was not easily accessible to or readable for the general population, which likely affected how widely disseminated and understood the reports could be.

Attempts, including by the presidential media division, to publicize snippets of the reports especially on online platforms like social media were reportedly shot down, likely because Gotabhaya Rajapaksa administration may not have understood the significance of media and public campaign efforts.[215]

Ultimately, despite spending a colossal amount of funds and time on them, it seemed the fact-finding reports were not put

215 Interview by author with a member of the presidential media division, September 22, 2022.

to good use. Lack of effective and widespread publicization and dissemination of the reports resulted in a number of Sri Lankans succumbing to disinformation, fake news, and conspiracy theories about the bombings. Many reportedly remained ignorant and unaware of the factual truth regarding the origins of the attack and evidence-backed recommendations provided to address pertinent gaps and lapses identified in its wake.

Report Takeaways

Within a nation's borders, a vital component needed for stability is national security. This was also the vulnerability exposed by the Easter Sunday attack. Indeed, as established in the PCoI, institutional failures, and political instability—namely the absence of an effective judicial legal system, lack of good governance, and a platform for the circulation of ideas—are all factors that play an essential role in the spread and development of political violence.[216] With the growth and advent of radical ideologies, provisions must be enacted to curb extremism and exclusivism spread particularly by deviant religious groups. Key takeaways and recommendations from the fact-finding reports in this regard have been listed below.

1. To govern effectively, the development of a community-based approach to tackle threats and advance national security is needed. Religious spaces are fragile and should be tightly regulated to prevent infiltrators from breaking up communities. To prevent and counter exclusivism leading to extremism, the authorities should work with the religious fraternity (e.g. religious leaders and bodies, scholars and teachers, mosques and madrasahs),

[216] Interview with a member of the presidential media division.

educational institutions, and the media to raise awareness and disseminate pertinent information.

Exclusivists and extremists should be mainstreamed, and their best should be transformed into champions of harmony and peace. Furthermore, firm action should be taken to investigate and prosecute those threatening unity and inciting division. To snuff out ongoing radicalization, government cooperation, collaborations, and partnerships with the private and non-profit sectors are essential. Without investing in community engagement and custodial rehabilitation, hate, terrorism and violence will endure.

Unless moderation, toleration and coexistence are promoted, and exclusivism disrupted, extremism will inevitably take root—leading to terrorism and violence. To sustain religious harmony, governments must create diverse presidential councils which include religious leaders of different denominations and sects. Religious integration is a vital cornerstone of building resilient communities and cohesive societies. Failure to do so could expose vulnerabilities to exploitation and risk of violence.

2. Build a core of leaders in national security where threat intelligence is not neglected. In every country, security is dynamic; past stability does not guarantee future security. Since the threat constantly evolves, security posture should also change. The intelligence community should constantly review and revise its assessments of the operating environment. To govern with foresight, political leaders and officials should understand the subject of national security and the vital role intelligence plays in detecting and neutralising threats. The intelligence community should brief their leaders to renew government and

partners' capabilities. Political interference in the security and intelligence apparatus can gravely damage any country. Thus, only trained, and seasoned professionals should direct and staff the services.

Future and emerging leaders should be educated within the law enforcement, intelligence, and military core. National security is the foundation of social harmony, political stability, and economic prosperity and should therefore be taught accordingly. A proper process should be established to nominate, select, and confirm leaders with the right competence and attitude for high office, particularly key positions of defence secretary, the CNI and other apex appointments. Wise leaders should be open-minded and have a thirst for learning. Effective governance, especially for those serving the security sector, is a learning journey. The mentality that we defeated 'the world's most dangerous terrorist group' will not help.

3. The backbone of national security is intelligence. To secure national interests, it is essential to develop a diverse mix of perspectives to effectively tackle the issues of national security on all fronts. Services should broaden their remit and recruit clerics, economists, health experts, sociologists, psychologists, statisticians, international relations specialists and mass media and tech professionals. Unless there is an active threat of combat, the numerical strength of the armed forces should be reduced and more specialized units such as intelligence and anti-riot units must be strengthened.

   Services should report directly to the executive leadership, a minister, and a secretary. In Sri Lanka's case, perhaps the SIS should not be administratively, financially, or operationally subsumed under the police.

As intelligence is paramount, the chiefs of the two premier services, the SIS and the DMI, can be elevated to and brought on par with the service commanders. There must be an exchange of personnel between intelligence services—where the SIS and special branch officers serve in the military services and vice versa. Joint projects from training to operations and building common databases should be encouraged. Those from outside the intelligence community should not be 'parachuted' to helm the intelligence services. Intelligence chiefs should be appointed from within the services.

4. Establish a national security mechanism with a National Security Act, Office of the National Security Adviser (NSA), National Security Council Secretariat (NSCS), and National Security Advisory Board (NSAB). As threats can be diverse and impact multiple domains (e.g. organized crime—especially terrorism and narcotics, geopolitics-geoeconomics, cyber and information), an NSA with a cabinet rank should be appointed to work with key ministers, secretaries, and departments. To secure both the traditional domains of security as well as new and emerging domains of security, an NSA should mitigate a range of risks and threats from economic security to energy security, health security and climate change security and resource security to supply chain security. An NSCS—with subject specialists with expertise and experience—is vital to provide recommendations and policy options, and to monitor and report if the NSC decisions are being implemented. Meanwhile, the NSAB can identify gaps, loopholes and weaknesses in the national security structure and propose initiatives, alternative options, and solutions to close them.

5. Formulate and continuously upgrade strong legal and policy frameworks to secure domains that impact national security. It is necessary to formulate and implement laws to protect the religious space, which is continuously infiltrated by religious fanatics or extremist ideologies. To promote harmony, and especially deter hate speech including incitement into violence, a Singapore-style maintenance of a Religious Harmony Act can be considered. Similarly, to protect the population from fake news, an Online Falsehoods and Manipulations Act is essential. Likewise, to provide measures to prevent, detect and disrupt foreign interference in domestic politics conducted through hostile information campaigns and the use of local proxies, a Foreign Interference (Countermeasures) Act is needed. Geopolitical actors operating under the pretext of advancing human rights, democracy, and religious freedom reportedly give grants to destabilize cultures, promote divisive ideologies, and break up communities. This needs to be countered and regulated accordingly.

A Public Order Act is also needed to prevent and deter attempts to disrupt social harmony or public peace. Freedom of speech, assembly, and political expression should not harm stability needed for economic survival and prosperity. When it comes to national security intelligence, safeguards should be established through a National Security Act to preclude the play of personal and party politics. If they do not respect the maintenance of the nation's interests, the nation-state will be crippled.

In a strong organizational culture, national security must remain the priority and national security intelligence functions including operations should be protected by law. Some may say that, in any domain, politicians can play at the peril of a nation, but when the national security system is compromised, the country will likely pay the ultimate price. To fight back, it is paramount to send an unequivocal message to the community so that they will not support terrorism and violence; this includes immediate proscription and dismantling of violent and extremist groups, especially in the wake of the Easter carnage.

Global Realizations and Ways Forward

The Primacy of Leadership

In a rapidly changing fast-paced dynamic world, securing nations requires leadership at all levels to mitigate national security risks. Visionary and decisive leadership is of paramount importance to govern countries with faultlines and vulnerable communities. Rather than let events take their own course, the outcome of events should be steadfastly shaped by government and community leaders. Leaders need to be agile and up-to-speed to be multifunctional and influence multiple domains. To rise to the occasion and act, they need to be constantly briefed and primed. They should be continuously educated and trained to groom them for adequate leadership too.

It is said that the Easter attack may be considered a failure of leadership in governance and politics, and more of an operational failure rather than an intelligence one. The Sri Lankan case illustrates that, to govern a nation effectively, political leadership and bureaucrats must keep abreast with the evolving threat landscape. Rather than follow a 'wait and see' approach, swift measures are needed to counter and respond to national security threats.

Victims and Survivors

Relevant government and non-government actors—such as law enforcement, intelligence agencies, the private sector, civil society, healthcare facilities, religious institutes, and schools—should work together to mitigate the impact of shocks after traumatic events like the Easter attack. Countries should develop multi-disciplinary crisis response teams and plans to respond to these harrowing incidents—and the victims and survivors left in their wake.

In the immediate aftermath of the Easter attack, a champion of harmony, Aamina Muhsin, recalled how a survivor lost his entire family. 'All three of his children died, but he noticed in his wife's eye, a flicker of movement. Keen to save her, he carried her out of the church in Katuwapitiya and drove his tuk-tuk to the nearest hospital in Negombo. There, he was told that they didn't have enough doctors to save her. He then had to travel an excruciating [three] hours with his dying wife all the way to Karapitiya in Galle. That's where she received her treatment, only to later succumb to her injuries. Would she still be alive had he not had to drive her across the country to receive medical attention?'[217]

Another survivor, whose son, Kieran Shafritz de Zoysa, was severely injured while dining at the Cinnamon Grand Hotel, was admitted to a hospital.[218] A straight-A student, Kieran, who was eleven years old, did not survive. His mother, Dhulsini de Zoysa, mentioned that 'despite requesting it countless times', she and Kieran's father, who was a heart surgeon, never received information on what procedures were performed on their beloved son. She took him to the hospital to save his life and when he died in hospital care, all they wanted was 'information', added Aamina.[219] The healthcare system was not prepared for massive

---

[217] Aamina Muhsin, interview by the Easter Attack Survivors Project, September 28, 2022.

[218] Jason Hanna and Carma Hassan, 'A US fifth-grader was at breakfast when he was killed in the Sri Lanka bombings', *CNN*, April 25, 2019, https://amp.cnn.com/cnn/2019/04/23/us/sri-lanka-sidwell-friends-fifth-grader-killed/index.html.

[219] Muhsin, interview.

national or regional shocks. It has been over three years since that awful day, Sri Lanka has witnessed three different governments since then, and yet survivors like Dhulsini de Zoysa have reportedly not received a formal apology from the government or a note acknowledging their pain.

It is the duty of the state to protect its citizens. It is the duty of the government that represents the state to ensure that its citizens' rights to safety and life are not violated. If anyone comes to harm from the consequences of state neglect and national security, it is their right to call for accountability and, at the very least, expect an apology. Wide-ranging victims and survivors of terror attacks—including wives and children of suicide bombers who were either abandoned or brainwashed—require adequate support and consideration too.

If the state fails to protect its citizens, and they lost their lives due to that failure, it is the duty of the state to memorialize those lives that were lost. In line with international standards, this is a basic requirement to be adopted after wars, terrorist attacks, and other conflicts. And yet, where does Sri Lanka stand when it comes to shaping the outcomes of the largest attack yet outside the Iraqi-Syrian theatre? There is reportedly no official memorial site or official documentation process of their stories.

International Dimension

The international community should work together to dismantle operational threats and ideological threats. There are existing and well-developed cooperative partnerships aimed at fighting terrorism. However, collaborative mechanisms to contain, isolate and eliminate the ideology are reportedly in their infancy. There needs to be greater commitment, resources, and effort, especially from the countries of the Middle East, to defeat exclusivist and extremist threats. National and regional observatories should also be established to map strategies and address the precursors of political violence.

Sri Lanka lacked the legislation to arrest Zahran in his formative ideological phase. However, after the Easter attack, the international community came together to demonstrate solidarity. For instance, Singapore's Law and Home Affairs Minister Kasiviswanathan Shanmugam and India's Prime Minister Narendra Modi visited Sri Lanka to demonstrate their support. In addition to INTERPOL, a dozen law enforcement and intelligence services gathered in Colombo to extend assistance to their counterparts. Officers from leading security and intelligence services—from the American FBI and Central Intelligence Agency to the Israeli Mossad, Australian Secret Intelligence Service, and Singaporean Internal Security Department—flew into Colombo to understand what went wrong. Likewise, the world's largest intelligence alliance, Five Eyes, reportedly realized they had not intercepted threat intelligence on the Easter Sunday attack and thus discussed how to deepen and widen their coverage and sharing through their partnerships outside the Anglo-Saxon arrangement. These—as well as the joint operations to track and, eventually, successfully eliminate the IS' apex leader Abu Bakr al-Baghdadi—are just a few examples that demonstrate the feasibility of enhanced cross-country coordination and collaborations within the threat landscape.

Uprooting the Ideology

While law enforcements can dismantle terrorist support and operational infrastructure, disrupting its precursor—the ideology—is a complex task. Stemming it from the root requires a range of actors—including religious, educational, digital, and political leadership—led by the intelligence community who, in turn, will guide the public and help build community understanding.

Contrary to popular belief, ideology is often the real principal driver of violence. Ideology and ideas crystallize into support and operational cells that create the environment and personalities to mount periodic attacks. In the case of Sri Lanka, both Salafi-Wahhabism from the Middle East and Jamaat-e-Islami from the subcontinent supplanted local and traditional Islam, which had peacefully coexisted with other faiths for decades. Driven by its rivalry with Iran, the ideology that Saudi Arabia is said to have promoted damaged the security and stability of many countries, including Sri Lanka. While Iran supported Shia Islam the second largest branch of Islam, the Saudis promoted Sunni Islam the largest branch of Islam followed by 85 to 90 per cent of world Muslims. With the spread of extremist Salafi-Wahhabism by the Saudi government to counter the Iranian influence, more Muslims worldwide embraced an exclusive form of Islam. Extremist Salafi-Wahhabism surged, sub planting local and traditional Islam that had coexisted for centuries with other faiths. Since then, Saudi Arabia, under Crown Prince Mohammed bin Salman, has reportedly cracked down on Salafi-Wahhabism. Though, it may be worth noting, the ideology continues to be practised in Sri Lanka.

Until the Easter Sunday attack in April 2019, Saudi Arabia witnessed over sixty terrorist attacks by the IS and al-Qaeda, of which twenty-five occurred with the emergence of the IS in 2014.[220] More than 200 citizens and policemen have been killed in these terrorist attacks.[221] The commentary of Saudi leaders have reportedly changed to reflect the threat too. According to Sheikh Khalid Ali al-Ghamedi, Imam of the Grand Mosque in Makkah, on [8 July 2016], '[t]he greatest and most appalling of all sins is

[220] The Embassy of the Kingdom of Saudi Arabia, *Saudi Arabia and Counterterrorism*.

[221] The Embassy of the Kingdom of Saudi Arabia, *Saudi Arabia and Counterterrorism*.

for anyone to deliberately and premeditatedly shed the blood of innocent people, wreak chaos and havoc and undermine security and stability in order to achieve the evil goals of criminal gangs and sectarian terrorist organizations.'[222] It is said that religious and political leaders have since spoken out and taken measures to incarcerate Salafi-Wahhabi clerics unwilling to change their views on mainstream Muslims and non-Muslims.

'The Kingdom of Saudi Arabia is determined, God willing, to strike with an iron fist those who target the minds and attitudes of our youth,' said King Salman bin Abdulaziz, Custodian of the Two Holy Mosques, on [5 July 2016].[223] The Saudi measures mention that the Ministry of Education has also revised its school textbooks to ensure that they do not include intolerant language, and regularly audits these textbooks and curricula to ensure that teachers do not espouse intolerance or extremism.[224] Imams who preach intolerance or hate towards others are to be dismissed, punished, or retrained as well.[225]

The National Dialogue Forum of the King Abdulaziz Centre for National Dialogue was instituted in June 2003 to debate reform and suggest remedies following the al-Qaeda terrorist attacks on 9/11. Each of these meetings takes place in a different city in the Kingdom. The Centre's objective 'is to combat extremism and foster a pure atmosphere that gives rise to wise positions and illuminating ideas that reject terrorism and terrorist thought'.[226]

In May 2017, Saudi Arabia inaugurated the Etidal Global Centre for Countering Extremist Ideology, a counterterrorism hub focusing on promoting a media and online culture of

[222] The Embassy of the Kingdom of Saudi Arabia, *Saudi Arabia and Counterterrorism.*

[223] The Embassy of the Kingdom of Saudi Arabia, *Saudi Arabia and Counterterrorism.*

[224] The Embassy of the Kingdom of Saudi Arabia, *Saudi Arabia and Counterterrorism.*

[225] The Embassy of the Kingdom of Saudi Arabia, *Saudi Arabia and Counterterrorism.*

[226] The Embassy of the Kingdom of Saudi Arabia, *Saudi Arabia and Counterterrorism.*

moderation and preventing the spread of propaganda. The Centre is headquartered in Riyadh and has developed innovative techniques that can monitor, process, and analyse extremists' speeches with high accuracy.[227]

Although Saudi Arabia's political and religious leaders have taken steps to address the issue, it seems Sri Lankan Muslim leaders and religious institutions have yet to take similar, decisive steps to curb radical Salafi-Wahhabism, especially with proscribed organizations continuing to preach even after the Easter Sunday attack. Authorities should work together with relevant actors to reform the religious, educational, and digital space. Otherwise, virulent and vituperative ideologies by aggressive and manipulative leaders may persist, grow—and ultimately lead to another attack in the future.

Shaping the Domains

Religious, educational, and digital domains play a major role in governance to shape outcomes, including in times of crisis. It is the obligation of organizational leaders functioning in these domains to ensure that no one in their community misuses or abuses these spaces to harm others. It is the duty of these organizations to encourage diversity and cross-sectoral interactions. Key and influential figures in these domains can play a huge role and shoulder a massive responsibility to participate in anti-terrorism and counterterrorism efforts.

Several studies have been done by various Muslim intellectual groups calling for the regulation of the Islamic space. For instance, renowned Muslim scholars have investigated how madrasah educational institutions can be regulated. There is a wider consensus among the members of the community regarding this, including:

---

[227] The Embassy of the Kingdom of Saudi Arabia, *Saudi Arabia and Counterterrorism.*

1. Re-naming the madrasahs as Islamic educational institutions or Moulavi training schools;
2. Making it compulsory for all students to study general syllabus or secular schooling and subjects for at least until sixteen years old and banning those who are unwilling to do so; and
3. Monitoring the funding, syllabus, teachers, and students of the madrasahs.

After the Easter attack, the natural reaction may have been to immediately expel foreign Arab preachers and close madrasahs, which would not have been helpful. Such arbitrary and unreasonable actions could create dissent within the community and may lead to greater conflicts and problems. When closing Salafi-Wahhabi and Jamaat-e-Islami institutions, the students and their future should be considered. There should be a mechanism to register the madrasah, similar to how Buddhists have *pirivenas* and Catholics have seminaries. The Muslim community needs Islamic educational institutions, of course, subject to strict monitoring and regulation. If the education ministry is unable to monitor the institutions, a unit under the DMRCA can be set up.

To address the challenges Sri Lanka faced in the lead-up to the Easter attack, perhaps it can be made mandatory for those enrolling in the madrasah system to simultaneously continue mainstream education. This will ensure that large numbers of youth have the necessary skills or knowledge to get employed elsewhere or excel in different professions as well. Systematically, the government should work with religious institutions to regulate the madrasah system. It could be made an equivalent of 'Dhamma school' or 'Sunday school'. Similarly, texts that are used for madrasah education as well as their syllabi or curricula should be regulated or standardized by the Ministry of Education.

With religious terrorism threatening to distort Islam, Buddhism, Hinduism, and Christianity to spread hatred and incite violence, the government can also work with religious authorities to issue licenses for the teaching or preaching of religion. This practice of licensing can be developed and made mandatory for all clergy across religions and, should any clergy step out of line, the license can be cancelled, and disciplinary action should follow.

Temples, churches, *kovils*, and mosques may also be built only with approval from the respective Grama Niladhari divisions. While, in some cases, western NGOs were said to have funded the construction of churches and conversions, there are also cases where Gulf countries and NGOs reportedly funded the construction of mosques and madrasahs to teach ideologies that could be damaging to Sri Lankan unity. Such foreign-funded projects can and should be approved by the ministries of religious affairs, public security, and defence before being implemented.

The curriculum of moulavi training institutions should also be standardized. For instance, the moulavi should learn Sinhalese and Tamil before learning Arabic or Persian. To navigate harmoniously in a multi-religious country, a moulavi should learn or at least be made aware of other religions, not just Islam. Otherwise, the tendency for the moulavi to condemn other faiths will be existent, and could create tier-one radicalization. When equipped with knowledge of other religions, the moulavi can draw commonalities between the religions. Unless moderation, tolerance and coexistence are taught, madrasahs, mosques, and similar religious institutions may continue to produce exclusivists who could develop sympathies and support for extremist and violent groups.

However, it is important to note that ideologies will not be defeated with discipline alone. Effective engagements with the wider Muslim community to resolve key issues—just as then

Defence Secretary Gotabaya Rajapaksa did with the Halal and Grease Yaka crises, among others—is also important. Regular dialogues, consultations, and exchanges between the government and community leaders can help the authorities map out better strategies for combatting extremism and refining community engagement strategies.

Rehabilitation and Reintegration

No one is born an exclusivist, extremist, or terrorist. Every detainee suspected of extremism and terrorism has the potential to transform into a champion of peace. Similarly, every sentenced prisoner can be transformed into a peaceful and productive citizen. The effectiveness of rehabilitation and reintegration interventions will determine the transformation of the heart and mind. Both the detention environment and post-sentencing prison environment should be like a school where the detainee or the prisoner learns.

In a custodial setting, rehabilitation should start from day one. All inmates should be assessed and categorised based on the risk and threat they posed. A case officer should be assigned to engage every inmate. Daily custodial services and programmes should enable the reflection and reformation of the beneficiaries. Irrespective of whether a detainee facilitated or directly participated in the Easter attack, rehabilitation should be implemented. The detention environment should promote wasathiyah, which is a central concept in Islam.

A part of the far-reaching approach of working together to end violent extremism is the engagement and treatment of victims and survivors. Having perpetrators and supporters listen to the heart-wrenching stories and experiences of loss and suffering of victims and survivors may also stir their hearts and provide them with broader understanding of the consequences of their actions, and thus change their perspectives on the situation.

The detention period is the golden window; the ideal and oftentimes only period beliefs of exclusivism and violent extremism can be changed and anyone harbouring an incorrect understanding of his or her faith can be reformed. Enlightened clerics can mainstream the detainee's thinking. After release, they should be assisted to carry on with their lives without recidivism. Simply resorting to punishment and release upon the termination of their detention or sentence will likely not solve the problem. If they are not rehabilitated in custody, the radicalization could exacerbate in a custodial setting.

Ideologies cannot be killed through punishment or retribution alone. Those radicalized should be identified as beneficiaries and given opportunities to start their lives anew—for instance, through education. When they finish their terms as beneficiaries, they can go back and positively contribute to society and their families. Since they will likely be criminalized, they should be trained by the private sector and perhaps assisted with employment upon release. To be able to integrate well and not rejoin violent and extremist groups, beneficiaries should have a stable home to return to. The social and family rehabilitation programme should prepare both the beneficiaries and their families so that the former feel welcomed and treated well. Unless those reintegrated find a community that accepts them and a sense of belonging, they can and may gravitate towards deviant groups again. The strategy is to shift focus from calling for justice to supporting individuals to change their mindset. By transforming them into peaceful and productive citizens, future stability and security can be achieved.

It is also worth noting that the UN identified and positively acknowledged the rehabilitation programmes in Singapore, Saudi Arabia, and Sri Lanka.[228] An internationally recognized

---

[228] Sabariah Mohamed Hussin, 'Strategic Counterterrorism, Terrorist Rehabilitation and Community Engagement: The Singapore Experience', *United Nations Asia and Far East Institute for the Prevention of Crime and the Treatment of Offenders*, March 2018,

rehabilitation programme, the existing rehabilitation framework can be developed and implemented throughout the remand and prison system to benefit those detained and sentenced for terrorist and criminal allegations and offences. If it enlists enlightened Sri Lankan Muslims to staff and guide its rehabilitation programme, Sri Lanka has the potential to build a world-class model to rehabilitate Muslim exclusivists, extremists, and terrorists. It may also be the dawn of a far-reaching approach and a multipronged strategy to effectively prevent and pre-empt violence, extremism, and exclusivism in Sri Lanka.

Networked Government

The post-9/11 era witnessed complex attacks by networked cells, groups, and movements. Threat entities expanded their operations from the physical to the digital space. The surge of religious exclusivism, extremism, and terrorism in the early twenty-first century shifted the global focus to detect, disrupt, and dismantle the terrorist infrastructure. Law enforcement's traditional and commonplace strategy of conducting investigations and bringing culprits to justice reportedly failed to deter and defeat the contemporary wave of politico-religiously motivated violence. Although it is necessary to punish perpetrators and supporters, the focus should be to prevent and deter violence.

To fight the current and emerging wave of violence, governments should develop multi-pronged, multi-agency, multi-dimensional, and multinational capabilities. Rather than working in isolation, governments should work both within and outside to build capabilities and capacities to influence the human terrain. The government should shift from a whole-of-government to a whole-of-society approach. For instance, in an effort to pre-empt

---

https://www.unafei.or.jp/publications/pdf/RS_No104/No104_8_VE_Hussin.pdf.

the Easter attack, the government reportedly did not share the threat intelligence with the churches and hotels. Despite retired and former officers from the security and intelligence community serving in the community organizations and private sector, it seems that the government has not yet built trusted partnerships with either the private sector or community organizations.

With the diffusion of threats and infiltration of communities, managing security requires outreach campaigns to co-opt both the private sector and influencing community organizations. Without shaping the thinking of the general population, governments cannot administer security effectively. Creative and innovative leaders should move from security cooperation to collaboration and partnership. The operating principle should be to move from a 'need to know' to a 'need to share' approach.

A good practice followed by the Sri Lankan police was to give foreign law enforcement authorities, security, and intelligence access to interview Easter Sunday detainees and examine their electronic devices. In addition to INTERPOL, FBI, and Australian Federal Police had full access and their investigations and analysis concluded that the attack was mounted by the IS Sri Lanka branch. Furthermore, they examined the crime scenes where the attacks took place, and their findings and forensic analysis were of exceptional value.

Working Together

To create a common operating threat picture, the intelligence jigsaw must be fitted together as terrorism and extremism present a common threat. The future of law enforcement, military and intelligence are in shifting from networking and cooperation to collaboration and partnership. The components are:

1. Exchange of personnel
2. Common databases

3. Joint training
4. Joint operations
5. Sharing of resources and technology
6. Sharing of experience and expertise.

Outside the Five Eyes countries, the progress to build and sustain security and intelligence platforms has reportedly been alarmingly slow. The IS-inspired Marawi siege in the Philippines from 23 May–23 October 2017 created Our Eyes, an ASEAN intelligence sharing platform modelled on AUS-CAN-UK-US-NZ. Just as INTERPOL has provided a global law enforcement mechanism, the world desperately needs an international intelligence capability to prevent and pre-empt threats in the making.

What the Future Holds

Likely Developments

In a borderless world, the internet enables ideologies to indoctrinate the like-minded and the vulnerable. The modus operandi of threat actors is to remotely connect, communicate, and influence their followers to strike. Away from the glare of the international community, the IS inspired a group of religious fanatics to mount attacks worldwide. The emerging model for terrorism is capacitating followers of foreign ideologies to mount long-range deep-penetration attacks. By communicating their ideology to die for God, the world's deadliest threat actors, al-Qaeda and the IS, inspired and instigated attacks worldwide.

Just as al-Qaeda's worst attack outside Afghanistan was 9/11, one of the worst attacks staged by the IS outside Iraq and Syria was the Easter Sunday massacre in Sri Lanka. With Afghanistan falling back to the hands of the Taliban on 15 August 2021, its ally al-Qaeda could mount similar attacks remotely, exploiting local franchises and like-minded affiliates.

Governments should be aware of the threat entities' footprint and modus operandi if they are to effectively counter the threat. The first phase of activity—propaganda and recruitment—can be detected and disrupted by the government enlisting the support of community partners especially religious, educational, and media institutions. In the threat spectrum, the government approach should be to dominate. To deliver a full spectrum response, the intelligence community should keep law enforcement authorities and military forces up-to-speed. Similarly, the government should invest in outreach to strengthen community relationships critical to preventing and pre-empting attacks. If the terrorists succeed, government and partners should be prepared and ready to manage the consequences of a catastrophic attack.

Shaping Outcomes

The Easter Attack inflicted severe damage, but it is believed that the failure to shape its outcome may have been what truly caused irreparable damage. Sri Lanka was reportedly unable to stop the carnage and shape its outcomes. The successive leadership did not manage to curb or control the threat, which is said to have almost brought about the near collapse of a nation-state. Although terrorism is not new to Sri Lanka, the emergence of religious exclusivism, extremism, and terrorism presents a new set of problems. Unless the issue is recognized by governments worldwide and countermeasures are developed, other countries could suffer the same fate as Sri Lanka.

Three decades preceding the Easter massacre, radical Salafi-Wahhabi and Jamaat-e-Islami ideologies separated Muslims from non-Muslims. Foreign ideologies supplanted Sri Lankan Muslim heritage. These virulent ideologies crystallized, forming operational cells, networks, and groups that gravely damaged national unity. Although several groups were banned, others continued to function. For instance, the Jamaat-e-Islami student wing is banned but its main branch operates. Similarly, many of the banned Wahhabi groups continue to operate either clandestinely or by infiltrating like-minded entities.

Unless addressed, the situation could worsen and Sri Lanka may become another country where religious hostilities and violence are a persistent challenge. It can go the way of conflict zones and countries where there are sporadic attacks. They include Bangladesh, Pakistan, India, Afghanistan, Indonesia, Philippines, Nigeria, Libya, Israel, Iraq, Syria, Yemen, Lebanon, and the Palestinian territories.

Without government and community partners worldwide taking firm steps to develop and sustain a zero-tolerance approach against radicalization, the global threat of religious hostilities will grow. What is vital is to transform places of religious worship and education into centres for interfaith dialogue and religious knowledge. In Sri Lanka, unless Muslim radicalization and reciprocal Buddhist, Hindu, and Christian radicalization is firmly dealt with, the threat will continue and may even grow. As a strategically positioned regional hub, maintaining Sri Lankan security is paramount for international travel, trade, and commerce.

Can Sri Lanka Come out Stronger?

After Easter Sunday 2019, Sri Lanka can come out stronger if it takes the right steps. If a country wishes to recover after a devastating attack, the first step is to develop a common approach. By departing from confrontational politics and forging a national agenda, the government and the political opposition can work together to develop bipartisanship in national security. First, create a legal and policy framework to reverse radicalization by promoting moderation, tolerance, and coexistence. Second—and in parallel—is to build capabilities within the military, law enforcement, and intelligence to prevent and pre-empt attacks.

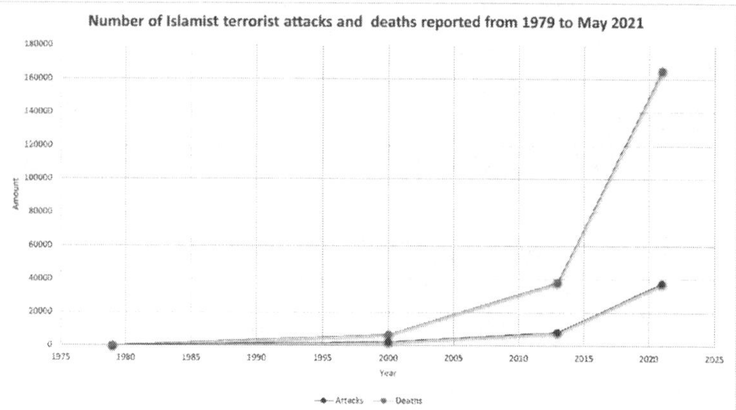

Number of terrorist attacks and deaths reported from 1979 to May 2021
Source: Global Terrorism Database - https://www.start.umd.edu/gtd/

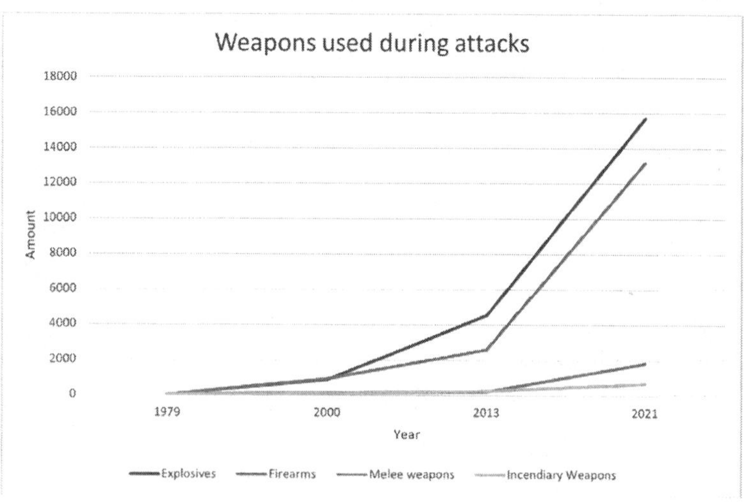

Weapons used in terrorist attacks from 1979 to May 2021
Source: Global Terrorism Database - https://www.start.umd.edu/gtd/

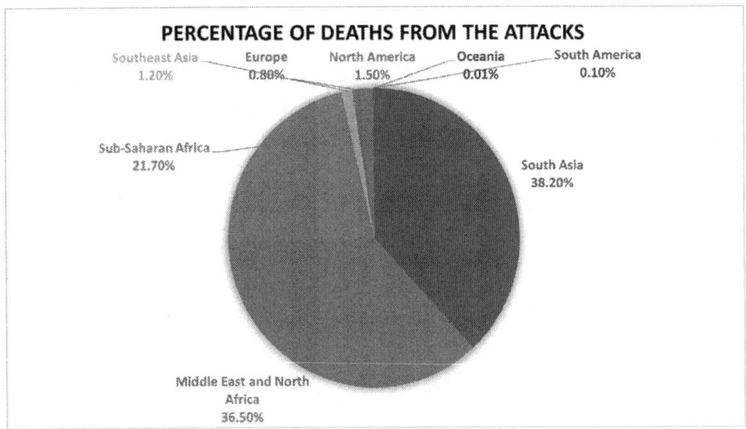

Percentage of deaths by region of terrorist attacks from 1979 to May 2021
Source: Global Terrorism Database - https://www.start.umd.edu/gtd/

By investing in ethnic and religious integration, Sri Lanka can restore harmony and maintain social cohesion which are preconditions to securing a multicultural country. Similarly, by investing in and developing speciality in religious exclusivism and extremism within the security forces and the intelligence community, the threat of terrorism can be mitigated. A key lesson is to engage religious leaders and institutions that can influence communities against hate speech and incitement into violence.

Conclusion

The Easter Sunday attack and failure to shape its outcomes cascaded, which likely destabilized Sri Lanka alongside what seemed to be unclear leadership and an inadequate national security framework. Economic mismanagement and the three shocks—a catastrophic attack, a pandemic, and war in Europe—plunged Sri Lanka from crisis to chaos.

In an age of conflict and turmoil, the leaders entrusted with national security should ensure a safe and secure environment. To administer a government and to govern a country, a skilled leader and his or her team must govern with a great deal of deliberation. Without statecraft, a safe and secure nation cannot be chiselled and created.

Social and political stability, which is fundamental to economic prosperity, comes from the appropriate maintenance of national security. Sri Lanka reportedly lacked integrated leadership and bipartisanship, which has resulted in a culture of confrontational politics. All parties should work together to formulate national policies to build Sri Lanka. To prevent policy paralysis, policy coherence through awareness is essential. This will ensure that all parties have ownership of the policy—especially national security and foreign policy.

The Easter Sunday attack demonstrated a number of gaps, loopholes and weaknesses in the national security framework—and changed everything. Will there be a similar attack in the foreseeable future? With enhanced globalization, ease of travel, migration, communication, and technology, will remote and distant threats from far away theatres move stealthily, take root, manifest, and materialise? Every successful and failed attack is a lesson for politicians, bureaucrats, military forces, law enforcement authorities, and intelligence services. If Sri Lanka learns from its weaknesses, it can come out stronger. If the international community learns from Sri Lanka's experience, the international security and intelligence community can build a more secure and safer world.

Acknowledgements

The Easter massacre changed the lives of many colleagues, friends, and thousands others. This is the inside story of how a catastrophic attack was planned, prepared, and executed, and what governments and society should know to detect and disrupt its repetition. On threat and response, I had unprecedented access to information from intelligence services, law enforcement authorities, and military forces. This included reports by Sri Lanka's foreign counterparts and technology partners. In an effort to build a rehabilitation programme, I also interviewed those arrested after the Easter attack. In addition to reviewing terrorist seizures, I travelled six times to Kattankudy, the ground-zero of terrorism, to interview detainee families.

I am indebted to many for supporting the research seeking to dissect the attack. I would like to acknowledge the steadfast support of Penguin Random House SEA especially Nora Nazerene Abu Bakar and Amberdawn Manaois. I am grateful to the Konrad-Adenauer-Stiftung for funding the research project and especially to Christian Echle and Dr La Toya Waha for their continued support and the latter's valuable comment.

My research assistant Anargi Jayakody from King's College, University of London, edited the book manuscript with inputs from Aamina Muhsin, co-chair of the Sri Lanka Reconciliation Movement, and Rashane Jude Pinto, a national security analyst formerly with the Institute of National Security Studies, Sri

Lanka. In addition to arranging meetings with the family members of the Islamic State (IS) and other detainees in Kattankudy and Colombo, Dinithi Dharmapala and I jointly interviewed the IS leaders, members, and supporters. My doctoral student, Clifford Gere, Rajaratnam School of International Studies, Nanyang Technological University, Singapore reviewed the manuscript together with Inuri Hettithanthirige Tennakoon of the International Law College (Faculty of Laws), Panthéon-Sorbonne and Queen Mary School of Law, University of London, and Kavindhya Wickremesinghe from the Faculty of Law, General Sir John Kotelawala Defence University, Sri Lanka.